PRAISE FOR DELIVERY MANAGEMENT

"A truly engaging and story-driven book that answers important questions about Delivery Management, offering valuable insights for experienced and new product practitioners. Jonny paints a clear picture of an emerging discipline that can help teams to realise their potential."

Janna Bastow, Co-founder, ProdPad & Mind the Product

"Jonny has delivered just as he always does: open, engaging, and incisive. There is huge richness for all leaders in this book shaping a conversation around an evolving environment with systems and humans at the core. A great read whether a seasoned Delivery Manager, or new to leadership."

Roxane Heaton BEM, Chief Information Officer, Macmillan Cancer Support

"This is THE compendium on modern delivery leadership. Jonny builds on the shoulders of giants, weaving together contemporary product delivery approaches and articulates both the value of delivery roles as well as providing a useful toolbox for aspiring and experienced delivery leaders. A go-to book for those involved in helping product teams to release value for their users."

Aaron Jaffery, Director General, Digital Experience & Client Data, Service Canada

"It's rare for an agile book to correctly capture and align all the conceptual elements, underpinning values and principles, but Jonny Williams has managed it in Delivery Management. Understanding these is far more important than rigid adherence to a framework for any Delivery Manager, new or old. But this isn't just theory because the book gives all the practical techniques to manifest the essential behaviours and approaches for successful delivery. It strongly reflects how the best of modern Delivery Management is done in practice. Essential reading for anyone seeking to master Delivery Management."

Barry Traish, Head of Role for Agile Delivery, Department for Work and Pensions

"This book authentically and intelligently captures the core ethos and philosophy of agile Delivery Management. It's full of techniques that work and is the reference book I expect even experienced Delivery Managers to use. It's a great starting point for someone new to the role, or someone who wants to understand more about how Delivery Management can help their organisation."

Nick Smith, Head of Profession, Agile Delivery, Government Digital Service

"I've worked with a lot of Delivery Managers over the years. The ones that were new to the role often thought it was a bunch of techniques; formulas to spray about and charts. That's just a tiny part of it. This book gets to the heart of the role quickly with personal experience, insight, and technical skill. Jonny has told you exactly what you need to do, and why. Let's get rid of those 'roadmaps of doom' shall we?"

Sarah Winters, Author of Content Design & Founder, Content Design London

"This book is going to help solve so many challenges that myself, and others, face as leaders of delivery departments. I see this book as must read material for all delivery professionals, and potentially for other team members in a product team, to build empathy and understanding for the role. By providing a common language and a gamut of practical tools, I'm expecting it to set forward the practice several years."

Laura Burnett, Head of Delivery, Made Tech

"This is a thought-provoking, considered, and enlightening guide, based on real-life learnings and experiences, that will help those who are curious about Delivery Management through to challenging those who consider themselves an expert. The focus on enablement, delivering quality and value over quantity, and helping to articulate clearly in a digestible way what Delivery Management actually is, are just a few reasons why this is a recommended read!"

Zara Powell, TechWomen100 Award Winner & Delivery Director, Zone

"This book has all the information I wished I'd had access to when starting out in Delivery Management. Jonny's details are thoughtful, entertaining, useful, and practical - an absolute joy to read and I'll be referencing this for years to come."

Jon Rhodes, Director & Co-founder, Paper

DELIVERY MANAGEMENT

"One will weave the canvas; another will fell a tree by the light of his axe. Yet another will forge nails, and there will be others who observe the stars to learn how to navigate. And yet all will be as one.

Building a boat isn't about weaving canvas, forging nails, or reading the sky. It's about giving a shared taste for the sea, by the light of which you will see nothing contradictory but rather a community of love."

ANTOINE DE SAINT-EXUPÉRY

DELIVERY MANAGEMENT

ENABLING TEAMS TO DELIVER VALUE

JONNY WILLIAMS

VULPES
PRESS

Vulpes Press publishes in a variety of print and electronic formats and by print-on-demand. Some material included in standard print editions of this book may not be included in eBooks or in print-on-demand.

Cataloging-in-Publication data available upon request.

Cover and book design: Vulpes Press
Edited by: Annabel Hill

Paperback ISBN: 978-1-7391862-0-3
Hardback ISBN: 978-1-7391862-1-0
eBook ISBN: 978-1-7391862-2-7

To Claudia,
My best friend - you make life amazing.

BRIEF CONTENTS

CONTENTS

INTRODUCTION

Tired. The kind of tiredness that three strong coffees won't fix. I'm in the middle of the town square. My feet ache and my head hurts. But these fences need moving.

Wedging my fingers into the metal mesh, there's enough to grip, but not comfortably. Fences are awkward, but we must have moved at least fifty by now. The town is getting quiet as people leave the festival for the weekend. Day three. Nearly finished.

I'm half expecting a few people to down tools and decide they have done enough. Part of me would love to stop, but it doesn't feel like an option. The whole team is on their feet and we are synchronised. There are no words being spoken, but we all understand the rhythm of our actions and where we need to be.

It's been a long day after a series of long days. Only ten more fences to go and then we're finished. I can feel every step as steel toe caps press into the tips of my toes and the arches of my feet droop onto hard soles. It's less of a walk across the square now and more of a shuffle, but nobody is complaining.

Two fences left, nearly there. This hasn't taken as long as I expected. My boots don't feel so heavy on the walk back and even the fences feel lighter. We pick them up together and stride towards the pile of woven metal. Every part of the festival is packed down now. This is the final job of the weekend, and we all know it.

As we release the metal bars, they impact fences below and chime across the town. We're done. Everyone takes a breath. We inspect the empty space around us and admire the contrast between quiet evening air and the bustling crowd of people that were here only hours before.

Taking a seat for the first time in what feels like forever, I am relieved. I won't have to do work like that again for a while. But part of me wants to. Part of me already misses it. Not the early mornings, or cleaning up after other people. Part of me already misses the team. We made something special happen this weekend. We made people happy. Somehow, I'm not tired anymore.

Working for my friends' event management business that summer as a fresh faced twenty year old, I was only really fussed about getting some cash before heading back to university. I didn't realise that the experience would be so transformative and shape my beliefs about work and life. For the first time, I truly understood the power and value of people working together, as one team.

Seeing the outcomes of collaboration made it abundantly clear to me that organisations rely on people. I realised that one person alone rarely keeps an organisation afloat. The vast majority of businesses depend on teams. They are the source of delivery. They are the ones who make things happen.

For teams to be effective, they need the right environment to work in. I imagine you have ideas about what a good environment looks like, and hopefully haven't experienced too many bad ones. Creating the right atmosphere can be a challenge.

Organisations are not always equipped to create space for teams to thrive; they are often set in their ways, and can struggle to change. However, with the right conditions and support, teams can be set up for success.

That's where Delivery Management comes in.

This book will introduce you to the approaches, practices, and skills required to enable teams, and help them to uncover ways of working that support their ability to make amazing things happen.

If the teams you work with aren't quite hitting their stride, and delivering value still feels like a distant aspiration, then Delivery Management can help.

WHY THIS MATTERS

In my time as a Delivery Manager, I experienced exciting moments with teams where we did impactful work that made a real difference in people's lives. I built strong relationships with colleagues whom I still speak with almost every day even though we no longer work together. It is an incredibly rewarding role that enables you to foster strong bonds with people and contribute to teams that are tackling significant challenges.

This was more true than ever during the pandemic. Dropped into a new team working on the impossible, or at least the improbable, the service was award-winning but built on a foundation of sand. There were layers of unnecessary technology strapped together with the digital equivalent of elastic bands. Nonetheless, it was a key part of national infrastructure, designed to ensure you only need to report a death once to the government. It was our job to fix it.

Admin is a headache at the best of times, but when someone you love has died, admin is the last thing on your mind. This service mattered, but we didn't know at the time how much more it would matter as the number of cases continued to climb. Each day brought new pressure, delivering change while collectively processing the enormity of everything happening around us.

We met twice a day remotely, and collaborated in the hours between. There were levels of complexity we had never experienced before, and our context was a less than delicious cocktail of difficult technology, volumes of dependencies, and intense organisational pressure. But we all played our part. I shielded the team from noise to ensure we had a clear run at success, helping us to find time for humour and optimism in challenging times. We refined our forecast, defined our goals, and delivered value.

We worked as an ensemble to tackle the biggest challenges. All of us were dedicated to non-stop collaboration as a single unit. The new solid foundation we had built was working for us, but we needed to get it in the hands of real users. As we pushed the product into the outside world for the first time, an expectant mix of anxiety and joy washed over me. Until finally, we had our first user.

We were successful.

On the first day we had two hundred users. Each day the numbers continued to climb, and I was elated to have enabled our team to improve such a vital service. Something so many people had said was impossible to do. The elation lasted until I had a sobering realisation: each new user meant someone had lost a person they loved.

One year later, a Delivery Manager I was working with experienced a death in their family. They took some time away from work. I didn't expect to see them ask on Twitter whether anyone knew who had worked on a service that let them report a death to the government. "I just want to say that you have done really, really good work that helps people at a really horrible time."

That is the real power of teams in action. Creating products that improve other people's lives. I cannot think of better evidence to show you how rewarding it feels to support a team to do something impactful. That is the opportunity that every Delivery Manager has.

As a leader of other Delivery Managers, I have grown to understand the breadth of this discipline, and also the chances that exist to help others explore what it means to be a Delivery Manager.

While working as Head of Delivery, I got to see the discipline from many different perspectives, working closely with people who had a broad range of experience and plenty of views on what it means to deliver value. I saw first hand the vibrant passion that many Delivery Managers have for the teams they support and the work that they do, alongside a consistent willingness to help others learn and develop.

Sometimes, Delivery Management can be a challenging career path to pursue because of the fact that it is poorly understood by many people and lacks a universal definition. A singular interpretation of the discipline might undermine the flexible and adaptable approach that Delivery Managers have to employ, but it can cause a lot of stress when you are speaking cross purposes with someone about your role or the things that you are responsible for.

This frustrating experience is especially common because almost everything an organisation does relates to delivering value in one form or another, so Delivery Managers are at risk of being held to account for it all. I am determined to bring a new level of clarity to this space to ensure that other people don't have to relive those types of conversations as many times as I have done.

There are several common misconceptions about Delivery Management. One of these is that it is the same as Project Management or Service Delivery Management. While there are some similarities between these disciplines, there are also several key differences that we will explore. This book will help you to understand how each is distinct.

We will also consider the misconception that Delivery Management involves managing people. This is not the case, as it supports self-organising teams that can ultimately manage themselves. It is aligned with empowerment rather than command-and-control behaviours.

Delivery Management can be found in organisations around the world. The discipline has been growing in popularity over the last ten years as a prominent component of product teams across the public and private sector.

Its adoption has been aided by acknowledgement from influential people such as Marty Cagan. In his book *Inspired*, he explores why many teams fail and how successful product teams work. One aspect of this is a suggestion to embrace Delivery Management as a way to ensure success, especially by reducing the burden of impediment removal.

The discipline is most commonly applied by Delivery Managers, although you might also encounter an equivalent role found in many teams; Delivery Lead. Some organisations expect people in related roles, such as Product Managers, to be proficient in Delivery Management, but this can limit their ability to be effective.

Many people with experience of working alongside product teams wonder how Delivery Management is connected to accountabilities such as Scrum Master or Agile Coach. We will consider how they are related, although there are some obvious distinctions; specifically a lack of alignment to a singular methodology or framework, including Scrum.

Delivery Management is all about enabling teams to deliver value, whether that is through achieving shared goals or meeting business outcomes. It is considered to be a vital role in many organisations, and there are some essential skills you will need to be familiar with if you're going to be successful.

This book will provide a valuable resource to gain knowledge about Delivery Management and as a conversation starter to share ideas with others, from exploring coaching approaches, to applying new ways of working.

Above all, it will enable you to enable others.

WHO THIS BOOK IS FOR

In Oslo, 1944, a dutiful civil servant is preparing for another meeting. This would be his third of the day, and little progress had been made in each committee session thus far.

Somehow, targets were being missed on a regular basis, and pressure was mounting. The Reichskommissar himself had expressed dissatisfaction with the seeming incompetence of the bureaucrats around him. Of course, he was equally mindful of how this would impact his reputation in Berlin.

As the meeting began, the civil servant took a seat among fifteen other colleagues. A long set of introductions were the precursor to any valuable conversation.

Finally, they could begin. Someone started working through the minutes of the last session. All was going well until they reached line seven: "Rural production capacity and exports." A decision from the week prior about how many potatoes were being shipped each month was drawn into question.

After a long, rambling speech about the efficacy of shipping in barrels rather than crates, and exporting over land versus sea, a new agenda item was created. Nobody quite understood how Anders Nilsen had connected his family's holiday home to the potato trade, but it had obviously been an important aspect of his argument.

The session progressed in a similar fashion. Maybe this was just plain old bureaucracy at work. Every word was picked apart, and every topic was open to further consideration. Not a single conclusion was reached, or decision made.

Quite remarkably, nobody considered how many civil servants sitting around the table were actually members of another group: Milorg, the Norwegian resistance movement.

Their anti-Nazi views made them the perfect citizen saboteurs. However, their method of sowing chaos would not involve breaking machinery, or brandishing guns; their weapon of choice was purposeful stupidity.

This approach was defined in the top-secret Simple Sabotage Field Manual, created by the American Office of Strategic Services, the body that would lay the ground for the Central Intelligence Agency, or as you might know it, the CIA.

The manual set out a set of simple instructions to cause maximum disruption through dysfunction. Working slowly, complaining frequently, and giving promotions to the worst employees were all recommended practices.

Of course, it's unlikely that many contemporary organisations have been infiltrated by citizen saboteurs, but organisational dysfunction can be an effective form of sabotage nonetheless. It can limit the flow of work and stop teams from achieving valuable outcomes.

For many of us, the clever approaches employed by these civil servants might bring a smile, followed by the uncomfortable realisation that we are working in companies afflicted by the same chaos carefully orchestrated by the allies during World War II.

Have you ever found yourself feeling restricted by dysfunction? Maybe you've experienced mismanagement? Do you believe that there must be a better way? If so, this book is for you.

Delivery Management contains a multitude of concepts that increase clarity, reduce disorder, and support effectiveness. Ultimately resolving dysfunction to increase the likelihood of value delivery.

This resource has been created to help people apply Delivery Management effectively, and one aspect of that is to help others understand what this discipline involves. In my experience, the more that people understand something, the easier it becomes to make a meaningful contribution and crack on with what you need to do.

This book exists to support people who apply Delivery Management, including aspiring and current Delivery Managers. It's also for people who work alongside them, whether you are a team member, manager, or colleague from anywhere across an organisation. If you aren't yet applying it to your work, I would urge you to look at life through the lens of someone who is going to do so while you're reading, and get a taste of what it involves.

If you are an experienced Delivery Manager, you might not agree with everything you encounter in this book, and that is a good thing. It is not designed to be a prescriptive immutable framework or to provide a methodology, but it should help you to gain clarity about the discipline, even if that clarity emerges in opposition to the ideas I am sharing.

As you read further you will find that there are some topics where you might be left wanting more. However, this book will act as a guide to enable you to discover enough ideas and content to further your learning. It is my goal that the ideas I focus on and amplify provide direction for where to go next in your Delivery Management journey.

Because this book is designed to be read by a wide range of people with different levels of experience in Delivery Management it provides a broad overview of the discipline. Every circumstance and situation is different, so there will never be a single source of truth for precisely how it should be applied, or how to be a Delivery Manager.

Your application of these ideas and others, built from your experiences and knowledge, are essential. Delivery Management is underpinned by the unique skills you possess. However, to help you on your way, the inclusion of various tools, tactics, and techniques should prove to be valuable in the process of enabling teams to deliver value.

HOW TO READ THIS BOOK

We are going to start our journey into Delivery Management with some of the basics. How is it defined? What does it involve? What skills does it require? After this, we're going to explore some of the accountabilities that it incorporates, including coaching and leadership, alongside the ways that it directly enables the delivery of value.

Once we're on solid ground with a foundational understanding of the discipline, we will start to consider the people, approaches, and systems it can be applied alongside and the contexts where enablement can have the most impact. If that wasn't enough, we will also think about what a career in Delivery Management might look like, including preparation to land your first role or progress your career.

If you're new to Delivery Management, I suggest reading the first two chapters of the book that introduce the discipline and its core skills in order to get a broad overview before you consider skipping ahead to any areas of interest. You should find plenty of thoughts to expand upon, whether the ideas that you generate take the form of post-it notes you keep for yourself or blog posts you share with a wider community.

If you're an experienced Delivery Manager, I would recommend that to get the most out of this book, you read it in a similar way to how you might approach working with a team. Start with an open, non-judgemental mindset and work through the text. Consider the various ideas on offer, using your own relevant experience to interpret and build on the content at hand.

Before we dive into the content you're waiting for, I want to say thank you for choosing to read this book about Delivery Management; whether you picked it yourself or were given a copy. As you read further, you will be able to explore what Delivery Management involves from many different angles, uncovering useful insights along the way.

I have seen first-hand the magic that happens when teams are given the environment, culture, and resources to be effective. Delivery Management plays a key role in making that happen. My ambition is that more people will be given the opportunity to help teams find that same magic, and I hope you get to experience it for yourself if you haven't yet. Enjoy the book.

CHAPTER 1
INTRODUCING DELIVERY MANAGEMENT

It's Thursday. It's the middle of July, I'm in Manchester and it's sweaty. A proper summer day. Rocking up to a shiny new office building gleaming in the sunshine. Full of opportunity. I'm wearing my midnight blue suit and my lucky tie. The one littered with yellow origami birds. I'm ready.

Stepping through the revolving glass door, I'm hit with a wave of refreshing, cool air. I'm hoping it might help to dry the beads of sweat that are gathering on my forehead. I pretend it's just the summer heat, and not the nervous energy I feel right down to my toes. That feeling of blurriness, nausea, excitement. We all know how important a single conversation can be. How life changing. I was hoping this would be one of those days. I'm ready. Suited and booted for my first Delivery Manager job interview.

If only I really knew what a Delivery Manager was.

Scouring Google, hunting Glass Door for tips, watching YouTube videos and trying to unpick what exactly I'm applying for. I can't be completely sure if the role will be what I'm after, but I know I'm ready for change.

Two hours later. I'm back outside. My tie is a little looser, but its luck remains intact. Fortunately for me, my beliefs about enabling others, willingness to get stuck into challenging work, and instant enthusiasm for putting post-it notes on the walls culminated in an exciting job offer, a new adventure, and an open door for learning and opportunity.

Still, I can't help wondering how much easier that interview might have been if I had a clear picture of what to expect.

Delivery Management is a term that's been used in the technology industry for many years. But what does it mean, exactly? If you ask ten different people to define Delivery Management, you'll get ten different answers. How can a role or a discipline that doesn't have a fixed definition be effective? How have Delivery Managers been able to consistently enable and support teams to deliver value in a sustainable way without a universal definition?

In this chapter, we're going to examine some of the important concepts that define Delivery Management. If you're working in this arena, it always helps to have an understanding of what others might expect from you, and what the role should entail. That's especially true if you're reading this while putting on your lucky tie or waiting in the foyer of an office building with tall glass doors before your first Delivery Manager interview.

DEFINITIONS

Emily Webber, the former Head of Agile Delivery for the Government Digital Service, wrote in 2016 what is now a well-known blog post throughout the British Delivery Management community, that has often been referenced as a valuable starting point when attempting to define the Delivery Manager role.

This definition aligns closely with how the discipline has been adopted across the United Kingdom public sector, but, as a result, it is not all encompassing.

It has helped to shape my understanding of Delivery Management, and provided a foundation for creating my own definition that we will explore later in this chapter.

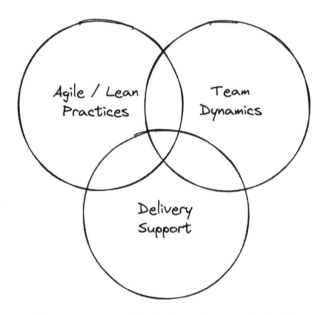

Figure 1.1: Aspects of the Delivery Manager role adapted from Emily Webber

While Emily herself has acknowledged that the definition she created is imperfect, it is a great place to begin. In the blog post, Emily frames Delivery Management as the role of a servant leader, who keeps pace with the introduction of relevant agile and lean tools and techniques, and removes obstacles and blockers that might get in the way of delivery.

She breaks down the role of a Delivery Manager into three

areas: Agile and lean practices, team health and happiness, and delivery support. (Figure 1.1)

Agile and lean practices - You are responsible for ensuring that the team is applying agile and lean practices. Agile is an iterative approach to delivery, and lean is an approach to creating value while minimising waste. You work with the team to make sure that they're constantly improving and that they're delivering value to their colleagues, customers, and users; the people who are affected by the work.

Team health and happiness - You are responsible for creating a positive working environment for the team. This includes making sure that the team has everything they need to be productive, that they're properly trained, and that they have the resources they need.

Delivery support - You are responsible for making sure that the team has everything they need to do their job. This includes supporting activities such as requirement gathering, financial tracking, risk management, and release planning. However, Emily suggests that if this work takes you away from the first two areas of responsibility it can be supported by another person, inside or outside of the team, highlighting agile and lean practices and team health and happiness as a Delivery Manager's primary areas of concern.

While functional information about Delivery Management existed in the United Kingdom public sector prior to Emily Webber's blog post, this definition has been celebrated as an easier to understand explanation of the role, extending beyond the basic United Kingdom government definition which states that a Delivery Manager is accountable for the performance of the team. The accessibility of Emily's definition has made it easier to offer people who have never heard of Delivery Management a basic understanding of what it involves.

In a subsequent 2021 blog post by Emily Webber about progression frameworks for multi-disciplinary organisations, she redefined Delivery Managers as people who enable teams to have a consistent, smooth pace of delivery. This alternative definition is not aligned to particular approaches such as agile and lean, and alludes to a broader perspective on delivery that does not depend on any specific ways of working.

This short definition accommodates the variety of circumstances you might end up working in as a Delivery Manager, whether that is delivering a product from inception to retirement, or ensuring a team is able to reliably support a service. There is also scope in this definition to include times when you might be responsible for enabling other delivery professionals, or liaising with colleagues, customers, and users to ensure that their needs are met.

One negative aspect of this shorter definition is that delivery is not explicitly aligned with value. As a result, it would technically be possible for you to adopt this definition without enabling valuable outcomes to be achieved. For example, if you supported a team of copywriters to type letters at a consistent, smooth pace, then you would be aligned with the role, regardless of whether the letters formed recognisable words in any form of legible sentence structure.

Emily Webber's definitions both have merit, and her blog post describing the aspects of the Delivery Manager role has been hugely helpful to countless people working in the United Kingdom public sector. Based upon my first hand experience of seeing these definitions being discussed, they have offered a valuable resource to share with others, especially during challenging conversations, due to their clarity and simplicity.

However, these definitions raise consistent questions with people working outside of a public sector context. The first definition is often seen as a reinterpreted variant of the Scrum Master accountability, or being too similar to the role of an Agile Coach. We will expand on these ideas in chapters two and seven to consider how Scrum Mastery and Agile Coaching are aligned with Delivery Management, but also what makes it a unique discipline.

An alternative definition of Delivery Management that approaches the discipline from a different context can be found in Marty Cagan's book *Inspired* and in his posts on the Silicon Valley Product Group blog. As an established product leader with over twenty years of experience with well known companies including eBay, Hewlett-Packard, and AOL, Marty is well placed to offer a definition of Delivery Management that reflects how it has been applied in leading technology companies.

Marty frames Delivery Management as a special type of Project Management that incorporates a mission to serve the team by removing obstacles, also known as impediments. He suggests that these impediments could involve other teams, including functions that are not aligned with products. As a result, Delivery Management might include liaising with people in marketing to get something approved, or working with another Delivery Manager to prioritise a key dependency, alongside dealing with multiple other comparable roadblocks.

Delivery Management is defined as being all about helping teams to get stuff live faster, not through domineering or autocratic behaviours, but by removing obstacles that get in the way. This could include adopting the accountability of a Scrum Master, but Marty is clear in his blog that in his view the role is not about discovery, or coaching on process; it's all about getting stuff pushed live. He suggests that if for any reason people might give up on having someone dedicated to chasing down and removing impediments, Delivery Management could help to turn things around.

While I support the majority of what Marty Cagan suggests about Delivery Management, my personal feeling is that presenting the discipline as a flavour of Project Management creates the risk of undermining the role due to the expectation that traditional Project Management accountabilities will still exist.

Many of these traditional accountabilities, such as task allocation and timeline management, are incompatible with the aspects of Delivery Management that enable value delivery to be accelerated and impediments to be removed. This is potentially less of a concern in high performing technology organisations where traditional cultural approaches, dominated by inflexible bureaucracy, are less likely to be seen or expected.

A NEW DEFINITION

My own definition of Delivery Management began to truly emerge when I started to coach and mentor other Delivery Managers. Hearing their experiences and understanding where my perspective of Delivery Management was more narrow than I realised helped me to capture broader universal truths and refine my understanding of the discipline.

Building on the work that Emily Webber and Marty Cagan have done to shape and define Delivery Management provided me with fertile soil to have rich conversations with other Delivery Managers. My experience as Head of Delivery, working closely with a delivery community of practice in a public sector organisation going through significant change, offered me a full spectrum of views on what Delivery Management is and isn't.

Overall, I believe that Delivery Management is about enablement above anything else. It enables teams to deliver value. I realised that teams might be able to deliver value without me there, but their chances of achieving their goals were much higher with my involvement. There are three aspects of enablement that I have consistently seen in action. (Figure 1.2)

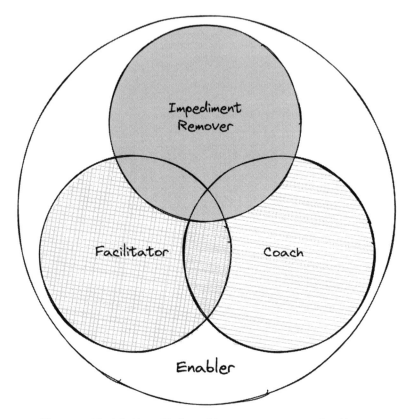

Figure 1.2: My definition of Delivery Management as aspects of enablement

Removing impediments - Although I didn't always realise it at the time, the vast majority of my effort as a Delivery Manager was invested in removing impediments. These were blockers that the team could not remove for themselves, and even as I became a manager of other Delivery Managers, I invested the bulk of my time in ensuring teams could get on with the job of delivering value without anything getting in their way.

Facilitating - One of the most rewarding aspects of Delivery Management for me has always been facilitation. Spending time with groups of people and teams in order to make decisions and define a course of action can be exciting and challenging. The satisfaction of enabling people to overcome the challenges of complex and complicated work through engaging and open practices is an essential aspect of the discipline, and, for many, it is one of the joys of this role.

Coaching - While this aspect of enablement became more prominent as I progressed in my career as a Delivery Manager, coaching skills were still essential when working at a team level. Supporting others to adopt new approaches, and maximise their potential, while advocating for self-organisation and self-management are fundamental to Delivery Management.

The balance of these aspects of enablement is not always equal. There were times when I found that I was doing almost nothing but removing impediments with a small amount of time spent on facilitation and coaching. However, my experience of Delivery Management showed me that I needed to invest in all three of these areas otherwise my ability to be flexible and adaptable in a variety of scenarios would begin to suffer. For example, when I did not invest in my ability to adopt a coaching stance, I could easily revert to telling people what to do rather than enabling the team to be autonomous.

Delivery Management is fundamentally about enablement; however, this definition has been shaped by my experiences, so there will be organisations where this picture does not align perfectly. There are also a number of contributing factors that will impact the application of this definition. Let's explore them a bit further.

COMPLEXITY

Ambiguity exists everywhere, but in order to process the world around us, we all seek simplification. We constantly make subconscious choices about our perception of reality in order to exist, often foregoing complexity to generate a coherent image of existence.

Simplification is a dominant mental model because acknowledging the true complexity of the world is uncomfortable and difficult. However, our filtered interpretation of reality can cause a number of problems; we ignore ambiguity.

The Cynefin framework, created by Dave Snowden, is a tool that can help people acknowledge ambiguity and respond effectively to the situation they are in. (Figure 1.3) It introduces five domains:

- Clear
- Complicated
- Complex
- Chaotic
- Disordered

Our bias towards simplicity leads us to believe that much of the world fits into the clear domain, where cause and effect are obvious. For instance, opening a door; if the door does not open, we can presume it is locked and respond accordingly. However, very few things actually exist in this obvious place, especially in the world of work and teams.

The majority of situations sit between the complicated and

complex domains, where cause and effect can be understood with analysis and the application of expertise, or it can only be understood retrospectively due to the unknowable. Fixing a computer is complicated; it requires expertise, but with sufficient analysis it is predictable. Working with people is complex; it is not fully knowable or predictable. People are ambiguous.

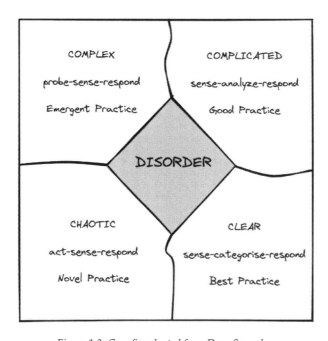

Figure 1.3: Cynefin adapted from Dave Snowden

Jonathan Smart, author of *Sooner Safer Happier*, suggests "Organisations are heterogeneous, not homogeneous. Organisations are emergent, not predictive. Organisations are complex adaptive systems." You can never be entirely certain of the cause and effect that will occur with people, and teams, in an organisation, and over time these variables will continue to change.

One of the key reasons why Delivery Management is difficult is because of this inherent organisational complexity. People are the essential ingredient; without people there are no teams, and with no teams there is no value delivery. People are fundamentally complex; they operate in an organic system of interactions and decisions that is constantly shifting.

As such, all teams work in a complex environment, often undertaking complicated and complex work. They are operating with a significant volume of unknown information. For instance, this might include the implementation of software that the team has never used before or working with a group of users that they are unfamiliar with.

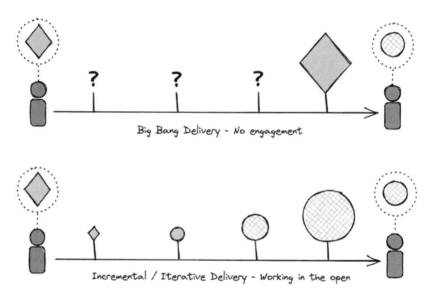

Figure 1.4: Incremental / Iterative delivery adapted from Henrik Kniberg

When so much information is unknown, many factors can change over time. It is impossible to predict everything that will happen. Iterative and incremental ways of working can help the team to deal with uncertainty by inspecting their situation and adapting to change. (Figure 1.4) Delivery Management enables teams to adopt this approach in order to deliver value even in the face of complexity.

Incremental delivery breaks work down into parts rather than delivering one large thing that might or might not be valuable once it is delivered. Iterative delivery uses a sequence of activity to accumulate outcomes that deliver value. By combining both approaches, it is possible to deliver smaller outcomes on a regular basis that gradually accumulate over time to result in the delivery of something larger and more valuable.

These ways of working are in contrast to some traditional approaches that define a set of requirements up front and allocate a set of tasks to individuals to complete over a fixed period of time. When that window of time has expired, the individuals inspect their combined output and see whether they have completed the work that was defined at the outset of the time period, with the expectation that it will still deliver value.

For a lot of people, adopting an approach that lets them continuously inspect the work they are doing and make decisions based on what they find rather than being tied to a fixed plan feels like common sense. In complex environments, taking small steps towards an outcome, while gathering frequent insights, reduces risk by ensuring that the work undertaken will deliver value.

When I worked in traditional teams before I became a Delivery Manager, I would advocate for evidence-based decision making and was baffled when someone senior would leap in and suggest we couldn't change course because it wasn't on the plan. Why would we deliver something that we knew wasn't what our customers wanted? In my experience, there is nothing quite so disheartening as creating something over the course of months or years that nobody wants and delivers no value.

During my time as a Delivery Manager, it was amazing to see teams testing their assumptions and getting something into the hands of users as soon as possible so that we could actually see whether we were heading in the right direction. Iterative and incremental ways of working reduce impediments by making work visible, and by encouraging frequent inspection and adaptation.

Effective ways of working amplify the impact of Delivery Management, while ineffective ways of working diminish it. Strengthening this foundation is essential. Coaching teams to adopt ways of working that support the overall delivery of value, and facilitating their application, are key aspects of Delivery Management.

Delivery Management positions ways of working as a deciding factor in whether a positive working environment will exist for the team. Without this environment, a team will be less likely to deliver value. A negative working environment can present complex impediments to delivery including team conflict, a lack of transparency, siloed working, and other challenges, each of which we will explore in later chapters.

The adoption of effective ways of working enables a culture of trust and collaboration. This culture helps teams to overcome any issues that might limit value delivery. As a result, the volume of internal team impediments is likely to be reduced, and effort can be increased in the reduction of blockers that extend beyond the self-organisation of the team.

Because Delivery Management is focussed on enabling the delivery of value, it is important to understand the variety of factors that can cause obstructions that might prevent the team from working effectively. Enabling work to flow in a sustainable manner is a helpful way to frame many intentions behind Delivery Management.

REMOVING IMPEDIMENTS

Marty Cagan's definition of Delivery Management amplifies the importance of removing impediments. If a team is being coached to improve internally, and their ways of working are being supported through effective facilitation, it is still possible for them to be completely blocked in their ability to deliver value.

Delivery Management is distinct from pure coaching disciplines that do not have a level of responsibility for outcomes. It retains a level of ownership for challenges that a team is facing. As a Delivery Manager, I still had skin in the game; I had a level of responsibility for the team's effectiveness.

Impediments can take many forms. If something blocks or restricts the team from achieving valuable outcomes, then it can be considered an impediment. Delivery Management enables these roadblocks to be made visible and removed.

Examples of impediments can include a lack of specific skills in the team, cross-team dependencies, pressure from management, or even indecision within the team. However, if the team can resolve an issue without intervention, or if the impediment is not impacting the delivery of value, these blockers should not be the focus of Delivery Management efforts.

I would suggest that roughly 80% of my time was consistently spent on removing impediments of one variety or another, while the remaining 20% of my time was invested in coaching and facilitation. However, I believe that this distribution aligns with the Pareto principle.

The Pareto principle was developed by Joseph M. Juran in the context of quality control and improvement. It states that for many outcomes, around 80% of consequences arise from 20% of causes. The principle was named after Italian economist Vilfredo

Pareto, who demonstrated that 80% of land in Italy was owned by 20% of the population.

As a Delivery Manager, the 20% of my time spent on coaching and facilitation led to 80% of the valuable outcomes I was involved in. In contrast, the more significant amount of time I spent on identifying and removing impediments only had a direct impact on 20% of the value realised by the teams I supported. (Figure 1.5) Removing impediments requires a large investment of time and effort, and the results are not always guaranteed. However, without Delivery Management that investment would need to be made by the wider team.

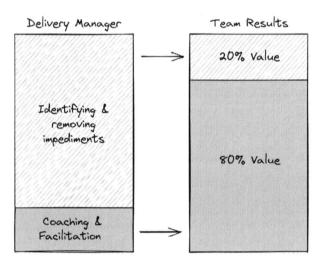

Figure 1.5: Pareto Principle of Delivery Management enablement

Impediments can be significant and complex. Effective Delivery Management requires flexible and adaptable approaches that enable the removal of dependencies in a broad range of scenarios. This can sometimes involve asking for forgiveness rather than permission in order to minimise the time and effort invested in removing or reducing a blocker.

It is highly unlikely that a team will ever work with zero impediments, but if the team can self-manage effectively, they may not need a specific individual person fulfilling this role. Coaching and facilitation can enable the team to mature to a point where they are able to remove blockers independently.

However, reducing the cognitive load that would otherwise be placed upon a team to identify and reduce impediments is a key benefit of Delivery Management. No team should ever be worse for having someone who is committed to enabling the team to deliver value.

POSITION IN THE TEAM

Delivery Management provides a form of leadership that works in service to the team and the wider organisation. Servant leadership is a non-traditional leadership approach that leverages practices and behaviours focussed on the well-being of those being served. Each of the enabling aspects of Delivery Management contribute to servant leadership.

The term 'servant leader' originates from Robert K. Greenleaf's 1970 essay *The Servant as Leader*. In this, he describes an individual who is naturally inclined to serve and makes a conscious choice to aspire to lead. Servant leaders increase and enhance personal involvement and teamwork, distributing decision-making across an engaged environment where power is not concentrated in one person's hands.

This aligns with the enabling aspects of Delivery Management. The discipline is not aligned with autocratic leadership styles, or dictatorial management. Instead, Delivery Management is centred upon advocacy for self-organisation. The team should be able to manage their own work and operate in any way that results in value delivery.

If the team is stuck, Delivery Management advocates for supporting the team to uncover their own solutions and better ways of working. If there is no route forward, then there is an opportunity for intervention in order to remove impediments, but this does not include adopting an authoritarian stance inside the team to drive change.

Delivery Management incorporates the removal of obstacles that limit or restrict the team, but this is ultimately an aspect of enabling the team to pursue self-sufficiency. While this task might never be complete, Delivery Management is aligned with a focussed effort to ensure teams work effectively to deliver value at a sustainable pace without outside imposition.

Servant leadership does not mean undertaking every activity for the team, even when they are blocked. Attempting to do so creates risk as it can result in the creation of new impediments or dependencies. Effective Delivery Management mitigates the creation of bottlenecks, as such it does not advocate absolute ownership of activities within the team.

Over-reliance on individuals is an impediment for many teams; as such, Delivery Management advocates sharing knowledge beyond competency-based boundaries resulting in cross-functionality, and the ability to leverage skills across different disciplines.

Sometimes, leadership is perceived as being a singular role within a team. However, servant leadership within a Delivery Management context aligns more closely with the principles of a leader-leader culture rather than a leader-follower culture, as described by L. David Marquet in his book *Turn the Ship Around*.

A leader-leader culture reflects an environment of trust, safety, openness, and feedback where everyone within the team has a level of ownership. This does not remove specific responsibilities that individuals might have within the team, but it does enable collaboration in pursuit of shared outcomes.

Being a leader who serves does not mean being the only leader in a team, and definitely does not mean saying yes to everything people might ask for. Delivery Management enables and encourages others to realise their full potential.

Delivery Management is not team management. Instead, it involves managing the environment and context around the team. This can include supporting the team to adopt new practices such as feedback loops or information radiators, facilitating workshops or meetings to enable engagement, influencing the creation of a standard operating environment with all of the tools and technologies the team requires, or removing blockers that are affecting effectiveness, each of which are ideas we will explore further in later chapters.

Training is an aspect of Delivery Management aligned with coaching. However, this does not include training or coaching others in disciplines that are not aligned with Delivery Management. For example, Delivery Management does not incorporate training someone in how to apply a programming language. However, these types of training requirements could constitute an impediment that needs to be removed.

Ensuring that people have what they need is fundamental to the enabling function of Delivery Management, including pathways to learn new skills. This enablement can also extend to supporting the physical environment of the team, including hardware or home office equipment if this would otherwise create an impediment.

Delivery Management does not substitute the role of a Manager for the individuals on the team. Managers are ultimately responsible for ensuring that people are fully supported and properly trained, and therefore they are often the escalation point for specific impediments.

Managers should ensure that everyone in the organisation has the tools they need to be successful. This should include training in the company's policies and procedures, as well as supporting their development. There is also an expectation of Managers to provide support to individuals if they have issues that extend beyond the responsibilities of the team such as illness or a change in circumstances. By providing this support, Managers ensure that individuals are able to be effective at work.

This highlights that Delivery Management does not remove the need for additional supporting functions within an organisation. Access to mentoring and coaching outside of the team context are fundamental to an organisation's long term success. Delivery Management forms part of an organisational ecosystem that is intertwined with other functions and roles. Working with people across the entire business is an essential element of enabling teams to deliver value.

COACHING

Can we have a chat? Four words that have struck fear into my heart on more than one occasion. From a simple query about something mundane, to news of a tragic event, this open question can be the precursor to a broad range of conversations. In this instance, I had a feeling what the chat might be about.

I'd noticed a few things that weren't quite right in the team and the disconnect between a few individuals was starting to become visible. Frustrations were boiling over in retrospectives. Unhealthy conflict was increasing each day. Fortunately, no punches had been thrown yet.

I trusted the team, but it was unclear how much they trusted each other. Maybe this conversation with Tom, one of the Engineers, would paint a picture for me.

I listened carefully. "We're being told what to do each week. We don't need to be assigned tasks by a Product Manager that doesn't know what they're on about. This isn't working for me." I could feel his frustration. "You're the Delivery Manager, what are you going to do to fix this?"

This was an important moment. His question provoked all sorts of ideas in my head. I could have a word with the Product Manager, maybe I could mediate a conversation between everyone. Before I could open my mouth and start solutionising, the silence that was hanging in the air while my brain whirred was filled. "I'm sorry mate, it's a bit harsh to put all the pressure on you to fix this. I'm really stressed at the moment and hate working on this product alongside all the other stuff I'm expected to handle."

The silence had created space for the conversation to open up. After another pause, I asked "What do you think we should do?" I could see that Tom was struggling with this situation, but I had faith that the best solution would come from him navigating his own way through this challenge.

An hour passed quickly, and after listening intently while peppering our conversation with a few more questions, we reached a point where I asked "What's the first action you're going to take?" With assured confidence, Tom shared a plan that he had full ownership of. The plan would increase trust in the team and reduce the pressure on everyone to manage an unsustainable workload.

I was an enabler of his ideas, but I didn't fix these problems for him. It was rewarding to see a member of the team open up and share how they were feeling, but it was twice as fulfilling to witness Tom's determination and resilience to improve every-one's circumstances. You never know where a chat might lead, but it's always worth saying yes to one.

Coaching is only one aspect of Delivery Management, but it can prove to be an incredibly powerful method of enablement. Effective coaching can be an enabler for the removal of impedi-ments and create a context where facilitation can be more productive. It supports the emergence of new and better ways of working and can support the catalysation of change. It is fair to say that coaching is one of the most impactful elements of Delivery Management.

Coaching plays an important role in helping to create an environment with high levels of trust where team members feel safe to experiment and take risks. This helps the team to be more agile, enabling them to rapidly pivot towards effective decisions. As a result, they are able to become more proficient in delivering value to customers, colleagues, and users. Coaching supports teams to become psychologically safe.

Psychological safety is a term used to describe a mutual level of trust that leads to a belief that it is safe to take interpersonal risks. This means that team members feel safe to share and implement their ideas without fear of judgement or punishment. It creates a level of understanding that puts people at ease and creates an environment where people feel comfortable when working together.

This does not mean that everything will always be easy or that everyone will always agree, but it does mean that people have trust in each other to provide support, listen to ideas, and attempt to maintain a healthy environment for everyone's bene-fit. Creating a psychologically safe environment is one of the most important things that Delivery Management enables within teams. It is a theme that is woven throughout many of the concepts we will explore in later chapters.

Improving circumstances for the team also involves working beyond the team boundary. Delivery Management includes coaching and educating the wider organisation on effective ways of working. By doing this, it is possible to build the environment needed for the team to be successful.

Organisational coaching can involve engaging with senior Managers regarding alternative management styles, as well as educating people on values and principles that can support teams to deliver value. Without this engagement, new ways of working might not be able to flourish within the organisation.

Coaching the wider organisation can be challenging and requires courage, especially as Delivery Management does not always align organically with the traditional hierarchy of many organisations.

In many ways, it is fair to consider Delivery Management as a transitional discipline. When Delivery Management enables people to adopt new ways of working and align around the delivery of value, the team might be in a position where a specific enabling role is no longer needed.

Just as not every person who exercises needs a personal trainer, not every team needs Delivery Management, and some just might not be ready for it. However, if there is space for improvement in a team or organisation, then having an enabling advocate is unlikely to be a bad thing.

Delivery Management should enable teams to be self-sufficient. It is not designed to create dependencies. Effective Delivery Management should leave the door open for a team to stand on their own and deliver value without needing a designated enabler.

VALUE

Delivery Management enables people to work together and deliver what others need, including customers, users, and colleagues. This means that Delivery Management does not incorporate everything that makes it possible to deliver value, but it does help others to be effective and productive.

Rather than focussing on outputs such as features or items, the intent of Delivery Management is to enable teams to achieve valuable outcomes. Value can be defined in many different ways: it could mean delivering something that meets a user need, reducing support costs for users, saving the organisation money or time, or it could simply mean improving someone's experience when using a product.

When organisations are not focussed on value, it can be easy to prioritise output rather than outcomes, resulting in teams building features that do not solve problems for users. This approach to delivery can be described as a feature factory due to the parallels between traditional factories and this mode of operation in teams.

Factory workers assemble features without considering their broader contribution to a product. The team is focussed on churning through work rather than delivering value. Feature factories can also prioritise the pace of work to generate increased output. This can lead to a situation where the team is not able to focus on the quality of their work, and they may end up releasing things that are defective or unreliable.

As a result, teams are not able to consistently deliver value. Delivery Management helps to prevent this from happening by coaching the team to focus on the quality rather than the quantity of their work. (Figure 1.6) It is better to deliver the right thing at a slower pace than the wrong thing quickly.

It is important to acknowledge that without output it is impossible to achieve outcomes. If nothing is created then there is no value. Delivery Management enables sustainable, consistent delivery in order to ensure that there is sufficient output to realise valuable outcomes.

Facilitation plays a key role in helping teams to discover where the investment of their effort will have the most significant impact. Delivery Management provides an approach to support conversations and exploration of potential opportunities by encouraging the engagement of an entire team in pursuit of a strong, validated selection of ideas for what to do next.

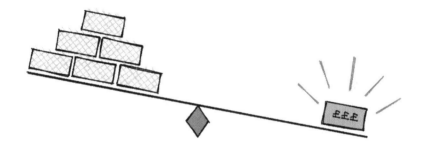

Figure 1.6: Deliver quality over quantity adapted from Henrik Kniberg

RELATED DISCIPLINES

Helping a team to consider what they plan to deliver and when they might work on it is reminiscent of Project Management, but it is worth emphasising that Delivery Management and Project Management are not the same.

Project Management has existed as a distinct discipline since the 1950s, and it has been instrumental in countless significant organisational accomplishments over time. It requires the alignment of context specific details with the application of planning, processes, people, and power.

Project Management involves taking sole ownership of team coordination in order to deliver something. This includes adopting responsibility for planning how others will deliver the scope that has been defined, as well as liaising with other groups of people, including colleagues, to make sure that everyone gets what they need from the project. A 2020 study published by the Association for Project Management found that people management and stakeholder engagement were considered to be the most important skills for project professionals to develop.

In contrast, Delivery Management does not involve adopting sole ownership of a team. Collective team enablement is the primary function of Delivery Management in order to support the team to deliver value. It enables everyone to understand what they require to be successful, and decide how they want to collaborate to achieve valuable outcomes.

Delivery Management highlights that the team is ultimately responsible for their work, and therefore, they should own the choices that they make when planning or executing delivery. This does not involve any individual owning how or when things should be completed; the team decides as a whole.

While Delivery Management might leverage some valuable elements of the traditional Project Management skill set, it is focussed on enabling teams to achieve outcomes regardless of whether this happens within the boundary of work that is normally limited by time or scope, more commonly known as a project.

Delivery Management is focussed on the team rather than a project, and enables others to deliver value regardless of how the team structures their work.

In his Silicon Valley Product Group blog post about Delivery

Management, Marty Cagan reflects on why Project Management is struggling in so many organisations. He reflects that the Project Management "brand" is potentially damaged beyond repair. Unfortunately, for many people Project Management has become associated with a host of negative connotations, such as inflexibility, micromanagement, and a lack of technical expertise.

Marty shares that Project Management is often seen as the root of many problems within companies, and as a result, some have gotten rid of the Project Manager role altogether. While this may seem like a drastic measure, sometimes organisations feel that it is the only way to improve performance within a team.

By removing Project Management, organisations believe that they can eliminate the source of many conflicts and allow team members to work more cohesively. However, Marty notes that distributing Project Management responsibilities elsewhere can cause even bigger problems.

As organisations increasingly shift their focus towards the delivery of products that are not limited by time and scope in the ways that traditional projects have been, it can be challenging to position Project Managers effectively. I believe they still have an important role to play in organisations. However, they are likely to be most effective working outside of teams, aggregating information, and enabling coordination between different business functions where a traditional skill set can be applied in a productive and positive way.

Delivery Management is an effective way to bridge the gaps that a transition away from traditional Project Management might leave behind, without reducing the capability of teams to self-organise and make autonomous decisions about their work in order to maximise the value they deliver. Delivery Management is especially effective at minimising the likelihood of a clash between the perspective that a traditional Project Manager might have, compared to the approach of a product team leveraging agile or lean ways of working.

Although Project Managers might require a shift in mindset and perspective in order to adopt Delivery Management approaches, there are many ways for Project Managers in transition to gain relevant experience. The aim of this is to support them to demonstrate their abilities as effective team and organisational enablers that are able to remove impediments, provide facilitation, and offer coaching.

In many organisations that apply information technology service management (ITSM) approaches, Project Managers that deliver IT or digitally aligned projects will step away from a product once it has reached a fixed point of completion aligned with time or scope. The product might then be handed to a Service Delivery Manager who will manage the activity of a team to sustain it.

Although both titles are similar, Service Delivery Management is distinct from Delivery Management. Delivery Management does not involve managing a service or the team itself. Instead, it is focussed on supporting the team to develop their own approaches that will result in the continuous improvement of products.

Technical Programme Management is another Project Management adjacent discipline. A Technical Programme Manager is responsible for every aspect of a technical programme's success. A programme can be understood as a defined business objective comprising multiple projects. Technical Programme Management establishes what work will be completed when, by whom and what resources are required.

Because programmes have broader scope than projects, Technical Programme Management is a more extensive discipline with broader responsibilities for scoping work and ensuring quality checks have been performed. They have a responsibility for prioritising business and technical needs as part of every programme so need to have sufficient knowledge of both technical and business domains.

Delivery Management at a more senior level, working across multiple teams, can align with some of the responsibilities that are found within Technical Programme Management. However, Delivery Management is focussed on enabling others rather than directing them. Equally, Delivery Management does not always require deep technical or business knowledge as other roles within the team are more likely to accommodate this such as Tech Leads and Product Managers that we will consider in chapter six.

Delivery Management is frequently compared with Engineering Management due to the team enablement function of both disciplines. However, they are distinct from each other due to Engineering Management involving a blend of people management, project management, and technical capability.

Engineering Management includes the curation and enablement of diverse teams, bringing together people with appropriate skill sets in order to achieve outcomes or deliver projects. It can support the discovery, design, and delivery of products within teams, but also frequently incorporates a broad selection of oversight activities to ensure teams operate within scope and budget.

While it is an enabling discipline, it predominantly focuses on planning, coordination, and the application of technical practices, while adopting a supervisory approach across individual or multiple teams. This contrasts with Delivery Management which does not take ownership of these activities, or managerial accountabilities.

Although Engineering Management is often aligned with the

management of projects, it can play a role in product teams applying incremental and iterative ways of working. Effective application of the discipline includes team coaching and facilitation, so there are times where it will overlap with Delivery Management from an enablement perspective, sometimes being complementary when applied in unison.

From an organisational perspective, it is essential that people are comfortable with the distinctions between these disciplines, and their associated roles. Words matter, and it is important to create clarity. If an organisation believes that traditional Project Management will be the most appropriate approach for their environment, then they should hire Project Managers. It is always best to align job titles with the discipline that someone will be expected to apply.

CONCLUSION

Delivery Management is a unique discipline and role that does not need a singular definition to be valuable. While working as a Delivery Manager, various definitions were more applicable at different times in my career, and each offered alternative perspectives on how the discipline could be applied. The understanding of Delivery Management that I developed over time is that it is fundamentally about enablement.

Although a universal definition has never been required for Delivery Management to be effective, my perspective on the discipline as an enabling capability helped me to form my own definition. This has given me the opportunity to communicate about my own experience of the role and the wider set of accountabilities I have adopted, while also leveraging this definition as a tool to have deeper and more meaningful conversations with other Delivery Managers, and people interested in what the role entails.

Through the removal of impediments, facilitation, and coaching, Delivery Management enables teams to deliver value. It is not about managing teams or dictating how things should be done. Delivery Management supports people so that they can find new and better ways of working, while ensuring an environment exists that enables a sustainable approach to achieving valuable outcomes.

There are a whole host of skills that can enable you to make a positive contribution to teams, many of which we are yet to explore. As a result of these skills and a broader Delivery Management approach, you can help an organisation to deliver outcomes more effectively and improve experiences for colleagues, users, and customers through the impact of your efforts.

Questions for reflection:
○ What are the three aspects of enablement?
○ What value does Delivery Management offer?
○ How can Delivery Management enable teams?
○ How can Delivery Management impact an organisation?
○ How are Project Management and Delivery Management distinct?

CHAPTER 2
THE DELIVERY MANAGEMENT TOOLBOX

You've done it. After months of dedication, weeks of focus, and hours of invested effort, you've finally achieved your goal. You've actually done it. How good does that feel?

Excited, relieved, triumphant. This was the feeling I had when I achieved a certification I had been working towards for a long time. Professional Scrum Master III.

At the time, there were less than one thousand people around the world who could say that about themselves. Congratulations poured in on LinkedIn when I uploaded the certificate. Satisfying. What a feeling, I had done it, I had reached my target.

But when I went back to work the next week, nothing had changed. A few people reached out to say congratulations. The study group I had helped pull together were pleased for me and were keen to see what tips I had for the exam. Nothing really changed. I had a nice new badge on my LinkedIn profile, but beyond that my knowledge and abilities were the same as the week before.

I had managed to reach the pinnacle of Scrum Master certification, but the Sprint Planning I helped to facilitate that morning ran the same as before. The calls with colleagues that I attended were still focussed on our progress towards the same outcomes. The team trusted each other to the same extent.

My fancy new badge didn't suddenly have people begging for my time, or hoping I would join their team. I was the same Delivery Manager as the week before.

Although some new Scrum aligned super powers might have been nice, deep down I knew nothing would change when I got that certificate. It wasn't the badge that mattered. It was the months of dedication, the weeks of focus, and the hours of invested effort. That was what enabled me to support the team.

The learning journey I had been on taught me about facilitation, conflict resolution, removing impediments, teaching, mentoring, coaching, and how best to apply these skills in a real organisation. But it was only when they were applied with actual teams that I truly gained knowledge, and understood I could adopt and adapt skills that would enable the people around me to deliver value.

Over time, I have refined these skills, and studied them from multiple different perspectives. There isn't one approach to rule them all when it comes to being a Delivery Manager.

This certificate was just another rung on an endless ladder of learning, and I still had a long way to climb. Fortunately, that means I have the opportunity to set new goals continuously, and as a result, I still get those moments where I hear "You've done it!"

At this point, you should have a good sense of how to define Delivery Management, but you might be wondering what your approach should look like, and what skills you should be learning. How can you facilitate communication, remove obstacles, coach individuals and teams, and work to enable others? What tools do you need in your toolbox?

When you apply Delivery Management, you are accepting a mission to support people to work together so that they can deliver value sustainably. You are like a coach for a football team. People could get on the pitch and kick the ball without a coach's involvement, but their support should be something that makes it easier for the team to be effective.

While you might not be the person putting the ball in the back of the net, you are still an integral part of the team's success. People achieve more because of you.

It is essential to have a broad array of skills that allow you to support people in the most appropriate way. Someone wouldn't coach rugby players in the same way as cricketers, and the swimming team don't want to apply exactly the same training methods as equestrians. Every team and circumstance is different, so you need to be flexible and adaptable in order to support people fully.

Not all Delivery Managers carry the same tools in their toolbox, everyone will have their own unique twist on how to approach challenges, so don't forget to consider what works best for you. This chapter will explore some of the most valuable skills that will enable you to apply Delivery Management.

CRITICAL THINKING

There are an assortment of skills possessed by the vast majority of knowledge workers that enable them to engage with complicated ideas, solve problems, and deliver value in complex environments. These skills fall under the banner of critical thinking, and they are essential to Delivery Management.

Even a relatively simple task such as inspecting the environment around the team, and considering whether it is enabling or limiting, requires critical thinking skills such as inference, analysis, identification, and curiosity. Critical thinking lays the groundwork for facilitation, coaching, and impediment removal.

Developing critical thinking skills also results in the cultivation of a rich resource of information that you are able to share with others. If you can analyse challenges and understand limiting factors, while retaining an open approach to working with others, you have the opportunity to distribute this information and engage a wider audience. This generates transparency.

A Spanish study in 2021 indicated that people who are disposed towards critical thinking demonstrated higher levels of openness, with greater levels of acceptance towards diversity and challenge. Cultivating openness makes it easier for everyone to feel included, regardless of their role in an organisation. This openness helps to build trust and psychological safety.

Openness and transparency are foundational aspects of an environment that enables teams. They are essential because they ensure that people know what is happening with ease at all times, both inside and outside of the team.

Transparency helps to highlight progress, as well as making impediments and dependencies visible that might slow down a team. We will explore facilitation and communication skills that will help you to create transparency.

Skills that encourage openness and transparency are vital for effective Delivery Management. Critical thinking abilities underpin both of these skill sets. This will also assist you with understanding when it might be most appropriate to apply the other skills we will discuss in this chapter.

It is also valuable to apply these same skills in relation to your own capability in order to assess your level of competency. You should always be open and transparent with a team about the skills you bring to the table, and where you might not be the person they need to work with in order to resolve a specific challenge.

AGILE COACHING

The intersection between Agile Coaching and Delivery Management is substantial, and it provides a helpful resource for uncovering specific skills that can support you to be effective, especially in relation to the coaching and facilitation aspects of Delivery Management.

Agile Coaching helps organisations, teams, and individuals to adopt agile approaches. While it can also be applied in order to enable teams to deliver value, it is distinct from Delivery Management, especially as Agile Coaching lacks an explicit competency related to the removal of impediments.

The Agile Coaching Competency Framework created by the Agile Coaching Institute outlines eight core competencies for Agile Coaching, all of which can prove to be valuable in different contexts. (Figure 2.1)

Each of the eight competencies of the framework is relevant to Delivery Management to varying degrees. For example, the quadrant related to mastery is more likely to be applicable if you are working in a complex domain or supporting change across an organisation, while facilitation is a fundamental aspect of Delivery Management.

The extent to which you choose to apply the Agile Coaching Competency Framework as a complementary artefact to support Delivery Management is likely to correlate with the scope of influence or the level of responsibility you have. This is a concept we will explore further in chapter ten in relation to progression.

In my experience, when I supported teams to deliver value in environments with greater complexity due to factors including large scale dependencies and challenging colleagues, I applied more aspects of the framework. Business and transformation mastery were especially relevant as they enabled me to coach the wider organisation to experiment with new ways of working. As a result, I could enable multiple teams and remove impediments on a larger scale.

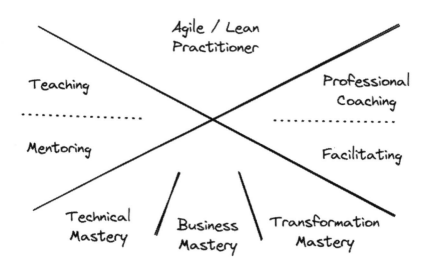

Figure 2.1: The Agile Coach Competency Framework adapted from Lyssa
Adkins and Michael Spayd

AGILE AND LEAN PRACTITIONER

The framework starts with the competency of being an agile and lean practitioner. This supports each of the aspects of enablement within Delivery Management due to the various tools, techniques, and approaches that agile and lean practices offer to support removing impediments, facilitation, and coaching.

Agile and lean are different approaches to the delivery of value that are aligned in many ways. Agile is a people-focussed, iterative approach to work that is applied in order to achieve strategic goals. Lean is the application of a focus on continuous improvement while working to increase trust in the people that do the work.

A good starting point to learn about agility is the *Manifesto for Agile Software Development*. This document emerged in 2001 when a group of seventeen people met to discuss the future of software development and the challenges presented by existing ways of working. In only sixty-eight words, this group made a significant contribution to the way that countless people now work.

The manifesto states: "We are uncovering better ways of developing software by doing it and helping others do it. Through this work we have come to value:

- Individuals and interactions over processes and tools.
- Working software over comprehensive documentation.
- Customer collaboration over contract negotiation.
- Responding to change over following a plan.

That is, while there is value in the items on the right, we value the items on the left more."

The agile manifesto reconciled the views of people involved in defining multiple frameworks including Scrum, Extreme Programming, and Crystal Clear. However, the manifesto is only a starting point to consider how you might best adopt an agile mindset and consider the people-focussed values that were integral to the manifesto's creation.

By applying the principles of the agile manifesto and aspects of the various frameworks curated by the group of manifesto creators, you will uncover many different approaches towards enablement, including plenty of techniques and methods. Experimenting with these approaches will help you to develop a broader set of skills aligned with agile and lean practices.

Some of the core skills include being adaptable and flexible to change, challenging things that might obstruct a team, putting people at the heart of everything you do, tackling risks up front, working collaboratively, and helping others to prioritise value and outcomes over deliverables and output. We will consider how to apply these approaches in more detail in chapter seven.

These skills can be valuable in many different contexts, but it is important to recognise that agile and lean practices extend beyond frameworks or methodologies. These practices suggest that your mindset and values also have a substantial impact on your ability to remove impediments, coach, and facilitate.

PROFESSIONAL COACHING

Agile Coaching includes professional coaching as one of its competencies. This is a distinct set of skills that are more specific than a broader coaching approach. It is helpful to recognise the differences between these approaches.

Professional coaching is sometimes recognised by people as what they might label leadership coaching or business coaching. It does not require direct experience of the domain that a person or team is working in. Instead, professional coaching applies three key skills to unlock people's potential; active listening, asking powerful questions, and self-awareness. Skills that we will consider in more depth in chapter four.

The coaching aspect of Delivery Management is not specifically aligned with professional coaching and reflects a broader coaching approach that includes other Agile Coaching competencies such as teaching and mentoring alongside the application of elements of the mastery quadrant. However, professional coaching still provides a valuable enabling skill set that can be leveraged in many contexts.

Developing professional coaching skills allows you to partner with people in a creative way that enables them to discover and fulfil their personal and professional potential. Professional coaching requires you to focus on individuals as a whole, creating the space for them to consider how their professional and personal lives intersect. This relates to the idea that people's underlying potential is intrinsically linked to their entire integrated self, where their thoughts and feelings are not segregated by their context.

Learning about professional coaching, and the skills professional coaches apply with their clients, can enable you to make a valuable contribution to the team that does not provide all the answers. Instead, you are able to use these skills to help the team discover answers and solutions for themselves.

If you want to apply professional coaching skills with individuals or teams, you should be transparent about what you would like to offer and seek their support before proceeding. It is essential not to leverage professional coaching approaches without consent, especially as some people might not want to engage with you in this way.

FACILITATION

Facilitation has a consistent definition in relation to Delivery Management and Agile Coaching. It can be described as the practice of facilitating others to understand and achieve their goals through collaboration. Facilitation increases the effectiveness of communication throughout the team.

Facilitation is an important skill set that reflects your role in the team as a leader who serves. You aren't there to make decisions for the team or be the boss. As a neutral process holder, you are in a position to guide the team through the use of activities or workshops that help them arrive at their own solutions. Facilitation skills can be applied in a variety of circumstances, from small group conversations to workshops across an entire organisation.

You are not bringing content to the table in a facilitation role. Instead, you are focussed on providing a structure that enables the team to reach conclusions independently. Much like professional coaching, facilitation is a set of skills that are reliant upon impartiality. You should contribute unprejudiced opportunities for others to develop their own thoughts and ideas.

Facilitation and professional coaching both rely upon practice and consent, so seeking opportunities to refine these skills with people who are willing to help you learn is a good idea. Facilitation is often aligned with agile and lean ways of working, so your skills as an agile and lean practitioner might blend with your abilities as a facilitator.

MENTORING AND TEACHING

Mentoring and teaching are two competencies that incorporate a variety of skills that can be valuable for you to develop. Both of these competencies are aligned with the coaching aspect of Delivery Management, but they can also play a key role in supporting the removal of impediments. This is especially true if the team or wider organisation lacks knowledge in a domain that you have expertise in.

While both of these competencies relate to your knowledge and perspective, teaching is about instruction or showing someone how to do something while mentoring is about relaying your own experiences to help someone else grow and learn as a result of hearing from you.

Both of these competencies rely upon a similar set of skills including listening, encouragement, goal setting, empathy, patience, story telling, and adaptability. However, teaching includes additional skills such as being able to instruct others, while mentoring is not about providing direction.

It is important to only contribute mentoring or teaching to a team when they agree that it might be valuable. Nobody likes people who preach about best practice or constantly force information upon others, it should always be optional, otherwise you are not taking a people-focussed approach.

Opportunities to develop mentoring skills can start with a regular conversation that opens the door to sharing your perspective. Teaching skills can be more challenging to develop as you don't want to assert a power dynamic on relationships or act in a patronising way. Offering knowledge that you would like to share in the context of open sessions that anyone can attend or during team workshops can be a great way to develop your skills as a trainer or teacher.

MASTERY

The final Agile Coaching competencies are aligned with mastery. Technical mastery, transformation mastery, or business mastery. Technical mastery generally relates to technical expertise, especially from hands-on experience in a role such as Engineer or Architect. Transformation mastery aligns with expertise as an organisational change catalyst, enabling businesses to adopt new approaches and evolve. Business mastery refers to expertise in the domain of customer focussed innovation and value-driven product creation.

The skills that are aligned with mastery will be specific to your experiences of each domain, and will be skills that you have cultivated while developing your expertise. An example of this could be financial planning skills aligned with business mastery that you have developed from working across different business functions in the past or learning from experienced practitioners.

These competencies can support you to remove impediments. Knowledge related to their corresponding domains will assist you in understanding the causes of blockers. However, your level of experience will have an impact on your ability to apply mastery in any of these areas. This is also something to be mindful of in relation to the coaching aspect of Delivery Management, as a lack of mastery can restrict your ability to coach, except for the application of professional coaching.

Generally, it is not expected that you will be a master in all three of these domains, or that you will be able to apply all three competencies equally. However, having skills aligned with any of these areas can be incredibly helpful. For example, I have a higher level of proficiency in relation to transformation and business, while my technical knowledge is not at a level of mastery. Nonetheless, the technical knowledge I do have has helped me to be effective when working with different types of teams, so it has been worth investing effort in.

There is a difference between technical skills and technological skills, so do not devalue a technical skill set that you might have even if it is not technological; for instance, experience as a Business Analyst might enable you to have more detailed conversations with the team or the wider organisation and apply specific tools and techniques that require expertise in order to understand additional levels of detail.

Skills aligned with mastery might enable you to support a team to adopt new ways of working or help them to get buy-in from people outside of the team. Mastery in some of these areas is also likely to overlap with the competencies of other people in the team. As a result, you might find opportunities to support team members with specific aspects of their role. We will consider the roles that are likely to be in the teams you support in chapter six.

COMMUNICATION

A common thread throughout the Agile Coaching competencies, without being explicitly noted, is communication, it is a fundamental set of skills that supports the application of each of the competencies. This is relevant to Delivery Management, as each of the aspects of enablement are almost impossible to apply without effective communication skills.

Communication can take many forms. Not all communication is verbal, in fact research by Albert Mehrabian suggested that as little as 7% of communication stems from the words we use. Understanding the various facets of communication is an important element of fully realising these skills. Learning about body-language, tone of voice, and vocal cues can all help you to express your own thoughts more clearly, and understand others with greater accuracy.

However, it is equally important to be an effective communicator through other mediums such as email or instant message. Being able to leverage modern communication platforms is a reality of the modern workplace, so it is worth examining and refining your written communication skills to make them as effective as possible. Consider whether you can be succinct, clear, and purposeful in writing.

Communication unlocks enablement. If you can't interact with other people, there is no way for you to apply Delivery Management. For example, it is highly likely that if you attempt to remove an impediment without engaging with anyone else, you will either waste time and effort, create a new impediment, or cause the team to operate as if the impediment still exists.

Although impediments will be specific to the context you are working in, communication is often the best tool you will have to remove them. Blockers can vary as a result of the products or service the team is delivering, the organisation you are working in, or sometimes as a consequence of your approach to Delivery Management, but a conversation with the right person is often the key to unblocking the delivery of value.

You need to ensure that your communication skills are not limited to a single audience. If you can only facilitate sessions with one exclusive group of people, then you are less likely to be able to enable diverse cross-functional teams to deliver value, or to have the capability to engage with people across the entire organisation.

Teams will include people from different backgrounds, with a variety of skills and knowledge. When working with a cross-functional, multidisciplinary team, you need to be able to facilitate communication throughout the team in order to help everyone to understand each other and collaborate effectively.

If you want to enable others to adopt new ways of working, you must be able to articulate different approaches to delivering value. For instance, being able to explain the implications of iterative and incremental delivery in contrast to approaches where nothing is delivered for weeks, months, or even years will enable you to coach or teach more effectively.

It can be challenging for teams to work together, but you can play an important role in enabling this to occur. For this reason, being able to recognise and understand the different viewpoints of team members is a valuable skill.

Understanding others will enable you to more readily support the resolution of unhealthy conflict that might arise and cause impediments. This does not mean shutting down conversation, or delaying conflict. Your focus should be on creating a safe space where people are able to express themselves fully in a constructive manner.

When working with a multidisciplinary team, it is important to encourage different perspectives. This means that you need to be able to create opportunities for people to share their ideas, something that is often supported through coaching and facilitation. Developing trust and psychological safety within a team helps this to be an easier process, but it requires constant effort to nurture an environment of openness.

You should develop skills that make sharing easier. This can span from applying simple facilitation techniques, such as icebreakers, to more specific communication tools like Liberating Structures; a selection of over thirty facilitation methods created by Henri Lipmanowicz and Keith McCandless.

Some foundational skills that will benefit anyone hoping to create a more open environment include active listening, being present and mindful during conversation, self-reflection, and empathy.

One skill that reflects the ability to be open and honest is candour. The book *Radical Candor* by Kim Scott outlines how to apply candour to generate trust and innovation. It highlights the importance of being direct and honest without being offensive. *Radical Candor* also celebrates collaboration as the route to effective problem solving rather than dictatorial leadership styles.

Working with people who have different skills and knowledge also means it is important for you to be able to communicate effectively with both technical and non-technical audiences. This means that you will need to invest effort in understanding jargon, as well as being able to explain things in a way that is easy to understand. You have the opportunity to remove impediments by working as a translator across different organisational boundaries that might impact the team.

The language that you use can bring clarity to delivery. Words can be interpreted in different ways, so you should apply the skill of using language that is clear and unambiguous. If you are introducing concepts to the team, it is essential to ensure that they understand what you mean, rather than simply leading them to adopt new words. Language adoption is meaningless if it does not substantiate real change.

Asking questions and searching for information is the simplest way to acquire the knowledge you need to be an effective communicator in different contexts. When you leverage communication, you can help everyone to develop a common understanding of the work they are doing and the environment they are working in. A lot of organisations don't realise how many assumptions exist in their teams due to people not feeling able to ask questions and make information visible.

Communication does not stop inside of the team. You are well placed to be able to advocate for the team with colleagues, including senior managers. You are in a position where you can understand the work that is being done around you, and you can explain the value that this is delivering, while potentially having time and capacity to invest in relationships across the organisation.

As a result, you can also help to solve problems, remove impediments, and reduce conflict between the team and colleagues. This might mean providing reassurance to a colleague, or bringing new information and clarity back into the team. You can help to ensure that everyone is working towards the same, well understood, goal and that the team is able to deliver value that aligns with the reasonable expectations of others.

DELIVERY SUPPORT

The impediment removing aspect of Delivery Management can have broad implications on the activities you might need to undertake. If the team has dependencies or blockers related to business capabilities, then you might have to provide support. This aligns with the delivery support function described in Emily Webber's Delivery Management definition and the business mastery Agile Coaching competency. However, these skills are not specific to Delivery Management.

You should not be responsible for this type of work by default. It can introduce an admin overhead which can be detrimental to the team, even when it involves lightweight commercial or financial activity. If it stops you from being able to enable the team effectively, it can be considered a problem in and of itself.

You might not have all of the skills required to support these activities, so it is entirely valid to seek support outside of the team, and possibly move responsibility away from the team. This is especially true if you are doing something that you feel is not adding value. You should consider whether you have an opportunity to influence people to adopt different ways of working or communicate why certain activities might be more appropriate for someone else to undertake.

In some environments, you might be responsible for

ensuring that commercial management activity for a team is carried out effectively. Without this type of assurance, the team are at risk of commercial agreements, including contracts, becoming an impediment. The skills required for this type of work include negotiation, attention to detail, coordination, numeracy, decisiveness, and organisation.

It can be useful to be able to relay commercial decisions to colleagues, especially for the benefit of the team, and ensure that contracts are adhered to. You might also be able to help with ensuring that colleagues get regular updates on work where commercial factors are involved if this prevents the team from being disrupted or interfered with.

Some organisations might expect you to be able to support the team to understand the financial impact of the work they are doing. To do this, it is helpful to have skills that enable you to understand budgets, identify potential financial risks, analyse data, and report on financial information. The financial implications of the team's work can have a direct impact on the products the team delivers, so this is an area that a Product Manager is likely to have ownership of. We will consider the role of the Product Manager in the team in chapter six.

Financial management activities can reduce impediments that might arise as a result of poor budgeting or a lack of understanding around why certain activities need to be prioritised from a financial perspective. This is especially true if you are working in a team that is dependent upon partner organisations or contractors to support the delivery of elements of a product.

Having skills that enable you to support the team with business capabilities, such as the creation and management of budgets, can ensure that they are able to focus on delivering value. It is key that this activity does not happen in isolation and is shared openly across the team.

Limiting the flow of information can damage trust and psychological safety, although it is equally essential that you don't bombard everyone with so much information that they become overwhelmed. Make information open and accessible, but don't force it upon anyone in the team.

If at any point you are asked to provide delivery support that you are not comfortable with, then it is essential that you highlight this with the team or with relevant colleagues. Business mastery can be an enabler of effective Delivery Management but it is not a fundamental aspect of the discipline. As such, it is important that you feel confident in the tasks you are undertaking rather than creating unnecessary risks or impediments by struggling to do something specialised and complex like financial analysis.

PLANNING

Stretching out before us, the roadmap of doom. Parallel coloured boxes stretching beyond the virtual horizon line. Scroll far enough and supposedly the plan had an end date. Not one that I ever saw.

Milestones stacked upon milestones. Interwoven dependencies tracked in red lines knitted the plan together into a digital fabric of dependencies and assumptions.

This plan was on everyone's minds. colleagues asked if everything was on track to meet the deadlines three years from now. Teams anxiously adjusted delivery dates. I couldn't stop thinking how much time we were wasting every time we tweaked an intricate detail on this map of the unknown.

A best guess might be putting a finger in the air, but this was like jumping out of a plane with no parachute to declare which way the wind would blow next week. This mammoth plan. This monolith. Unless we had some secret oracle hidden in the stationary cupboard, I couldn't see it going anywhere.

The battle raged on over the roadmap. Teams would make an autonomous decision and be reprimanded at their weekly planning forum. "This wasn't on the plan, what are you doing?"

People were dedicated to the comfort blanket that had been stitched together with guesswork and a fine layer of bullshit. Assurance was the word used to describe the roadmap. Nonsense was the word teams whispered in defiance.

Finally, a team struck out. Their Product Manager bravely declared "We're only going to capture what we know, everything else creates too much risk." I could see their team nod in agreement. This didn't go down well with management. Private meetings and passive aggressive emails circulated.

But the team stood firm. They would only capture the known, albeit including the known unknown. The assumptions and best guesses on their segment of the roadmap gained question marks. They removed milestones and added open ended goals.

Then something amazing happened. In a board meeting with the big boss a question arose "Why is this section different?" After some explanation, three words would change everything: "That makes sense." The clarity and certainty of depicting facts had the Chief Operating Officer sold. Admittedly he had plenty of questions, but he said "I finally feel like someone's being honest with me."

My role in this rebellion was only a small simple act. I dared to question the roadmap, I was eager to ask why we were doing this, and what it meant. Once teams knew there was no answer beyond "It's what we've always done." their own spark of resistance grew. It didn't take long for the roadmap of doom to unravel. Fortunately honesty, transparency, and openness took its place.

Creating detailed predictive plans and timelines is an expectation that has been placed on me many times in the past, however this has occurred most commonly when people have made inaccurate assumptions about my role, such as believing that Delivery Management involves the same accountabilities as traditional Project Management.

In the world of Delivery Management, planning and forecasting is a team activity rather than an individual one. No single person is in charge. You are not there to manage the team, define scope, or direct people. Although ownership of artefacts such as roadmaps or backlogs usually rests with one key person in the team, most commonly a Product Manager, this does not remove collective responsibility for their creation.

A clear vision and common goals can help to ensure that the team is always working towards something that is collectively understood while keeping everyone engaged around shared ideas. You can leverage communication and facilitation skills, such as asking open questions and visualising people's thoughts, to help others to understand what they are trying to achieve.

Defining a vision and establishing goals can provide the flexibility that fixed plans often lack, while still enabling the team to create clarity around their work. A defined vision and goals provide direction, and support the ability of the team to forecast their work.

In many teams, you can provide direct support to a Product Manager who has a level of responsibility for providing direction in relation to what the team will deliver, and why. Although the process of defining a vision and goals should always be collaborative and involve the whole team, it can be beneficial to work closely with a Product Manager to help them increase alignment.

Although you are not directly accountable for planning and forecasting, it is essential that you can enable the team to self-organise and think about how they will deliver value. Most skills related to shaping a vision and goals are best learned by working closely with experienced leaders and Product oriented colleagues, alongside studying agile and lean practices. Developing this skill set will enable you to provide a greater level of support to others, especially Product Managers.

There is an important distinction to be drawn between the skills required to create a fixed plan that everyone is forced to follow, compared with facilitating a collaborative creative process of ideation and prioritisation that offers context to the work that the team think will achieve valuable outcomes. You should invest your effort in the latter.

It is key to remember that plans can often be taken as promises. As such, it can be valuable to provide coaching, teaching, and mentoring to help teams to understand this and avoid overcommitting themselves. Being open and honest about assumptions or the unknown is a valuable communication skill that can benefit the whole team if they are at risk of overcommitment.

As time progresses and the team gains a clearer picture of how their goals, vision, and forecasts might have to change and adapt, you will have the opportunity to apply skills such as reflection, analysis, and evaluation to support them with shaping and clarifying their ongoing direction of travel.

By leveraging the ability to ask open questions and consider the bigger picture, you can help the team to remain aligned with the wider organisation. If you can communicate how this perspective is incorporated into the way that they forecast and define their work, you can also reassure senior colleagues who might not be used to teams working in this way.

ADVOCATING CHANGE

Sometimes, you hear a story and it sticks in your head. This is one of those tales that I can't stop thinking about.

I still remember the first time I watched the film *Catfish*, and its depiction of internet-era deception. However, the reason that I can recall it so clearly isn't due to the mysterious journey the main character Nev embarks on. It's because of a short segment about how fish are shipped across America. Maybe you're not instantly hooked on that narrative proposition, but stick with me.

It turns out that the story originates from a pastor named Chuck Swindoll. Many years ago he noted that codfish suppliers had created a big commercial business in the northeastern United States, but shipping them much further than their east coast origin posed a problem.

At first, fishmongers froze the cod, packed them in ice, and shipped them. But, the freezing process took away any flavour from the delicate meat. Frozen fish clearly wasn't the way forward, so they experimented with shipping them alive, in tanks of seawater. That proved even worse. Once cooked, the fish became bland textureless mush.

Finally, someone had a creative idea. Why not try putting them in the same tank as their natural predator, the catfish? When the cod arrived at the market, they were as fresh as when they were first brought out of the ocean. There was no loss of flavour, and they remained firm and flakey. Some people even argued that they tasted better for the journey.

It's fair to say that every organisation has a few catfish in their tank. But whether we know it or not, they keep all the cod from getting soft and tasteless. Chuck explained that it's important not to resent the catfish in our lives as intruders while the chase continues. It's the tension in the tank that keeps everyone swimming.

Sometimes you might need to be the catfish. People might not love you for advocating a non-static state when swimming in a tank of still water, but, without some pressure to move, the end result of a long journey can easily deliver zero value and leave a bad taste in the mouth. Truly enabling others requires movement and change.

For modern organisations, change is often the only certainty. Technology has enabled information and ideas to move at a more rapid pace than ever before. However, some people will prefer to continue working in the ways they are most familiar with, even if they no longer deliver value. You can apply Delivery Management to enable teams to be flexible and adaptable to accommodate this modern reality.

Being an advocate for change requires courage. It can be a challenge for many people, and often creates a sense of discomfort. This is why it is important to have a blend of skills that support the change process. Critical thinking can help you to recognise opportunities for change, while coaching and facilitation will support the process.

You should develop skills that let you rapidly understand the challenges of different environments, and help teams to implement suitable and sustainable change. Finding people who are receptive to experimentation and have an open mindset across the organisation can lay the foundations for change before there is broader cultural acceptance.

The world around us is unpredictable. As a result, the team's work is likely to shift as the understanding of what they are delivering evolves. Constant change often means it is easy to make decisions that appear wrong in hindsight, so it is important to help others accept that they won't always get everything right. Being able to learn rapidly in order to adapt is more important than being correct the first time around.

Communication, coaching, and facilitation skills can help the team to reflect on their work, and develop a blameless environment where learning and growth is more important than pointing fingers. Welcoming conversation inside the team, asking questions, objectivity, and creating time to observe are all useful skills that support reflection. This can also enable the team to identify areas for improvement without waiting for external feedback.

You should never force changes onto a team. In the words of Jonathan Smart, author of *Sooner Safer Happier* "Surviving and thriving is not mandatory." If the team isn't receptive to change, you still need to be able to help them to understand why different approaches might be beneficial; sometimes change is the only way to remove an impediment. Developing influential communication skills can help to foster a culture where people are comfortable exploring new ideas and feel safe trying something different.

Finding ways to adapt to the challenges of a team with a fixed mindset is an essential skill. You can let people know that you are ready and waiting to coach, support, and guide if they decide to explore new practices or methods, but until that point you are happy to focus on facilitation and impediment removal. This ensures that you avoid driving change through command-and-control.

It is essential that your approach is flexible and adaptable. You can use self-reflection to ensure that you are able to accept constant change and develop skills that are versatile. This should mean that the way you work is not fixed, and you can adjust to different contexts. You should develop skills that enable you to suggest different approaches that suit the specific needs of the people you support. Sometimes, you will get it wrong, not all of your ideas will work, and that is okay.

CONCLUSION

There are a multitude of skills that can help you to apply Delivery Management effectively. These skills will always vary depending on the context that you are working in. Sometimes, you will have the perfect tool for the job, but that doesn't mean it is the only way to get the job done.

Investing time and effort in filling your toolbox with skills that you can use with confidence, while keeping an open mind to new approaches, is the best way to support the people around you to deliver value.

By building on a foundational framework such as the Agile Coaching competencies, you have the opportunity to develop new skills that directly impact your ability to enable teams, whether you are removing impediments, coaching, or facilitating.

If you are able to combine these skills with effective communication and an adaptable approach to work, then you are sure to be equipped to face any challenge that teams and organisations might throw in your direction.

Many of your skills will overlap with those of people in other roles, such as Product Managers. This commonality will help you to be a more effective enabler when applied in combination with your skills as a coach, facilitator, and impediment remover.

I was once told that the Delivery Management skill set you

bring to the table is a bit like baking a cake. There are some common ingredients that it would be wise to use; empathy, curiosity, communication, but there are also unique flavours you might choose to incorporate; public speaking, drawing, writing. It's up to you to define the recipe.

Whether you think about your skills as a book of recipes or a Delivery Management toolbox, you should be generous with them. Truly enabling others includes distributing knowledge and leveraging the skills at your disposal to support others to become self-sufficient and capable.

You should aim to discover and leverage whichever skills enable teams to be effective. Don't worry if your approach to removing impediments is unique, or your facilitation style is quirky. What matters is whether it works for the people you support. If you are enabling them to deliver value, then you're doing the right thing.

Questions for reflection:
○ Which Delivery Management skills are most important?
○ How can you develop Delivery Management skills?
○ Which Delivery Management skills do you already have?
○ How does Agile Coaching relate to Delivery Management?
○ Are there specific skills that support different aspects of enablement?

CHAPTER 3
A LEADER WHO SERVES

"One will weave the canvas; another will fell a tree by the light of his axe. Yet another will forge nails, and there will be others who observe the stars to learn how to navigate. And yet all will be as one. Building a boat isn't about weaving canvas, forging nails, or reading the sky. It's about giving a shared taste for the sea, by the light of which you will see nothing contradictory but rather a community of love."

These words by Antoine de Saint-Exupéry, translated from his 1948 book *Citadelle*, are believed to be the origin of a paraphrased quote that is frequently attributed to the author: "If you want to build a ship, don't drum up the men to gather wood, divide the work, and give orders. Instead, teach them to yearn for the vast and endless sea."

The original quote espouses the natural desire that individuals discover when they collaborate in pursuit of shared goals, while the modern adaptation adopts the perspective of a leader, guiding people towards the ocean.

Both perspectives reflect the magnitude of what teams can

achieve. Conquering the unknown, venturing into the expanse. But they do not attribute success to the way work is managed, or the dominance of a single person.

Purpose is what guides them; a collective longing for the sea. The leader is there to help them discover this purpose, and serve others in the process. Building a boat is the output, feeling the freedom of salt spray and rolling waves is the outcome.

Leaders with a servant leadership approach are in high demand. A study by the MIT Sloan School of Management found that when employees were asked what type of leader they would prefer, nearly two-thirds said they wanted a "servant" versus a "traditional" leader. But what does servant leadership really mean? What makes it distinct? And how can you apply this approach every day while enabling teams?

In this chapter, we will explore your role as a leader who serves the team. This will include consideration of different leadership stances, how they impact the delivery of value, and the reasons why a servant leadership approach enables teams. We will also examine different ways that you can effectively serve the team.

LEADERSHIP

A leader is someone who people follow willingly. It is important to recognise that leadership is not something that can be allocated. While traditional management structures will often attempt to assign it as part of senior roles, this does not guarantee true leadership.

You might not be perceived as a leader based on your job title alone, but you have the opportunity to become one by enabling others. It is all about your intentions. Within a team context, everyone should have the opportunity to adopt this responsibility at different times. In a team of equals, there should be no single leader.

Serving the team as a leader does not mean making everyone cups of tea or buying biscuits on request. Instead, you understand what others really need in order to be effective, and serve them by helping to ensure that those needs are met. This includes trusting the team to operate autonomously, with responsibility and ownership of their work.

Command-and-control management provides a valuable contrast to servant leadership. It is an approach that relies upon processes, standards, and structure. This style of leadership continues to be dominant in the majority of organisations.

At its core, command-and-control is a top-down approach, where one person gives the orders and everyone else has to follow them (Figure 3.1). In a context where people's hands are the vehicles of production rather than their minds, this enables one person to think while everyone else acts.

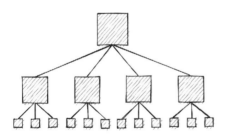

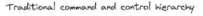
Traditional command and control hierarchy

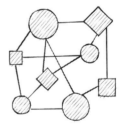
Network of servant leaders

Figure 3.1: Command-and-control vs networked servant leadership adapted from Lex Sisney

You can be a leader who serves others by supporting, facilitating, and collaborating, rather than directing or dictating. As a result, you should respect people as individual thinkers who can make their own decisions; they will be treated as adults. This means that you can apply your time to help other people achieve valuable outcomes, instead of just telling them what to do.

You can serve the team through your actions. By applying the aspects of enablement, you can help to make other people's work more impactful, and ensure that nothing is going to limit their ability to work effectively. Delivery Management without servant leadership is like a ship with a hole in the bottom; you might go some of the distance, but you'll have a very tough time staying afloat.

INFLUENCE

A defining aspect of servant leadership is the application of influence, rather than authority, to catalyse change. True leadership involves offering experience and knowledge for the benefit of the teams you serve, while accepting that nobody is compelled to follow the approaches you advocate. People choose to learn from you.

When practices are forced on people, they are unlikely to understand why things are changing or what they should be doing. In contrast, by teaching the team about different practices, and facilitating experimentation, you have the opportunity to serve the team as a leader. This ensures that they retain ownership for their ways of working, and have an opportunity to understand the requirements of their chosen approach.

You might propose ways of working that will enable the team to deliver value, but these concepts will be measured on their own merit, rather than being adopted by default. Your ability to influence might make certain practices seem more compelling, but regardless of your preferences, you are not making decisions for them. Servant leadership should enable self-organisation.

This stance requires you to accept that you cannot enforce ideas, and that sometimes your insights won't be accepted. As such, it is equally important for you to be personally open to change and to be willing to try new things in order to uncover approaches that align with the team's needs rather than exerting power.

The contrast between traditional command-and-control and servant leadership is clear to see when teams are asked why they have adopted certain ways of working. When teams holistically own their approach, and the practices they apply, they are able to define how they operate in a way that is optimised for their own effectiveness, rather than the satisfaction of someone external.

You can play an important role in enabling the team to discover and apply ways of working that allow them to achieve valuable outcomes. If you adopt a command-and-control stance, you will be more likely to force your ideas on the team rather than giving them the space to define their own approach.

However, being a servant leader can also involve influencing existing ways of working. You can't truly serve a team by enabling them to become more efficient at applying an ineffective approach. For example, if the team is comfortable with how they operate, but they aren't achieving valuable outcomes, and have lost focus on why they are working together, you should serve them by supporting them to adjust their practices.

It can be difficult to make this reality transparent across the team; comfort and familiarity is often alluring. Asking open questions can help to highlight the gap between how people are working and the delivery of value in a supportive way. Having the courage to ask whether they would like your support to experiment with different practices can help the team to redis-cover their purpose and unlock their potential.

ADAPTABILITY

Variety is inevitable; no two people, teams, or organisations will ever be completely identical. Applying Delivery Management in diverse contexts provides you with the opportunity to serve others in many different ways, as the needs of the people you enable will be unique. However, in order to do this effectively you have to be adaptable.

If you can only facilitate one type of workshop or leverage one approach, then you are reducing the likelihood of being able to serve the team in the way that they need. Applying the same practices in every context you encounter, regardless of their suit-ability, is not a sign of leadership.

It can be easy to become overly comfortable with a limited set of practices and ignore the complexity of your environment. If you always perform the same activities, you should reflect on whether you are doing this to serve others or to make life easier for yourself.

For example, I once worked with a Delivery Manager who wheeled out the same powerpoint slide every three weeks for a retrospective. Team engagement was almost non-existent, and the event had lost all of its purpose. Everyone was bored of going through the motions, and the Delivery Manager's attempts to facilitate this event no longer served the team.

True leadership requires acknowledgement that there is no such thing as a one-size-fits-all solution. Certain practices or approaches might have a higher likelihood of enabling the team, but nothing is guaranteed. In order to be a leader who serves, you need to uncover appropriate methods for the context you are in.

Meeting people where they are, and accommodating their needs, helps to build trust, which is fundamental to servant leadership. You are proving that you are invested in their success, but also respect their intelligence and capabilities, rather than trying to coerce them into adopting a predefined approach. It is your job to guide, not to control.

Sometimes, things won't go to plan, but this should not alter your ability to encourage, support, and enable the team to reach their full potential. You can serve them in this scenario by facilitating reflection, and providing consistent support. It can be challenging to stimulate empowerment, ownership, and transparency when things break or falter, but this is when your leadership can be its most impactful.

As teams mature, you should be mindful of what they need and adjust how you work accordingly. Recognising their progress as a self-organising unit can help them to feel valued and understood. If you can grow with them, and shift your approach, you will be able to serve them more effectively. Change is a direction, not a destination, so you should be prepared to adapt continuously.

Your contributions as a leader who serves the team should shift over time. For example, a team that is just starting out might need more guidance and coaching as they get used to working together. In contrast, teams that have been working together for longer might not need as much support, but they are still likely to appreciate your help as an enabler and impediment remover.

Enabling the team to mature is an act of servant leadership in and of itself. Accepting that your role will change over time is a selfless act that might make your position less stable and secure, but it is the right thing to do in order for the team to become more effective. Many teams have been hindered by leaders who did not want anything to change in order to ensure that they could continue to perform the same function, so it is important for you to avoid this trap.

CURIOSITY

Leadership expert L. David Marquet, author of *Turn the Ship Around,* suggests that curiosity is a desire for information in the absence of any extrinsic benefit. In his book, he describes becoming the Captain of a submarine that he didn't expect to work on with only two weeks' notice. This forced him to shift away from testing others by quizzing them, to asking questions that could enhance his own knowledge and performance.

Being truly curious meant that he had to stop pretending to be all knowing. He needed to accept that he wasn't the heroic leader of the ship who had all the answers, because pretending that he knew exactly what to do at all times would put the crew at risk. In turn, this highlighted other people's knowledge and responsibility. The whole crew was needed, not just the Captain.

It has been said that a leader is only as good as the questions they ask, and fortunately for Marquet, he had the ability to ask some excellent questions. This approach to leadership enabled him to unlock the knowledge and intelligence of the entire crew. Curiosity creates an environment for collective thinking by inviting others to use their brains alongside your own.

You can serve others by asking questions from a position of genuine curiosity. Whether this leads them to uncover information they had not previously considered, or helps to ensure that everyone is on the same page, your inquisitiveness can emphasise aptitude, autonomy, and alignment.

Curiosity also enables you to break free from pre-existing beliefs that you may hold, and programmed responses that you have accumulated over time. It allows you to think beyond what you know, and embrace complexity rather than disregarding it. All of which results in an approach that is centred around others rather than ourselves.

Humans naturally love classifications. The world is much easier to comprehend when the vast volume of information around us can be packaged into neat little boxes. This packaging process is essential for day to day life as it enables us to exist without becoming overwhelmed by the cognitive complexity of the world. However, it can also limit our ability to think beyond assumptions.

If you retain a fixed mindset, you are destined to avoid the reality of the context you operate in, including the needs of the people you are trying to enable. You cannot be a true leader who serves if you adopt this approach. You need to be able to think outside the box and consider multiple perspectives in pursuit of moving power towards the team. Embracing curiosity amplifies your willingness to enable collective collaboration and the dynamic exchange of ideas.

Having a constant sense of curiosity ensures that you are not prone to oversimplifying the environment around you. As such, you can avoid the over-application of pattern based thinking to situations that appear familiar. This will enable you to leverage the most appropriate practices and build genuine human connections rather than operating on a default Delivery Management mode at all times.

This mindset should extend throughout the work you do, incorporating the team, the organisation, and Delivery Management itself. There is always more to learn, and every new piece of knowledge will help you to grow as a leader, creating a clearer picture of how you can serve more effectively. Keeping an open mind will help you to avoid thinking that you have all the answers.

Ultimately, your curiosity can spark the same inquisitive approach in others. You can serve the team by enabling an open and engaged culture that creates clarity, something that we will explore further in chapter seven. A team that is willing to learn by listening to ideas and suggestions from diverse sources, with a willingness to experiment, will be significantly more effective at delivering value.

CHALLENGES

L. David Marquet's description of the heroic leader is of a person who knows all, gives all of the commands, and is always right. They have to be the hero, which is especially true in times of trouble. They are ready to throw on their cape and fly everyone out of a bad situation.

Even with good intentions, hero leaders are still exerting command-and-control behaviours, believing that they know the best resolution for every problem. They inadvertently rob the team of any opportunity to learn or grow, and limit self-organisation. Saving the day is often more about optics than long term resolutions. They treat the symptoms but not the disease.

Servant leadership is not about being the hero. You should endeavour to do whatever it takes to help the team to achieve valuable outcomes, but truly serving them means you don't seek opportunities to steal the spotlight. Your role as an enabler should not be to fix every problem, but to support others to discover fixes first.

In order to serve the team you need to avoid becoming a bottleneck. If the team would be unable to deliver value when you're on holiday, or nobody else in the team would know who to speak with about an impediment, then you are creating unnecessary dependencies that generate risk.

Engaging the team in the process of overcoming challenges is an essential aspect of being a leader who serves. Providing people with opportunities to think independently about potential resolutions to problems, or ways to remove impediments, helps to acknowledge their role as knowledge workers with their own unique insights. You should not force the team to adopt your approach. After all, there is more than one way to cook an egg.

"Don't force it" is a great mantra for leadership through service. Creating the space for people to work through blockers, and uncover how their actions might be limiting value delivery, is an essential aspect of team maturation. Sometimes people have to feel the heat of a hot stove to understand the risk of being burned.

However, serving the team does not involve being entirely hands-off. You are still a coach, facilitator, and impediment remover. It is important that you are ready to support them through the process of tackling challenges, and play your role as a proactive participant in the team. For example, they might benefit from your support if they believe a workshop with senior colleagues could help to clarify outcomes and priorities.

In that situation, the team might need further support if management is creating undue pressure. Working as a mediator or coach to support people outside of the team to see the impact they are having does not involve being a hero if the team defines a course of action that would benefit from your skill set. Let the team decide, and work from there.

You should be willing to support the team to address challenges at any level of the organisation. This might mean working with other teams across the business, or having discussions with people in senior roles. Sadly, this is not something that many people are comfortable with due to the pressure it can carry. As such, you could offer to serve the team by leveraging your communication skills.

Sometimes, certain situations can be daunting, but it is important that you remain committed to serving the team. Conflict is the perfect example of this. It can be uncomfortable to witness, and difficult to respond to. In this instance, you might be able to facilitate communication so that people can work through the issue themselves. This might involve asking open questions or vocalising what you have observed without applying judgement.

It's important for you to be aware of the team's dynamics and to be prepared to intervene if something does not seem right or conflict is becoming unhealthy. If things get heated, it's important for you to stay calm and rational, even if someone starts to raise their voice or use insulting language. This can help to de-escalate the situation and to get everyone back on track.

In order to serve the team, you should do your best to ensure that everyone is treated fairly and with respect, even if people don't agree with each other's perspectives. It can be useful to remember that disagreements are a normal part of working together, but conflict should never become destructive.

Limiting unhealthy conflict highlights the leadership aspect of servant leadership. Sometimes you might need to make a decision, based on what you know, at a time when nobody else is able to. However, this should always be communicated transparently in order to ensure that the team can disagree and make their own decision if they want.

LEADING BY EXAMPLE

Thank you. How many times a day do you hear those two words? Maybe we factor in some variance. Thanks. Cheers. Ta. I can't count how many times I heard those words every day when I worked for Ben.

Everyone was deserving of some form of thanks. That might not sound too remarkable, but Ben really meant it. It was genuine.

What made this unique was that in our line of business we were working with the full spectrum of society. From CEOs and Executive Directors, to caretakers and bin men. This didn't matter to Ben. Everyone deserved the same, heartfelt thank you.

For a good number of months this didn't really sink in. We would work in the office and I would take his lead on phone calls, following up politely "thanks for your time" and when we would venture into the outside world I would smile as Ben built bridges with everyone around us.

It was only outside of work that I realised this approach had made its mark. I was having coffee with a friend, and as the server placed a drink on the table my friend didn't even flinch. They kept talking, remaining more focussed on me than the person who had just done something for them. I glanced up, said thank you with a smile, and re-immersed myself in our conversation.

But this interaction played on my mind. Was everyday gratitude not as normal as I had become accustomed to? I decided to confront Ben. Recounting the coffee story he frowned, and gave a slight shrug. "I don't get it, it doesn't cost anything to be decent to other people."

I dug a little deeper and shared my slow realisation of recent weeks; that he engaged everyone with the same appreciation regardless of status or stature. "Why wouldn't I?" I remember that succinct point clearly because I couldn't find an answer to throw back. It was common sense.

Down the line, new threads of this conversation would emerge as I rationalised the belief system I had absorbed. Topics ranged from never knowing which postman might be sitting on a cool million in the bank, to contemplating how many Directors worked for companies on the verge of collapse.

It was impossible to know what someone was going through or where they had been. However, it was entirely possible to spare a moment and show genuine gratitude for someone I had interacted with. No matter how small the interaction.

I owe real thanks to Ben for that lesson. I learned a lot while working alongside him, things that still inform how I work to this day. None of these lessons were forced. They were part of the culture he crafted. An unspoken but constant set of values that were defined and shaped through everyday activity. That's still my image of real leadership. Present, supportive, hard-working, and authentic.

A true leader is respected and followed willingly, not out of fear or coercion. This involves setting an example that inspires others, enabling you to lead through actions rather than orders. When you serve the team in this way, you allow them to focus on their work rather than being distracted by somebody trying to tell them what to do. This helps to build trust, as they know that you have their best interests in mind rather than prioritising your needs.

By adopting this approach, you have the opportunity to become a trusted friend, a reliable coach, and a valuable ally to the team in difficult situations. You should aspire to listen without judgement and provide support, no matter what. This does not mean you always need to smile or be constantly happy.

It is far more important to be authentic than perfect if you want to build meaningful relationships.

When Matt Hicks became CEO of Red Hat, he shared an example of the leadership he had experienced as a teenager that shaped his approach to working with others. "We all empty the trash" were the words of his first ever manager. Everyone contributes, and nobody is too good for the tough jobs. By serving the team, you are setting an example for others to follow, where everyone is ready to support each other.

It takes courage to be a leader who serves. You will be working in ways that not everyone will be familiar or comfortable with in the wider organisation and beyond. This approach might be considered disruptive to an environment built around hierarchical models of power, or seen as confusing to people who only feel comfortable when they have a sense of control. However, your actions can start to redefine the organisation's culture, with a focus on respect and trust for others.

It is not only your approach to leadership that can set an example for others to follow. All of your actions can be influential. Whether your work as a coach inspires others to assume positive intent during challenging interactions, or your role as an impediment remover empowers people to reduce the impact of blockers for themselves, your acts of enablement can shift an entire team's mindset.

As a result, you should consider how your values and behaviours might influence the people around you. Self-care is a powerful example of this. It can help you to stay focussed and motivated. Small acts like taking a walk in the park over lunch, or ensuring you use your annual leave allowance to decompress can set a precedent of what is acceptable in the team.

If you prioritise your wellbeing at work, other people are likely to do the same. If everyone feels comfortable taking some time for themselves every day to recharge then they are more likely to work effectively and contribute more to the team. When you look after your own energy, you establish an example for the team to follow without forcing them to do anything.

Of course, everyone is different, and your idea of wellbeing might look vastly different from someone else's. Not everyone loves a team quiz. Your actions and behaviours should not impose upon anyone in the name of serving them. In order to keep growing as a servant leader, you should be open to feedback. Consider suggestions about your approach and invite people's thoughts, including any criticism, in order to improve.

SELFLESSNESS

Facilitation is a powerful aspect of Delivery Management. It enables you to drive engagement and distribute power rather than allowing any singular voice to dominate conversations. You can use it to support the creation of a collaborative environment where everyone is able to share their ideas and contribute to discussions. It lets you lead by serving others.

This highlights the selfless nature of servant leadership. When you are in a position to steer a conversation, it could be easy to become the presiding voice. In contrast, you should avoid this command-and-control style, and let the team offer their own thoughts and ideas first.

As a leader who serves, you have the opportunity to make others feel valued and heard. For instance, when it comes to presenting information to colleagues, you should create the space for other people to contribute, ignoring the spotlight or the appeal of being the hero. This helps to build trust and respect, but it can also have substantial positive effects on personal wellbeing when people know that everyone has a voice.

This is equally true when making decisions as a team. In many situations, a decision that is reached through consensus will be more effective in the long run because everyone will gain a level of ownership. You can serve the team by facilitating communication in a way that helps everyone to contribute and identify whether they are aligned.

These examples highlight how servant leadership involves putting the team first rather than taking a course of action that might feel easier for a lot of leaders. Doing all of the talking, or making decisions for everyone else to follow, is the way that a lot of people operate. It can feel like the simple option; nobody can let you down if you do everything yourself. However, this undermines trust and restricts everyone else.

You should always be looking for ways to help others grow and develop. This means sharing opportunities for them to demonstrate their abilities and strengths rather than considering how situations or activities will benefit you. Ultimately, investing your trust and effort in the team will be beneficial for the whole team as it will enable everyone to achieve more.

This extends to ensuring that you never take individual credit for the team's work. You should highlight the collaborative effort of the team instead, and celebrate collective achievements. This enables people to feel appreciated and respected. It also gives them the opportunity to recognise your approach as a leader who serves, which could set an example for them to follow in similar situations.

You can create a sense of camaraderie within the team and develop psychological safety by celebrating the entire team's successes. When you take genuine pride in the work of the people around you, regardless of whether you gain any type of recognition for it, you will strengthen your relationships and build the bridges that will help you to be a more effective enabler. Finding happiness in other people's achievements can be incredibly rewarding.

Although you are not responsible for organising social events or coordinating team building activities, there is no harm in suggesting a team lunch or dinner to celebrate successes. You could also share positive news with other people in the organisation to ensure the team's work is recognised and appreciated. It is important that this doesn't create a sense of hierarchy, so it should be discussed with the team.

You should endeavour to put the team first and avoid seeing yourself as the most important person in the room. Focus on what others need rather than yourself when possible. By doing this, you can create the opportunities for other people to lead, and serve the team in the process. A team that is built upon people putting those around them first will be more trusting, supportive, and resilient to change.

The collective values that the team cultivates will underpin a culture of servant leadership. For example, if the team adopts values of respect, courage, and commitment, they are likely to prioritise others over their own individual needs. It is hard to be selfish when you have values that are focussed on improving interactions with the people around you.

STEPPING BACK

Servant leadership involves working closely with people every day in order to gain a true understanding of their work and what matters to them. This includes recognising their priorities, what challenges they're facing, and the goals they're hoping to achieve. This information will enable you to help the team deliver value and fulfil their potential.

Your presence should assure the team that they can depend on you, whether you are there to answer questions, provide support, or offer guidance. Being available when the team needs you will ensure that you can uncover opportunities to coach, facilitate, and remove impediments in the service of the team.

However, there may come a time when the team no longer needs the same levels of support. This can be a sign that the team is doing well and that they're able to work effectively. If you have enabled the team by sharing your knowledge, and avoided becoming a dependency, it might be possible for the team to become self-sufficient.

It's important for you to recognise this and step back when necessary. This can be difficult, and might cause you to worry about your personal contribution to the team, but it's important that you allow them to stand on their own feet. You can continue to be available when needed while actively encouraging them to self-organise and flourish.

In the book *Drive*, Daniel H. Pink explains that the keys to motivation are autonomy, mastery, and purpose. Being prepared to step back from certain activities creates an environment where people have control of what they do, the opportunity to develop skills rather than relying upon you, and make a contribution towards achieving a shared vision. Your willingness to let go can motivate the team to achieve more.

This can also open up new opportunities to work as a leader who serves. Less of your time will be constrained by day to day work with the team, and you can start investing greater effort in the wider organisation. This work will still involve the aspects of enablement but on a broader scale. However, this effort can still serve the team, as environmental improvements around them can support their ability to achieve valuable outcomes.

If you avoid creating the space for the team to work autonomously without your constant involvement, you are unlikely to be serving them. You will constrain their psychological ownership, as you will be removing their autonomy and influence over the work they do. To be a true leader who serves you need to give control, and create an environment where others feel empowered to lead.

CONCLUSION

Adopting a servant leadership approach means that you are not there to control the actions of the team or tell them what to do.

Instead, you are willing to support the team in any situation in order to help them succeed. This is a fundamental element of Delivery Management, and underpins your approach as an enabler of value delivery.

Working with the team to find solutions to problems and prioritising collaboration over your own individual needs is a key element of being a leader who serves. You should let the team experiment and learn for themselves rather than attempting to manage them. This gives you the opportunity to be a coach and teacher, supporting others to grow and fulfil their potential.

By applying this approach, you can enable the team to be more autonomous and self-sufficient in the pursuit of valuable outcomes. Ultimately, it takes courage to have trust in the people around you and to invest your effort in helping them to be effective, but the culture this type of leadership creates can be incredibly motivational.

The default setting in many organisations is still command-

and-control management, but being someone who prioritises others and works in an authentic way to get support willingly is something to be admired. Adopting this stance contributes to everyone's success rather than just your own.

Questions for reflection:
○ What is the impact of dictating how a team should work?
○ How can you serve the people around you?
○ What are some command-and-control behaviours?
○ When have you seen someone lead by example?
○ When was the last time you were genuinely curious about something?

CHAPTER 4
A COACHING STANCE

"Well, the problem is that I can't do pair programming." As I listened intently, I could feel the frustration that Lauren was experiencing. I always admired her dedication to the team. Whenever we held a team review she was ready to share her work, and she was quick to celebrate other people's successes. I tried to shift my mind away from my existing perceptions and stay focussed on our conversation.

"What would you change?" I asked. She explained that she hated the pressure of having someone looking over her shoulder. She was worried that she'd be judged for opening up Stack Overflow or for mistyping something. Ultimately, she didn't want this to be a source of anxiety.

I paused while I prepared to ask another question. In that extra few seconds, I looked at Lauren and words came spilling out of her mouth. "I guess I haven't really told them about any of this before. We've all been so busy, but I pick up backlog items that nobody else wants to touch because it means I don't have to stress about pairing. It's not good, because I know it means nobody really gets to see what I'm up to."

She continued. Uncovering insights that had never crossed her mind about the team. From relationship dynamics between other Engineers to the impact a former Tech Lead had on her confidence. It was like a path unfolding in front of both of us. Finally, her thoughts seemed to reach an impasse. "I just wish I could make this work."

I could feel Lauren's passion for her work, and the deep care she felt for the team. But I also understood the anxiety of feeling unable to participate in something everyone else seemed able to do so effortlessly. I left the silence to sit for a moment, took a breath, and eventually asked "What's your plan?"

There is an unattributed story floating around on the internet about Sigmund Freud. Supposedly, one day Freud's son Ernst went missing. As his wife Martha began to panic, she begged Freud to help her search for the boy. He suggested that they wouldn't need to search at all if they wanted to find him.

Martha was dubious. "How on earth are we going to find him if we don't search?" Freud remained confident and repeated his assertion, followed by a question: "Did you tell him not to go anywhere?"

As Martha began to recall recent conversations she suddenly jolted, "The pond!" The couple immediately made their way downstairs and across the courtyard, until they reached the lawn with a distant view of the water.

Sure enough, Ernst was sitting, legs dangling over the edge of the pond, smiling in the afternoon sun. Martha had all of the pieces of information she needed to find her son, she just needed the right question to bring them into focus.

Lauren might not have uncovered a quick fix for her pair programming anxiety during our conversation, but she did decide on a course of action. She always had the ability to find a solution to the problem, but until we spoke she hadn't unpicked why this was an issue for her, or committed to do something about it. She decided that speaking to the team would be her first step.

Coaching enables people to maximise their potential. It helps them to uncover solutions to challenges, and provides a supportive structure for growth. You are in a unique position to enable others to deliver value, and this is precisely why coaching can be so impactful.

When you think of a coach a few names might spring to mind. Maybe you think of Alex Ferguson, Phil Jackson, or Vince Lombardi. But is this the type of coach we're talking about? Do these prominent sports coaches have the secret formula for effective teams? Or are there different coaching approaches that you can apply?

We have already considered some of the nuances of various coaching approaches, and explored Agile Coaching as a broader framework of competencies. However, in this chapter we will take a deeper look at the ways that you can successfully adopt different coaching techniques and approaches.

We'll examine how coaching can help the team to become confident in their ability to make decisions and self-manage their work while building trust. We will also explore how you can coach others when you might not have expertise in a specific domain.

COACHING MINDSET

People are often viewed as a commodity in organisations. When an organisation refers to people as resources, it can have a negative and dehumanising effect. It often makes people feel like their opinions and thoughts don't matter. Presenting someone as a commodity implies that they are expendable and that they ultimately don't matter as a person.

Coaching depends upon the idea that teams are made up of people, not resources. Everyone has value. This is especially important in the context of knowledge work as a person's ideas and identity will contribute to the overall success of the team.

It is important to remember that people have their own lives with unique motivations, challenges, and experiences. In order to be an effective coach, you should always be mindful of the reality that you are working with other humans, while also enabling others to recognise this fact.

Each person is unique and should be treated as such. What works for one person might not work for another. Equally, what works for one team might not be appropriate for everyone. The key is to find what works best for the context you are in. Your coaching style should be flexible and adaptable in order to work with different teams and help them to get the most out of the process.

Coaching can take many forms depending on the situation and the team that you are working with. It is not a one-size-fits-all approach, and nobody is the same. However, in all scenarios it is important to adopt a non-judgemental perspective, and consider the goals of the team or individual without preconceptions so that you can support them fully.

It is important to recognise that you are also unique, so you will have your own views and biases, both conscious and unconscious. This makes you who you are but can mean that it is challenging to maintain permanent non-judgment or neutrality. Leadership coach Lauren Cartigny suggests this is why we refer to having a coaching "stance" as it is something that we can step into rather than it being a constant mindset.

At its core, coaching is about building trust that enables people to achieve more. You are creating a space for someone to grow based on their own decisions. When you apply this stance, you are making a commitment to invest in a relationship where all parties need to be authentic and vulnerable.

Adopting a neutral approach while being authentic and empathic will help to develop the foundation of trust required for effective coaching. You need to be genuinely invested in people's well-being, including being open to calling out problems by objectively reflecting reality. You can't expect to help someone to grow if you are uncomfortable challenging them.

Coaching is the aspect of enablement that emphasises autonomy more than any other. It can only be effective if the person being coached, often referred to as the coachee, is willing to be honest with themselves and you, and to take responsibility for their own growth and development. This requires mutual respect, empathy, and openness.

PROFESSIONAL COACHING

Sports coaching is often the approach that comes to mind when people talk about coaching. These types of coaches instruct players' positioning, strategise tactics, and offer encouragement. They are often people with experience on the pitch, and have an ability to get stuck in.

In the context of a multi-disciplinary stream-aligned team, this type of coaching requires a large amount of experience. Not only would you require domain specific knowledge, but you would need expertise in varied skill sets in order to provide the type of training and guidance demonstrated in sports coaching.

Many teams can end up feeling disappointed by coaches that aren't a recognised expert in a relevant area. Even in a situation where you have knowledge of a certain domain, such as Product Management or Engineering, it is unlikely that you would also have the requisite knowledge to also apply the same coaching approach in other areas such as Content Design or User Research.

Sports coaching is mostly known for its directive elements; organising, teaching, advising, guiding, and supervising. However, coaches also undertake another set of activities. They empower, facilitate, validate, and support their players. These non-directive actions enable people to take ownership of their goals, and self-discover how to improve and grow. This is comparable to professional coaching.

The International Coaching Federation describes professional coaching as the process of "partnering with clients in a thought-provoking and creative process that inspires them to maximise their personal and professional potential." This partnership involves helping people to learn rather than teaching them. As a result, you are not telling a person what to change or trying to fix their problems for them.

Professional coaching can broaden your approach as an enabler, even when you lack expertise in a specific field. While you should aim to gain domain knowledge, it is important to recognise that you can't know everything, so finding methods that help you to support others to deliver value in different contexts is essential.

People that experience professional coaching can expect to gain an alternative perspective on challenges they face and opportunities for growth. Their approach to decision making is likely to mature, and they should experience a feeling of increased effectiveness and autonomy. However, this is all driven from within, as you are only supporting them through a process rather than providing direction.

Professional coaching must be consensual rather than being forced on anyone. As such, you should always seek someone's permission to explore this type of coaching relationship. When you apply Delivery Management, there is likely to be a level of expectation that you will coach the team, but this type of coaching relationship can be more intimate and require deeper trust, so agreement is necessary.

In a formal professional coaching relationship, consent is normally captured in the form of a verbal or written coaching contract. It enables you to agree on what yourself and the coachee hope to achieve.

The contract should establish clear boundaries and define a level of commitment. It might also include additional information such as the frequency of your sessions or how long the coaching relationship will last.

Working within the agreement of a coaching contract can help to establish trust, but it also provides a level of transparency so that the coachee can understand your approach.

Creating an agreement that articulates what someone can expect from you and what you should expect from them is especially helpful when you are part of the same team. It should reinforce the neutrality, trust, and authenticity you will bring to the table.

Creating a contract with someone in the team sounds like a very official process, but it can be as simple as a discussion about the type of conversations they might benefit from, how often you both want to catch up, and verbal agreement not to share anything outside of those sessions. The key element is holding each other accountable to those statements.

Being committed to a coaching relationship is fundamental to building trust and ensuring your approach will be effective. If you do not believe you can remain neutral or that you will feel obliged to report information back to other people in the organisation, such as senior managers, then you should reconsider your ability to support others as a coach.

Once you have created an agreement, you should work within its boundaries. However, as with any practice or approach, it should be frequently reviewed and iterated in order to be effective. If either of you feel that you are not getting what you need from the coaching relationship, you should work to renegotiate what is expected or required.

If challenges arise, such as a lack of consistent engagement, or that professional coaching might not be the best approach in a certain context, it is important that you and the coachee can be honest and open. You do not have to discuss issues within the context of a coaching session, but a healthy coaching relationship will address challenges rather than avoiding them.

It is helpful to understand professional coaching, even if you don't intend to apply it in an explicitly structured or formal setting. Many of the practices that we will explore later in this chapter are fundamental to professional coaching, but can still prove to be valuable outside of an explicit coaching relationship.

Be mindful that professional coaching is not the only coaching approach. For example, your expertise around different domains such as ways of working, impediment removal, and facilitation will enable you to offer more directive coaching to the team in certain contexts. Nonetheless, professional coaching provides a valuable set of complementary practices.

Being transparent about your approach ensures that you are providing people with options, and treating them as adults. Not everyone will benefit from professional coaching, and sometimes it won't be the right tool for the job. Acknowledging other approaches such as teaching, facilitating, or mentoring, ensures that people are able to make a decision about what they believe will enable them to be most effective.

COACHING TECHNIQUES

Whether you apply a directive or non-directive coaching approach, there are a broad variety of practices and techniques that you should have an awareness of. The majority of which are underpinned by one of the most fundamental aspects of coaching; being an effective listener. If you were to invest effort into one skill above any other as a coach, listening should be it.

For most people, listening ends up being about themselves. Instead of absorbing what someone is saying, they spend time considering their response, or thinking about what information they want to insert into conversation. This is a shallow form of listening. In a coaching relationship, if you can only think about yourself, it is unlikely that you are helping anyone else.

It can be helpful to consider listening as something that is typically defined at three different levels. (Figure 4.1) At the first level, you are listening to respond. This is the level that most of us operate at on a daily basis, where we predominantly consider nothing beyond the next thing to say. At this surface level of listening, we can miss key information and risk misunderstanding.

The second level is listening to understand. This requires a sense of motivation and focus as you are working harder to stay engaged while processing information. Sometimes, this motivation is easy to find, such as on a first date with someone you are attracted to and want to impress. However, you have to be self-motivated as a coach in order to apply the second level of listening with anyone you want to enable.

First and second level listening are less than ideal in a

coaching scenario as they both place a focus on you rather than solely being focussed on the coachee. Whether you listen to consider your response or to mature your level of understanding, it is likely that you will miss information because your brain will be whirring behind the scenes to analyse what you are hearing.

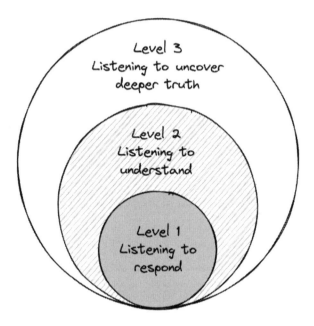

Figure 4.1: Three levels of listening

The third level of listening removes this impediment, because it is focussed on uncovering deeper truths. At this level, you are deeply engaged in what someone is saying verbally, while also paying attention to non-verbal cues in order to truly hear what they mean. This requires practice and dedication, and is often referred to as active listening.

Active listening involves fully embracing what someone is saying, and applying mindfulness to avoid getting distracted by anything beyond that point in time. The aim of this type of listening is to recognise the feelings and thoughts behind someone's words. Truly engaging with someone in this way can have a significant impact; your listening ability will often correlate with their ability to think.

Effective listening will enable you to apply other coaching practices. An approach that maximises the impact of active listening is the Socratic method. This is a questioning technique that can be used to help people explore their own thoughts and ideas. It involves asking short, open questions; for example, "What do you need?" "What will you do?" "What is stopping you?"

When you are fully engaged in what someone is saying you might feel the emotions they are going through, and be desperately inclined to help steer them towards a solution, but that can undermine their growth. Asking questions rather than offering advice, or giving direction, requires courage. You are trusting someone to find their own path, and develop their own wisdom.

In the book *The Coaching Habit*, Michael Bungay Stanier outlines seven powerful questions that can help you to truly enable someone to create their own solutions rather than jumping to offer advice.

- What's on your mind?
- And what else?
- What's the real challenge here for you?
- What do you want?
- How can I help?
- If you're saying yes to this, what are you saying no to?
- What was most useful for you?

He proposes asking these questions chronologically as a way to take someone through a journey of decision making and development. These seven simple questions can help people to engage with issues or identify opportunities, especially when partnered with active listening. As such, you should give people ample time and space to fully answer questions, and avoid interrupting, even with a new question.

Whether you start with these seven questions or develop your own, you can use this approach to help teams or individuals to increase their autonomy and ownership of both problems and solutions as they continue to grow. Most importantly, each question you ask helps others to uncover new information for themselves, rather than being asked for your benefit.

Almost any question has the potential to be powerful. For instance, asking "How might someone else handle this situation?" could help the coachee to gain an entirely new perspective. As a result, they might identify a different course of action, unlock new ideas, or develop a greater sense of empathy that enables them to mitigate conflict and build trust.

Applying the Socratic method can be challenging at first, in a similar way to active listening, as it does not align with normal conversational patterns. For example, once you ask a question, you should give the person answering time to think. If they need clarification, then they are welcome to ask but you should not attempt to fill any silences. Being comfortable with silence is important because it demonstrates that you do not feel the need to dominate the conversation.

Mirroring is another technique that can work in unison with the Socratic method and active listening. It is a simple practice that involves replicating someone's physicality, tone, and language. This can often happen naturally in the process of active listening, but even with second level listening you can develop an awareness of body language, or specific words that are being said and mirror the other person.

People don't always realise the emotions they exhibit through their body or their choice of language, but mirroring can help them to gain awareness. It enables people to witness their own emotions and reactions. If people are at ease with themselves, then they are likely to continue in the same direction, but sometimes seeing themselves reflected can be jarring and lead them to shift their mindset, even at a subconscious level.

It is a subtle way to provide someone with the opportunity to consider how they are approaching an issue and whether they want to frame it differently. It can also have a positive effect of strengthening the relationship between you and the coachee. Over time, mirroring might start to occur in the opposite direction, where someone aligns with you as an aspect of an evolving coaching relationship.

A more directive technique you might choose to apply is reinforcement. This involves reinforcing a behaviour that someone wants to embrace by providing neutral recognition when it is exhibited. This can encourage the coachee to gain awareness of the thought pattern or the emotions they experienced that provoked the specific behaviour.

For example, if someone wants to increase their self-confidence, you could draw attention to something they said that highlighted self-belief and ask them to consider what they think about it. This will help them to reflect on their actions and continue displaying the behaviour, as well as recognising potential progress. The behaviour could potentially be amplified and reinforced further through mirroring.

Reinforcement is an example of how a directive approach can be less explicit than relying upon teaching or mentoring practices. Although you are only using second level listening to find these opportunities for reinforcement, you are still supporting someone's growth, which is the most important thing. You could also use this technique in unison with your domain specific knowledge to steer someone in a certain direction without telling them exactly what to do. For instance, recognising an action they have taken to remove an impediment.

These coaching techniques are predominantly focussed on enabling people to reach their own conclusions about how to work, grow, and deliver value. This can support greater self-organisation and help you to avoid becoming a dependency due to people being reliant upon explicit, directive coaching. By applying these practices, you are not doing the thinking for anyone else; you are creating the space for them to think for themselves instead.

CREATING A SAFE SPACE

Effective coaching in any form depends on a safe space for information exchange. When you exhibit behaviours that help to build and sustain trust, such as non-judgement, active listening, or empathy, you support the creation of this space. However, maintaining and maturing it can be incredibly challenging.

Society is inherently judgmental, in part due to the analytical nature of humanity that has enabled us to adapt to our surroundings and interact with other people to form modern civilisations. This means that we are constantly assessing everything around us, including each other. Coaching requires you to mindfully separate yourself from judgement by leveraging self-awareness to be present and adopt a neutral perspective.

By creating a judgement-free environment, you are developing a space that provides the best possible conditions for personal growth. In this setting, the person you are enabling will not have to worry about the pressure of conforming to your beliefs or prioritising your opinions ahead of their own development. Humanistic psychologist Carl Rogers described the basic acceptance and support of a person regardless of what they say as unconditional positive regard.

It is important to hold unconditional positive regard for the people you coach even when you might not agree with them outside of a coaching relationship. For example, you might work with a team that is dead set on experimenting with practices that you believe are obsolete or unideal. Being critical in this situation is unlikely to enable them to achieve valuable outcomes.

If you are judgemental, it can make people feel uncomfortable and discouraged. This can lead to them feeling like they cannot open up and share information freely. I have personally seen potential coaching relationships crash and burn when the person in a coaching role expressed disdain for a small error the coachee made. In effect, this is a violation of trust that can fundamentally damage a relationship, and potentially erode trust with all of the other people you coach as well.

In contrast, unconditional positive regard allows others to feel safe and comfortable sharing information with you, and provides you with the opportunity to support their growth. When people can be truly open, genuine opportunities to learn and develop appear. This is especially important within a team context, as it provides fertile soil for collaboration and autonomy to emerge and flourish.

Creating a safe space is important because of the authenticity it enables people to demonstrate. Coaching is not aligned with the belief that people are fragile or immature and need protecting; this is arguably the mindset that drives many command-and-control behaviours. Recognising the people you coach as adults is essential, and shifts the concept of a safe environment away from protection and towards openness.

When people express themselves openly, it becomes twice as important to be mindful of their privacy. You should not disclose personal information they share with you without their permission, unless you believe there is a risk of genuine harm. In that unlikely situation, speaking privately with a trusted but neutral professional is advisable.

In a professional coaching context, privacy can form part of your coaching agreement. However, it can be helpful to let everyone in the team know that any conversations they have with you will be kept confidential by default in any coaching context. This can provide opportunities for other members of the team to have less formal or sporadic time with you to enable their growth.

When confidential information is shared without permission, it will inevitably undermine trust. However, it can also be twisted and exaggerated, which can lead to disagreements and conflict. Gossip can quickly erode relationships within a team as it causes people to distrust one another, and it can create a sense of paranoia. If you are willing to share and discuss one person's private information, then why would you not share someone else's?

You should help people to be mindful of each other's privacy on the path to creating a safe space. Teaching the team about the benefits of unconditional positive regard, while being aware of the harm that can occur if openness is abused, can enable everyone to support an environment where people feel comfortable sharing their thoughts and ideas freely.

MAKING COMMITMENTS

Following through on commitments is an essential element of any coaching stance. In the broadest sense, this can be achieved by establishing expectations and consistently meeting them. When you do this, it builds confidence that you can be relied upon, which helps to nurture trust.

It is important to be clear and concise when you set expectations, so that there is no ambiguity between you and the people you coach. For example, you could state that you will endeavour to ask valuable questions before providing answers, or that you will still aim to provide support and challenge if you lack experience around a specific issue someone is facing.

Being honest if you can't do something you have said you would do will enable you to maintain trust. It is crucial to be upfront about any limitations you have, and willing to acknowledge any that you discover. This allows everyone to be aware of any potential roadblocks, and to plan for them.

It's also important not to overcommit because this can lead to disappointment and frustration for you and the people you coach. Overcommitting yourself can only serve to damage the relationships you establish, and undermine the effectiveness of your coaching approach. It is usually better to under promise and over deliver.

When you apply Delivery Management, you are making a commitment to enable others to deliver value. Coaching is foundational to this because any type of coaching relationship is significant, and can have a distinct impact on people's lives. As such, you should make an effort to be reliable and trustworthy, with a willingness to invest your time and effort to help others to maximise their potential. Arriving at events on time, active listening, and maintaining confidentiality all demonstrate this approach.

In order to truly enable others to deliver value, you should also be committed to supporting them to self-organise. This should be reflected through your coaching stance. You are not there to dictate or direct the team's work. As such, you should support them to uncover the optimal approach to achieving valuable outcomes for themselves. If you cannot fulfil this commitment, it might be beneficial to seek external support with the team's consent.

Commitment is not a one way street in a coaching relationship. You should not collude with the people you coach to maintain things that might hold them back. This can include their own lack of engagement or dedication to development. While growth can never be mandatory, it could become an impediment for the team if one person has an adamantly fixed mindset.

It is important for you to be able to gauge how committed someone is to developing a coaching relationship. You might choose to establish a regular check point with people you coach where you could explore the topic of commitment through powerful questions such as "How do you feel about coaching?" This will help you to provide appropriate support and ensure that both of you are getting what you need.

If someone doesn't seem committed, you should maintain unconditional positive regard for them, but might need to explore what isn't working. You could do this through a combination of mirroring and the Socratic method, but an open and frank conversation where you don't apply a coaching stance could be more beneficial. Never jump to conclusions; for instance, a member of a team I supported no longer felt they needed one-to-one coaching with me because they had successfully gained a place on a talent development programme.

Getting frustrated if someone you are coaching misses sessions or judges your actions is entirely understandable; you're human. If you do express your frustration in a way that might not be productive, it is best to accept what has happened and move on. At the end of the day, nobody is

DELIVERY MANAGEMENT   101

perfect, and sometimes you won't do the right thing. Being authentic without disrupting a coaching relationship is challenging, but if your intentions are genuine, then this type of situation is a valuable opportunity for your own learning and growth.

Arguably, a sensible way to refine your approach, and uncover tools that will enable you to be more effective, is to receive what you are offering others; the best coaches have coaches. Seeking coaching for yourself can serve to reinforce your own commitment, and help you to remain engaged with a process of continuous learning. If you truly believe in the value of coaching, then surely it follows that you would also benefit from the support of a coach.

AN APPROPRIATE STANCE

Is your front door locked? Give it some thought before you answer. Perhaps this question is making you contemplate checking your door. Maybe you already have, and you're returning to your seat now.

What if I told you that I know whether your front door is locked at this very moment, and that I don't need any information other than the fact that you are reading this book in order to give an entirely accurate determination?

I'll ask again, is your front door locked? If you aren't sure, would you like to know? Surely you remember the last time you locked it. Turning the key, lifting the latch, or sliding the bolt. It must feel almost subconscious. One of many daily actions performed on auto-pilot.

You might be wondering what secret information I have acquired about your home, or are you busy applying some critical reasoning to this situation? "There's no way he knows!" But, what if I do? Wouldn't that be amazing, or maybe slightly bizarre?

I believe that somewhere in your mind you know whether your door is locked, and if you don't know yet, you know how to find out. But wouldn't it be easier if I simply gave you a straight answer? Or, even better, if I never cast any doubt on your door locking capabilities?

That's exactly how Holly felt. "Can you just give me some direction?" Having built up the courage to reach out to a Lead Delivery Manager for advice, she had hoped to gain some insights from them about how to reduce the amount of pressure that managers were placing on the team.

All she could assume was that maybe this Delivery Manager hadn't experienced anything similar before as her search for answers brought nothing but questions.

I spoke with Holly after a particularly frustrating coaching conversation, with management pressure mounting. It didn't take long for me to sense her fatigue as I tried to build a picture of what was going on. "What can I do to help?"

"Just give me some direction, what would you do?" As we talked through similar situations I had been in, the conversation contrasted to the one she had experienced a week earlier. She was asking the questions this time. "How did you influence them?" "Did your Product Manager say anything?" "Did you tell the team?"

It's important to note that I didn't tell Holly what she should do, I simply shared my experiences. I couldn't know every detail of her situation, much like there is no way I could know the details of your front door. Trying to tell her what to do would be like me telling you that your door is wide open when I have no empirical evidence that suggests it would be.

We spoke a month later. That conversation might not have

been the key to all of the challenges Holly was facing, but she reassured me that it had helped. It sparked plenty of ideas, and gave her a better sense of what she could do next.

Sometimes, the last thing you want is someone asking questions.

Knowing when to adopt a coaching stance, or applying a different approach entirely, is an essential element of effective enablement. If someone is looking for advice or direction, but you attempt to force a professional coaching approach on them, you probably won't actually be supporting them.

Recognising the distinction between non-directive coaching, directive coaching, and other approaches that are aligned with coaching as an aspect of enablement, such as teaching, or mentoring, can help you to adjust your approach to meet the needs and expectations of the team.

Although non-directive coaching might not always be the right fit, attempting to apply it as your default approach is advisable. It ensures that you don't restrict people's growth by falling into a command-and-control trap of undermining autonomy by giving directions to people when they don't need them. Starting with questions gives people the opportunity to request help if they want to.

Coaching can enable you to identify potential problems and impediments, but you should always give the team opportunities to address these issues themselves first, without intervention. You can help the team to acknowledge challenges, but it's important to avoid fixing everything for them, as this removes people's opportunity to learn, and the chance to think for themselves.

Thinking about coaching from a team perspective is important because it is unlikely that you will be fully supporting them to collectively achieve valuable outcomes if you only invest effort into a single coaching relationship with one person. You should aim to work across the team to enable everyone. This can include applying coaching techniques in a group setting and helping others to understand elements of a coaching mindset, or practices such as active listening.

Of course, it's important to acknowledge that your coaching abilities could also be applied at an organisational level rather than working exclusively within the team. Recognising the wider system of work around you is an essential element of Delivery Management, so coaching across the system can ensure the environment around the team improves rather than having a singular unit of effective value delivery operating as an island.

The coaching stance you adopt should be flexible and adaptable to ensure that you can work across the entire organisation. For instance, being able to support leaders who operate outside of the team can be one of the most effective ways to remove significant impediments, especially those that originate as part of a cultural dysfunction. Being able to see beyond the silo of the team is an important element of every aspect of enablement; context matters.

The best way to know whether your coaching stance is appropriate for the situation you're in is simple; just ask. Coaching is only one aspect of Delivery Management, and you have plenty of tools in your toolbox that will help you to enable teams to deliver value if your stance isn't quite the right fit. However, coaching techniques such as active listening and powerful questions can support the other aspects of enablement to be more impactful, even when you aren't explicitly applying a coaching stance.

CREATING A LASTING IMPACT

Growth takes time. Enabling people to unlock their potential is not an overnight process; arguably, it's a process that is never complete. This is the primary reason why you should give the people you coach the tools to continue on this journey, regardless of whether you still work in the same team or organisation as them or not. By doing this, you can have a powerful, positive impact well into the future.

Coaching can help people to work through specific challenges, and well defined short term goals can be valuable for personal development, but the effects of your work should extend beyond this. The practices we have explored can have a broader impact, whether that involves making someone feel truly heard for the first time, giving them the experience of being trusted to make autonomous decisions, or helping them to discover what happens when someone is invested in their success.

Investing time in relationships, and creating an environment where trust and respect thrive, can contribute to the long term effects of coaching and help you to create a lasting impact in people's lives. You can supplement this by refining your skills and improving your abilities. As a result, you are more likely to have a profound impact on the people you work with. Whether you undertake training, develop your active listening abilities, or take time to read about different practices, you will be better placed to enable others.

If you are not committed to creating a lasting impact, it is likely to be reflected in your approach. In the short term, it might lead someone to feel unsupported, or it could cause them to lose interest in the coaching relationship. However, the longer term effect is comparable to measuring the cost of a missed opportunity. If you had fully invested in the coaching relation-ship, how much could that person have achieved? You might never get to find out.

Hopefully the individuals you support will have experienced positive work environments in the past where they felt trusted and empowered. Sadly, for many people these circumstances are still rare. In the process of coaching, you are able to expose indi-viduals and teams to an entirely different world of work that can open their eyes to new practices and encourage them to consider their own approach.

Offering a safe space, built on unconditional positive regard, where you do not dominate conversations, can highlight the domineering command-and-control behaviours that people might be conditioned to accept. Once someone has experienced an alternative environment, it can change the way they work, and the things they prioritise, for the rest of their career. Over time, teams that have experienced effective coaching should be well positioned to not only deal with the issues they currently face, but also overcome unforeseen challenges in the future.

Coaching can also create long-term impact by helping people to influence the culture they are working in. You can enable people to have the confidence to self-organise and work more autonomously as they realise their potential. This has the capacity to plant a seed that impacts the wider organisation, as the people you coach become agents of change who improve circumstances for others by advocating new approaches based on their own positive experiences.

The positive effects of coaching are not celebrated simply because they make people feel good. As we have discussed, factors such as psychological safety have an enormous impact on a team's effectiveness. When people maximise their potential, they become more capable and competent in the pursuit of value delivery. Equally, a culture where people have the opportunity to learn and grow by default ensures that everyone can adapt more rapidly to change and be ready for new challenges that might arise across the organisation.

CONCLUSION

Coaching is a meaningful and valuable aspect of Delivery Management. It gives you the opportunity to have a powerful, positive impact on others by enabling them to unlock their potential. When you adopt a coaching stance, you are making a commitment to help people develop and grow.

This approach relies upon the belief that everyone deserves to be recognised as a person, with their own idiosyncrasies and complexities. As such, coaching includes an array of practices and techniques that you can apply in different contexts to support people in a flexible and adaptable way.

Effective coaching often starts with listening. By creating an environment where people are heard, you give them the opportunity to uncover solutions for themselves rather than being directed by default. You can amplify these effects by applying techniques such as the Socratic method that can help people to reframe challenges and consider different perspectives.

The safe space you cultivate for the people you coach should be underpinned by unconditional positive regard. A non-judgmental environment can enable others to embrace authenticity and openness, while also helping to build trust in the coaching relationship. As a result, communication and collaboration across the team can improve without forcing the behaviours or actions of individuals.

The impact of helping people to define their own journey as they uncover their potential can be significant. It can enable teams to gain knowledge and discover more effective ways of working while supporting each other, or it can plant a seed that catalyses change across an organisation as people adopt new approaches.

In many respects, coaching is the antithesis of a command-and-control approach. You are treating someone as an adult who is trusted to make their own decisions, while speaking frankly and openly. Of course, this does not mean leaving them to struggle through challenges. You can guide and enable people when they encounter an impediment they can't remove for themselves without undermining their autonomy.

Many people find coaching to be unlike anything else they have experienced. Having the opportunity to speak freely, explore novel ideas, and take ownership of decisions is something that many people won't have experienced before. In combination with the other aspects of enablement, you can provide a blend of challenge and support that enables teams to deliver value.

Questions for reflection:
○ What are some powerful questions you could start using?
○ When can you practice active listening?
○ Have you ever experienced a coaching relationship?
○ What makes a coach great in your opinion?
○ What is the difference between directive and non-directive coaching?

CHAPTER 5
THE TEAM AND BEYOND

When you read the word team, what image does it conjure in your mind? Maybe you see football players ready for kick-off? Perhaps you think of your colleagues gathered around a laptop?

The word team makes me think about one of my fondest memories. It's a Saturday morning in November. I'm sitting alongside my dad with our eyes locked on the television. The tiny clock on our equally tiny screen is clicking down.

Matt Dawson, number nine, makes a surprise break through the Australian line. Seconds remain as the ball is thrown to team captain, Martin Johnson. He swiftly goes to ground and Dawson gathers the ball once again.

As it leaves his hands and sails over the twenty-two metre line there is only one person we hope the pass will reach. Jonny Wilkinson.

This was the culmination of four years of hard work. A team regularly described as flattering to deceive, they had lacked consistency and never truly seemed to realise their promise.

But over the previous four years, this team had learned how

to win. They had discovered an adaptable style, leveraging flexible tactics suited to the specific challenges they faced. They were pragmatic and had absolute self-belief.

Although the team arguably had some of the best players in the world, they worked as a unit. Individual talent had space to thrive, but it was enabled by a collective willingness to leave nothing out on the pitch. Their work rate and game intelligence ensured everyone had a role to play.

Of course, those details are a blur as the ball drifts towards Wilkinson. He makes the catch. With no hesitation, he kicks. The white dot on our screen is heading for the posts.

It hangs in the air. We are on our feet, my jaw is on the ground. Twenty-six seconds remain on the clock as the ball passes between the posts. We shout, we jump. I cry.

The final seconds are agonisingly slow, and as the ball is launched into touch, the whistle blows. England are the first northern hemisphere team to win the Rugby World Cup. Pure elation. For a few moments we aren't jumping in front of a small green couch. We're there.

That's the scene I picture when I think of a team, and I can still remember how every second of it felt. A team I wasn't part of, but one that gave me a valuable memory I treasure deeply.

I'm not sure that any group of people I have the pleasure to support will ever experience the indescribable joy that the England team felt when they won, or how I felt sitting with my Dad in front of our tiny television. Nonetheless, I think that seeing a team achieve a valuable outcome they had been working towards for so long taught me a lot.

Collaboration and context were essential to their victory. Everyone had a part to play, but they also needed to understand the task at hand, and adapt their approach accordingly. It also proved that when well trained individuals align around a common goal they don't need to wait for someone to tell them precisely what to do.

All of these lessons are applicable to Delivery Management. It is a discipline built around enabling others to uncover effective approaches and fully apply their skills in the pursuit of collective accomplishment. Teams deliver value, value doesn't deliver itself.

However, no team is the same, so you might be wondering whether your skill set will be appropriate for a variety of contexts. How can you ensure that you are able to support different teams effectively? Are there specific factors that will enable them to be successful? Or should you treat every team the same way?

In this chapter, we will consider what it takes to work in a broad variety of contexts, and how you can leverage your skills in any situation to manage the impact that different team types can have on your role as an enabler; working to remove impediments, coach, and facilitate.

Hopefully you'll be left with a very clear picture of a team in your mind.

TEAMS, GROUPS, AND COMMUNITIES

Before we jump into discussing teams, it's worth noting an important distinction that exists between teams, groups, and communities.

A team is defined as a group of people who work together to achieve a common goal. They should be able to trust each other and have a shared understanding of what they are trying to achieve. In order to be effective, they should be able to work collaboratively and self-organise.

In comparison, a group is a collection of people who work

towards separate goals. They can be made up of people from different teams or organisations, but are likely to focus on individual effort rather than collective collaboration. Groups might exist as a result of organisational structures, physical location, or relationships built around common expertise.

Lastly, a community is a group of people who share a common interest or passion. They can consist of people from different groups, teams, or organisations. Communities enable people to collectively develop knowledge as well as creating a support network outside of a team context.

It is important that you are able to identify when people are working as a team or as a group in order to apply your skill set effectively. Attempting to treat them in the same way can undermine your impact; for instance, a group is likely to lack alignment, so having coaching conversations about pulling in the same direction might be ineffective.

If you are attempting to enable a group, then you could help them to explore whether they are willing to deliver value collectively by increasing collaboration. Groups of separate individual contributors can transition into a team state, but it requires effort and commitment. This process is easier when people recognise the benefits of working as a team, such as increased resilience, efficiency, and trust.

EMPOWERED TEAMS

Delivery Management is a form of knowledge work, where critical thinking and problem solving are fundamental to success.

The types of teams you enable will include countless other knowledge workers undertaking complex activity and uncovering innovative solutions to challenges. As a result, Delivery

Management is naturally suited to organisations with empowered teams.

Empowerment is a form of trust that allows people to thrive. However, empowerment is not something that can be given; declaring that people are empowered only serves to reinforce existing power dynamics. It can only be achieved through the creation of an environment where people have shared power.

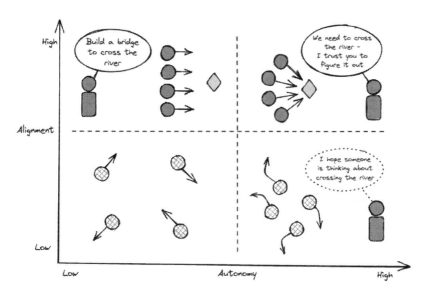

Figure 5.1: High alignment and high autonomy adapted from Henrik Kniberg

An empowered team should be able to choose how they work and what they work on in order to accomplish shared outcomes. This means that the team feels a sense of ownership and control over what they are doing. As a result, teams are more likely to be personally invested in their work. Motivation and autonomy often correlate.

Empowerment is balanced with shared vision, common goals, and a clear understanding of value. Effective teams will work with a high level of organisational alignment alongside a high level of autonomy. (Figure 5.1) You can enable the team to be aligned with the wider organisation while working autonomously by helping to foster mutual trust through open communication.

Effective organisations understand that they should not subject teams to approaches defined in industrial revolution factories. Management theories of this era, such as Scientific Management, often known as Taylorism, named after its creator Frederick Winslow Taylor, are built on the idea that people must be told exactly what to do. Management defines individual repeatable tasks that must be followed precisely.

This contrasts with vibrant organisational cultures that embrace the potential of human creativity and enable teams to apply the full breadth of their expertise and knowledge in order to deliver value. You can support this type of culture to emerge through the application of coaching and facilitation.

For example, you could facilitate sessions that enable impediments caused by a lack of empowerment and autonomy to be captured. This might include visualising hand-offs that cause delays to the flow of value due to work needing colleague sign-off. An outcome of these sessions could be the opportunity to have coaching conversations with business leaders to help them to consider how they can adjust their approach.

Sadly, your efforts will be less effective in contexts where teams are micromanaged. If a senior figure controls every aspect of the team's work or they suffocate the team with overbearing behaviours, it is less likely that you will be able to enable the team to deliver value.

Micromanagers believe there is only one way to work; their way. Attempting to teach the team about different approaches or questioning certain ways of working can be threatening.

However, micromanagers might not realise that their approach is suppressing the team's capabilities. It is a question of effectiveness or ineffectiveness rather than good or bad.

Micromanagement is an impediment to the effectiveness of the team. Tackling micromanagement requires courage, and addressing it should not be taken lightly. You should leverage cautious but clear communication and apply coaching skills such as asking open questions to inspect whether someone understands the impact they are having on the team.

In empowered teams, the whole team is accountable for their work. This contrasts with micromanagement approaches where one person often feels they are solely responsible for what everyone does. Singular responsibility incentivises unhelpful behaviours as it creates a power imbalance and can lead to an individual leaning towards a command-and-control approach. Empowered teams assume collective responsibility.

Because you will work across the organisation as an enabler, you can inadvertently become more visible than other members of the team. Liaising with colleagues to remove impediments, or facilitating workshops are clear examples of work that might cause this to happen. This can lead to people presuming that you have singular responsibility for the work of the team.

It is important to be a proponent of the team's autonomy and collective responsibility to mitigate the risk of people expecting you to be singularly accountable. While you should understand what the team is doing and how they are working, this is so that you can enable the team to deliver value. You are not there to own the team's work or become the team manager.

Pressure to assume a team manager role and take ownership usually increases when things aren't going to plan. If the team isn't working effectively or there are recurring issues, it might seem easier to take charge. However, this will only serve to undermine the empowerment of the team. Ultimately, this will change the team dynamics and limit any capacity for collaboration.

If there are problems with dynamics in the team, it can lead to a decrease in effectiveness. For a team to be able to collaborate they must communicate with each other, sharing ideas and feedback freely. If there is poor communication within a team, it can lead to frustration and confusion. A team that does not collaborate is not a true team, they are a group working on similar activities.

Your facilitation, coaching, and enabling skills can drive collaboration and create the space for positive team dynamics to develop. You can support the team to be open with each other. Openness fosters trust, and enables the team to have the confidence to advocate for their collective autonomy.

In stark contrast to an environment with empowered teams collaborating to deliver value are situations where someone expects you to work in total isolation. It is shockingly common to find organisations expecting Delivery Management to be applied in a context with no teams.

You cannot be accountable for delivery on your own. Whilst you might be an incredibly capable person, you would need to leverage skills outside of your Delivery Management toolbox in order to achieve valuable outcomes without a team, or in support of multiple teams. How can you enable, coach, facilitate, and remove impediments for a team of one that only includes you? Be mindful of these situations, and always seek an environment with teams.

TEAM TYPES

In order to enable teams to deliver value, it is vital to understand the structures and communication pathways that can exist across an organisation.

Removing impediments is easier if you have a sense of who might have responsibility for a road block, and coaching can be far more effective if you recognise the underlying purpose and function of the team.

The interrelation of teams plays a significant role in their success, which is why it is important to have a clear picture of organisational patterns and interactions. *Team Topologies* by Matthew Skelton and Manuel Pais provides an adaptive model for organisational design and team interaction.

Team Topologies defines four fundamental types of teams, and three core interaction modes. (Figure 5.2) We will consider the three interaction modes later in this chapter. The four team types are:

- Stream-aligned
- Enabling
- Complicated-subsystem
- Platform

Each type of team has its own unique challenges and rewards. You should help the team to navigate the context they are in and make the most of the opportunities that this can present. However, you might need to tailor your approach for each team type to ensure that you are enabling them in the most effective way possible.

Stream-aligned teams are aligned with a specific end-to-end stream of business value. This will normally involve ownership of a product. You can expect the majority of teams in an organisation to be stream-aligned, so it is the team type that you are most likely to be part of.

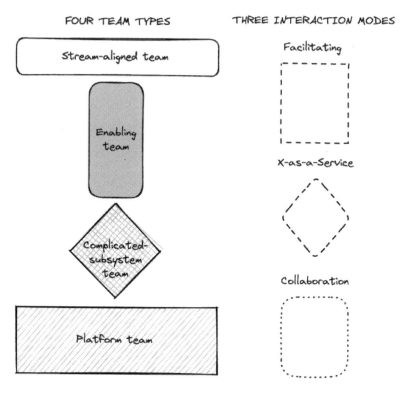

Figure 5.2: The four team types and three interaction modes adapted from Matthew Skelton and Mauel Pais

These teams should incorporate cross-functional skills and be able to operate autonomously to achieve valuable outcomes. As a result, you will be able to apply fundamental Delivery Management skills to enable them.

By supporting the team internally through coaching and facilitation, you can help them to develop clarity of purpose and remain aligned to the wider organisation. A key function that you can perform in stream-aligned teams is minimising the impact of anything external that could limit the flow of value.

Working in a platform team requires broadly the same skills that you will leverage to support a stream-aligned team. This is because platform teams also own a product. However, this product provides an internal capability for other teams in the organisation. The product takes the form of an underlying platform that should create a simplified curated experience for stream-aligned teams in order to reduce their cognitive load.

Because platform teams deliver value internally, they will need to interact with multiple other teams in the organisation. This can create competing demands on the team, so effective communication is essential. You might offer to support the team by facilitating workshops or sessions with people from across the organisation to ensure engagement is not dominated by any single colleague. This can enable you to build relationships across the organisation, which, in turn, can help with impediment removal.

The team is also likely to have a more specific technical skill set in order to curate what would otherwise be a complex experience for internal users. As a result, you should invest effort in understanding details of what this skill set incorporates. It is a good idea to tailor your coaching approach to recognise the technical skills that the team applies, while understanding that responsibility for an internal platform can create a high pressure environment. Everyone depends on these teams.

An enabling team also supports other stream-aligned teams to deliver value, but they don't usually have the same pressure placed upon them as a platform team. Enabling teams provide support and guidance to other teams who are looking to acquire new capabilities.

Enabling teams are composed of specialists in a specific

domain. They collaborate closely with other teams on a time limited basis, creating a purposeful, impermanent dependency in order to ensure that the teams they support have the capabilities and skills required to achieve valuable outcomes.

When you are part of this type of team, you should be willing to facilitate and enable the highly collaborative interactions that the team will have. You might have the opportunity to coach and mentor team members to adopt a teaching stance so that they can distribute knowledge more effectively during engagements.

The team type that you will be least likely to support are complicated-subsystem teams. These teams have responsibility for a part of the organisation that would be too complicated to be built or maintained by a conventional stream-aligned or platform team. They are reliant upon deep specialist knowledge.

Complicated-subsystem teams are at risk of having minimal interactions with other people due to the unique nature of what they do. However, it is key to remember that this type of team still provides a service for other teams that leverage their subsystem. If a subsystem isn't being used by anyone, then it doesn't need to exist. Why retain complexity if you can avoid it?

Your role in a complicated-subsystem team can be challenging due to the scale of extensive technical knowledge that is not simple to consume. Nonetheless, you should endeavour to educate yourself on what the team does. You can enable the team by removing any type of impediment that would make supporting the subsystem even more complex, and supporting the team to communicate the ongoing value of the subsystem.

Regardless of which type of team you support, being able to understand that not all teams are the same can help you to consider the skills you want to apply in different contexts. This can also enable you to define expectations, both from the perspective of being part of a team, but also what might be happening in the wider organisation.

It can be helpful to visualise information you gather about the different types of teams you are working with in order to create clarity for everyone involved and develop a common understanding. (Figure 5.3) Being able to articulate and document what a team's function is and how you might interact with them can help you to navigate an organisational environment.

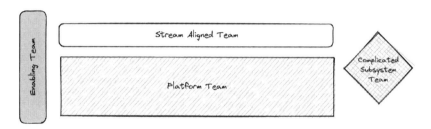

Figure 5.3: Map of different team types adapted from Matthew Skelton and Mauel Pais

This knowledge is invaluable when you are attempting to uncover how to support people in the most appropriate way. It is important to understand and acknowledge the nuances that exist between delivering value through externally facing products compared to internal enabling capabilities.

It is unlikely that you will ever work in all four types of teams, but you do have a higher chance of interacting with all of them. Being able to leverage a well-rounded skill set in combination with an appreciation for the specific benefits and drawbacks of each team type will help you to apply Delivery Management in any context.

Because of the different types of teams you might work with, you will meet individuals who have varied skills and who bring unique perspectives to the table. For you to be effective, you need to be able to work with a true variety of people. A team who all look, think, and sound the same is unlikely to deliver the best outcomes. You need to have an understanding of how different people work in order to be able to support them fully. We will explore this further in chapter six.

INTERACTION MODES

Unless you are working in a start-up environment, you are unlikely to find a business that only consists of one team. Every organisation exists as an organic network of relationships that influence how outcomes are achieved. The interactions between teams can be a defining factor in their ability to deliver value.

In *Team Topologies*, Matthew Skelton and Manuel Pais articulate two interaction catalysts; assistance to achieve a goal and providing or consuming a service. (Figure 5.4) This manifests in three interaction modes that reflect how teams communicate and work alongside each other:

- Facilitating
- X-as-a-service
- Collaboration

Collaboration involves teams working closely together to expand their knowledge and develop new skills. Teams should only apply this interaction mode for a defined period of time. Working beyond a fixed timeframe can create inter-team dependencies or develop an excessive volume of detail leading to increased cognitive load. This mode is most common between stream-aligned teams interacting with platform or complicated subsystem teams.

You can enable teams applying this interaction mode by

facilitating open communication and coaching them on the importance of shared goals. You could also help them to remove impediments that would limit their ability to collaborate with ease. This could include technical blockers, such as having access to the same systems, or organisational constraints, such as ownership of their time, in order to be able to adopt the same cadence of work.

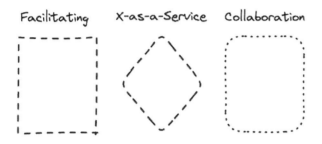

Figure 5.4: The three interaction modes adapted from Matthew Skelton and Mauel Pais

X-as-a-service is an interaction mode where one team is providing something for another team to consume. It is employed when a team's product can be used by another team as a service. This relationship is defined by the consumption dynamic. However, this interaction requires the team providing a service to be mindful of their role in an imbalanced partner-ship meeting another team's needs. Platform teams most commonly provide a service for stream-aligned or complicated subsystem teams.

In order to support teams providing X-as-a-service, you might coach the team on practices that enable them to work transparently in order to keep colleagues aware of progress and avoid conflict over potential competing demands. You might also enable them by facilitating workshops to capture internal user needs. If you work with a team consuming X-as-a-service, you might help the team to consider how to increase organisational psychological safety by developing a respectful relationship with a service providing team.

Facilitating requires one team to support or enable another team by removing impediments, helping them to learn, or teaching them about how to apply different practices. Teams that apply this mode of interaction should support the effectiveness of others; they are not actively creating anything themselves. This is the interaction mode normally applied by enabling teams with the other three team types.

If you work with a team that is facilitating, you could enable them by sharing Delivery Management skills that help others without actively creating something yourself. Coaching the team to adopt a servant leadership stance, as we discussed in chapter three, or various practices, such as workshops, found in chapter seven, can help the team to be effective facilitators.

Being aware of these interaction modes can help you to reduce unnecessary conflict between teams and make it easier for them to gain assistance or access services they need to achieve valuable outcomes. This can also enable you to gain broader organisational insights and work to remove large scale impediments or mitigate wider challenges.

Interaction modes should also be applied in a deliberate manner; teams should not need to communicate with every other team in order to deliver value. Relationships should be curated to mitigate the cognitive load and complexity that develops from a higher volume of interactions, as we will explore in chapter eight.

These modes should also shift over time. If teams are limited in their interaction patterns or the network cannot evolve organically, it can result in wasted effort or inefficiency. As teams learn and develop they will have different needs, so they might not require facilitation or collaboration. Even when a team consumes a service, this relationship should be reviewed as a comparable service might become available from a different team or even an external provider.

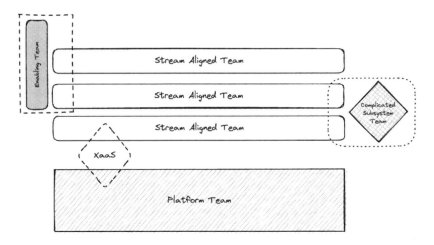

Figure 5.5: Map of different team types including interaction modes adapted from Matthew Skelton and Mauel Pais

The structure and communication pathways between teams is not trivial. It can significantly influence the way that work is conducted, as observed by Mel Conway in 1969. This phenomenon, now described as Conway's Law, indicates that there is a direct correlation between interactions among teams and the products these teams build.

Understanding the preferred form of team communication and, if required, reshaping organisational structures, are both essential to successfully creating products that deliver value.

Gaining knowledge of different team types and their modes of interaction enables you to support teams to align their vision and goals with the constraining factors of the organisational network they exist within. Visualisation of the different team types is strengthened with the addition of interaction modes. (Figure 5.5) This can provide everyone with a clear picture of what teams do and how they can collaborate most effectively, while highlighting potential impediments.

REMOTE WORKING

When you consider the way that teams interact with each other, it is worth examining the effects that working remotely can have in contrast to working in a co-located space. This does not need to be a binary distinction to have an impact as many businesses have adopted hybrid approaches to work.

Even in contexts with co-located, or in-office, teams, organisations might have a number of other teams working from different locations, whether that is a different city or country. As a result, these teams will also need to consider how they manage remote interactions.

It can be useful to consider how you might adapt your approach for these different environments. For example, you could experiment with virtual whiteboard tools to replicate a physical space, or consider how messaging platforms could support asynchronous communication.

Matthew Skelton and Manuel Pais have also created the *Remote Team Interactions Workbook* to support individuals and teams that are not physically co-located.

Remote teams might require increased support to enable effective communication due to interactions being mediated through digital tools, but this should not restrict engagement. You should support teams to explore how they can adopt practices that will enable them to deliver value in any context.

UNFAMILIAR CONTEXTS

Although you are most likely to work with stream-aligned teams that are responsible for products, this will not always be the case. For example, you might have the opportunity to help data management or marketing teams to achieve valuable outcomes. You should be ready to support them to deliver value regardless of their function.

Working in a new context does not change the purpose of Delivery Management; it is fundamentally about enablement. Your abilities as an impediment remover, coach, and facilitator are applicable in any situation, even when you lack domain-specific knowledge.

However, gathering information about any new environment can enable you to be more effective. You can adapt your approach and decide which skills to apply by uncovering organisational nuances. Understanding what has been successful in the past, or why certain teams exist, are examples of insights that can help you to thrive in a new context.

It can be challenging to work in unfamiliar circumstances for a number of reasons. It is important to acknowledge this challenge rather than ploughing ahead blindly.

For example, teams might have their own ways of working that are specific to their domain. It is also likely that you aren't familiar with a team's communication structures or relationships. You will have to be flexible and adaptable in order to adjust.

Alongside these factors, it is common to find that there is jargon you won't understand yet. You will need to learn about the specific product or domain that you are working in so that you can better understand the team's needs and how you can support them fully. It can be difficult to navigate these new waters, but with some effort, you can be effective and confident in any context.

Existing knowledge of a team or organisation might help you to hit the ground running, but it is not essential to your success. I have worked with highly technical teams operating in sectors I knew almost nothing about. By asking open questions about their challenges and taking the time to listen, they often discovered solutions regardless of my knowledge gaps.

One of the most effective ways that you can make working in different contexts easier is by applying a growth mindset. In her book *Mindset: The New Psychology of Success*, Carol Dweck explores two modes of thinking that can shape how we interact with the world.

A fixed mindset aligns with a belief that intelligence is static. As a result, individuals prioritise the appearance of knowledge, and apply a deterministic perspective. This can result in them avoiding challenges, choosing to ignore negative feedback and giving up easily as they believe that investing effort is largely a waste of time. Consequently, they are unlikely to achieve their full potential, while feeling threatened by the success of others.

In contrast, a growth mindset involves the belief that intelligence can be developed. It suggests that challenges should be embraced because setbacks are to be expected when you invest effort on the path to mastery.

This mindset welcomes feedback, including criticism, believing that there is always something to be learned from other people. Applying this mode of thinking can enable you to reach increasingly substantial achievements and attain a greater sense of influence over the world around you.

Working in an unfamiliar environment is an opportunity to grow. Although it might not always be easy, it is a chance for you to hone your craft and refine your Delivery Management abilities. If you keep yourself open to new ideas and approaches, you might find that there is a lot to learn. You should be willing to try new things and to explore alternative ways of working, even if they don't align with your previous experiences.

Adopt a non-judgemental perspective when you arrive in a new setting. This aligns with one aspect of professional coaching that we explored in chapter four; holding unconditional positive regard. This will enable you to provide support to the people around you from day one. Equally, it can help everyone to feel comfortable about your arrival, as they will also be experiencing change due to your presence.

Don't be afraid to ask questions, but remain open to information, and learn before teaching. Developing effective communication skills will ensure that you are able to collaborate in any scenario, and be ready to support people through change. Your ability to engage with others is fundamental to building trust, and trust is key to successful teams.

DEVOPS

When teams exist in a supportive environment, where they feel trusted and psychologically safe, it is easier for them to invest energy into the work they are doing.

This energy investment must be sustainable because organisations typically do not want to create products that instantly lose value after release. Devaluation can happen when products start to break or atrophy as soon as they are available to customers.

At a minimum, products should be maintained and supported after release, which requires an ongoing commitment to invest energy. To mitigate the need for this commitment from a single team, many organisations have a separate operations team that undertakes a support function. Traditionally, development and operations were kept separate where responsibility for a product would be handed from one team to another.

In this situation, it is possible to enable both teams to be more effective by supporting them to build relationships as early as possible. This helps to ensure that a product is easier to support and maintain in the future if it has not been handed over yet, as both teams are able to collaborate and define effective solutions. Early engagement can also prevent problems from arising at the point of handover, and ensure responsibilities are clear.

The traditional approach of handing products over to a different team for support is dependent upon a product reaching a fixed point of completion where creation stops and operation starts. This limits the delivery of value, because no product is ever perfect. Not only will there be inevitable defects, there will also be additional needs that emerge once the product has real users. If a product is near perfect upon its release, then value has probably been sacrificed in other areas by delaying launch in pursuit of perfection.

If the team that created the product continues to iterate it incrementally in order to fix defects and meet new user needs, then constant information handovers to the operations team will be required. This can be time consuming and inefficient. Even with knowledge transfer between teams, the best people to support a product are often the people who built it. Bringing development and operations approaches into the same team to enable products to be continuously improved aligns with the idea of DevOps. (Figure 5.6)

DevOps is an approach that increases collaboration. It removes the silos between development and operations in order to deliver valuable products that meet user needs and can be

supported sustainably. Although these functions do not necessarily have to sit in the same team, they should have shared
goals and purpose, enabled through effective interactions.

Although fluid collaboration between two separate teams
has benefits, they cannot be recognised as truly stream-aligned
teams. This is because neither of these teams owns an entire
end-to-end stream of value. If the team hands off responsibility
for such an essential aspect of the product, then they do not
have full ownership.

I saw this scenario play out in real life when a Director in an
organisation I was working with reached out to the Chief Digital
Officer to express her dissatisfaction with a data capture process
that was vital to a service she was responsible for. "Who do I
need to speak with to get this sorted yesterday?"

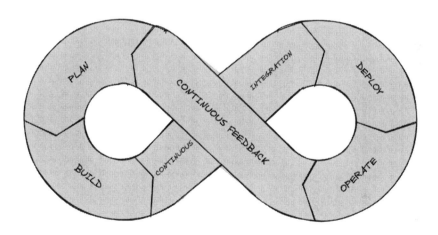

Figure 5.6: DevOps loop adapted from Atlassian

Because the teams were structured around projects, products
were handed over to an operations team once a predefined
amount of work had been completed. This meant that the data
capture process lived with operations. So, the Chief Digital

Officer reached out to them. "This needs sorting as soon as possible."

But the operations team didn't have the capabilities to change the data capture process. They were responsible for keeping it operational and making sure it stayed online, which they did successfully, but changes were a different story. Changes needed to go back to the development team. The Chief Digital Officer wasn't too concerned about this other than the growing list of people he had to engage to get a simple piece of work completed.

Sadly for him, once he submitted a request to the development team to make the necessary changes, it became clear that it wouldn't be that simple. The original group of people that had worked on the data capture process had been disbanded. There was no team left to reach out to.

He soon discovered that any of the individuals who had previously worked on the data project were now fully booked. They were working in new teams, delivering separate projects with defined scope and tight deadlines. More work for any of the old team would mean telling multiple Directors that their projects had to be delayed because something more important had cropped up.

One year later, a business case was signed off and a new team was gathered together to modernise the data process of a legacy application. When they started to inspect the code and compared it to any documentation they could find, they discovered that it had barely been touched. The operations team had successfully kept the lights on, but none of the potential improvements the original development team had hoped to implement were there.

In his book *Project Myopia*, Allan Kelly states that "disbanding high-performing teams is worse than vandalism; it is corporate psychopathy." Not least because it can take three months for a team to become effective, as stated in *Team Topologies*. This is common in the type of project focussed environment I experienced where teams are dismantled and reconstructed when they are assigned to a new project. (Figure 5.7)

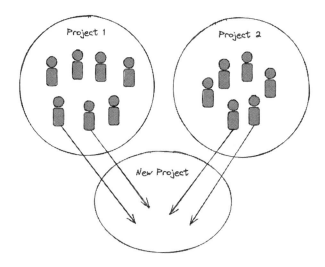

Figure 5.7: People get allocated to the work adapted from Mik Kersten

This stands in contrast to a secure environment where teams are long-lived and stable. (Figure 5.8) This enables work to flow to the team, rather than individuals being moved to the work. Of course, the context around any team will always be shifting, so it is important that teams are still able to change when necessary in order to continue delivering value. They should be stable, not static.

Witnessing the time it took for a product to be changed in order to meet user needs, and satisfy a senior colleague, convinced me that there had to be a better way. When I worked as part of a truly stream-aligned team that was committed to a long term vision and goals, it was clear what we owned. When we needed to change something to deliver value, we prioritised our work accordingly and made it happen. No delays, no hand-offs.

This same sentiment was reflected in 2006 by Amazon CTO Werner Vogels when he said "The traditional model is that you take your software to the wall that separates development and operations and throw it over and then forget about it. Not at Amazon. You build it, you run it." Stream-aligned teams build and run.

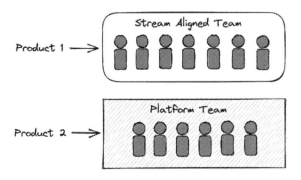

*Figure 5.8: Stable teams where work is allocated to them
adapted from Mik Kersten*

Bridging development and operations in a single, long-lived team ensures that insights about product usage and performance can be used to directly influence future iterations of products. This creates a shorter feedback loop between the people creating and using a product.

As a result, teams applying DevOps are able to continuously improve products. With an ongoing investment in iteration, organisations can commit to the principle that when improvement stops, a product should be actively retired.

WORKING BEYOND THE TEAM

Forests can be ruthless. Resources are limited, from nutrients in the soil to precious sunlight.

Natural competition is the deciding factor in which plants live and die.

In some tropical forests a number of species have developed a particularly ruthless growth habit.

Ficus, or fig trees, are well known for this habit. Their evolution in dark forests, with minimal access to the light they need to survive, caused them to find a unique solution.

At first, these fig trees don't take root in the ground. Their seeds are dispersed by birds and roaming creatures on top of other trees. As their shoots emerge, they climb towards the sun, reaching above the canopy. But, as this growth continues, their roots creep downwards, slowly enveloping their host.

These figs gradually strangle their support tree. Eventually, the fig becomes so dominant that the original tree will die. Although, it isn't all bad news for the host. It is believed that both trees benefit from their symbiosis during storms, as the strangler fig adds support and structure to help the original tree survive.

I shared an abridged version of this nature trivia with Steve, one of our senior colleagues. We were working together as part of a large scale organisational transformation. But what did trees have to do with our work?

The Strangler Fig pattern has become a well acknowledged approach to incrementally implementing change thanks to Martin Fowler. The pattern reflects the process of gradually adding to systems so that new and old components can coexist until the legacy elements can be removed, or strangled.

This involves a dramatic shift away from traditional projects where all of the changes are prepared in advance of a big-bang transition, and you have to hope everything works when the time comes. In contrast, the Strangler Fig pattern enables smaller outcomes to be achieved on a frequent basis until the original system no longer exists.

Our team was set on strangling the legacy products the organisation was using, including the organisational processes and structures built around them. But everyone else was looking for a fixed point of change.

Sharing the Strangler Fig pattern with Steve helped something to click for the team. He became our biggest advocate, and shared the pattern with people across the organisation. We went from being asked "When will the old system be gone?" to people asking about which aspects of the legacy products we might be able to strangle next.

Change was no longer framed as a one time thing. We weren't there to take out the old and insert the new, we were there to gradually iterate on solutions and deliver value on an ongoing basis. Of course, this support was amplified once we started proving how well our approach could work.

Much of your time will be spent working closely with teams, and enabling them to deliver value. But it is also essential to appreciate the importance of people in the wider organisation.

Engaging with colleagues in leadership roles outside of the team is a perfect example of this. You can enable senior colleagues to become visible advocates; providing support and making useful contributions that can result in greater opportunities to achieve valuable outcomes.

By working closely with organisational leaders, you can help them to understand the needs that people have, and consider how they can support others to be effective. This might involve working with them to ensure that teams have access to required resources, and that knowledge workers have the freedom to fully apply their skills.

You can also have coaching conversations with leaders. This will enable them to reflect on how they currently interact with teams and whether engagement can be improved. These conversations can provide opportunities to teach them about different ways of working, and help them to understand why people might be approaching challenges in ways that they aren't familiar with.

The effect of expanding your relationships into new areas of the organisation can be beneficial for multiple people. Not only can it increase alignment, it can also ensure that different expectations are more clearly understood by everyone. Helping others to see the benefits of your work occurring beyond a fixed boundary can often be the first step in extending your influence.

It is essential to have a broader organisational understanding of the context you are working in. The system of work and the various communication pathways that exist within it will include key individuals. Developing a picture of how teams interact with each other, but also with standalone colleagues, will help you to understand what is required to enable the team.

Working beyond the team can have a huge impact inside of it. It can provide you with a route to remove dependencies, or result in information being revealed that might influence the goals and vision for products. Just as teams benefit from fluid collaboration, you will also be more effective if you avoid working in a silo.

HELPING TO DELIVER VALUE

As an enabler of teams, your ability to remove impediments, coach, and facilitate will be impacted by your familiarity with various concepts including different team types, operational contexts, and the indicators of an empowered team. Your awareness of these areas will help you to apply your skills effectively in order to help teams to deliver value.

However, it is important to recognise and remember that delivering value is the fundamental reason to cultivate this area of expertise. You could become an excellent Delivery Management theorist, but unless you apply it in a practical context, you are unlikely to be able to support anyone in a substantial way. True knowledge lives at the intersection of theory and practice.

The impact of seeing these concepts in a practical setting will allow you to reach your own conclusions about what makes a team effective, and whether certain environments make it easier to achieve valuable outcomes. This will also help you to refine your toolbox of skills, and uncover your own tactics to have productive interactions that enable others.

You should be prepared to work with a variety of different individuals in various types of teams and beyond. If you are only prepared to work in one environment or with one set of people, you will find it difficult to apply Delivery Management. You might find that you have preferences towards certain industries or types of teams. This is not a problem, but you will always find a level of variability in any context that you should be ready to accommodate.

This variability can have a significant effect on how you remove impediments. Consider the difference between helping a stream-aligned team to remove dependencies by coordinating with another team, and supporting a complicated-subsystem team to rekey their secrets management solution without a quorum of unseal keys. If that second scenario seems intimidating, rest assured that both impediments could, arguably, be unblocked through effective communication. Nonetheless, context adds complexity.

The environment you are working in can become more complex if people are not aligned around a clear direction of travel, or if nobody understands what they are there to do. These types of situations can present some of the most difficult impediments to remedy as they combine factors including identity, knowledge, organisational structure, capability, assumptions, and beliefs.

Anything that negatively impacts the team's ability to deliver value can be considered an impediment. However, coaching and facilitation shine through as skills that can also remove roadblocks in these challenging scenarios. Asking open questions, organising sessions for reflection, and helping people to develop psychological safety can all help the team to achieve valuable outcomes even when they are starting from a point of maximum confusion.

You can make the process of removing impediments easier by remembering that all of the individuals you work with are people, regardless of their role or team. People generally want to feel included and valued, so treating them this way makes it more likely that they will support you as an enabler. Ensuring that everyone has access to information and that opportunities exist for people to feel heard are two ways you can foster a supportive environment with high levels of trust.

CONCLUSION

Understanding as much as you can about the circumstances that people are working in can have a significant impact on your ability to enable them. If you can comprehend the environment around the team, you will gain vital insights into the structures and communication pathways they need to navigate.

Every team will face unique challenges, but you will be better equipped to provide support if you can assess the function they are performing and recognise their levels of empowerment, autonomy, alignment, and ownership.

You will need to be flexible and adaptable if you want to leverage your skills in a broad variety of contexts. Having an awareness of different team types, and the scenarios they are likely to operate in will help you to apply a suitable approach.

Delivery Management recognises teams as the vehicle for delivering value. As a result, you should support them to adopt collective responsibility for their work and avoid any individual becoming isolated, including yourself. This will help teams to generate a clear vision, develop effective practices, and cultivate a healthy culture.

Teams should learn and grow together, defining their own goals in order to achieve valuable outcomes. However, their existence within a wider organisation is essential to understand. You should help them to recognise the role that other people can have in their success.

Working beyond the team is an important element of effective Delivery Management because so much of their work is impacted by the colleagues around them. You can coach and support these individuals to become advocates and adopt enabling approaches.

Team oriented knowledge does not guarantee the delivery of value, but it will enable you to be more effective in supporting others to collaborate and communicate. This creates a solid foundation for a team, consisting of unique individuals, functioning in a variety of roles, to work towards common goals in the pursuit of value.

Questions for reflection:
○ Which team types are visible in your organisation?
○ What are the indicators of an empowered team?
○ How would you describe the context you are working in?
○ How could you influence a colleague to become an advocate?
○ What do you think a healthy organisational culture should include?

CHAPTER 6
ENABLERS AND CREATORS

It was the best of teams, it was the worst of teams.

Fresh coffee in hand, still recovering from an early morning commute, we would congregate. Each day we looked at our plans, inspected our progress, and considered what we might be able to achieve in the coming hours. On the face of it, things were great.

We were getting so much done. It was always a good feeling when we delivered an update to colleagues about our progress. My manager would compliment me on how efficient the team had become, and I accepted the praise eagerly. We must be doing something right.

A few coffees later, I would walk with my head high towards the train station, staying a little bit later than everyone else to make it clear I was willing to put the hours in. Finding a seat on the late train was always easy, and with my headphones in I had no real distractions. If everything was going so well, why did I feel so stressed by the time I got home?

Finally, we got the chance to showcase our product. Through

all of the presentations and update meetings, we hadn't shown any real elements of our work to anyone. But we had been grinding away, churning through tasks, and increasing our output every sprint. Everyone was clearly busy, their daily updates made that abundantly clear.

The session did not go to plan. We had missed the mark completely, and for all of the work we had been doing, nobody seemed to know why we were doing any of it. colleagues started asking questions and underneath a layer of waffle and bluster we all knew we were bullshitting. We left the meeting deflated.

The blame game started. For all of our efficiency and hard work, all of the extra hours, and all of the caffeine, the team fell apart. Maybe we had never really been a team. Just a group of individuals pulling in a vaguely similar direction.

As we dissected our failures, we realised where we were treading on each other's toes. Three of us were having separate conversations with senior colleagues, people invested hours reworking the same code multiple times, and architectural diagrams lived in a folder that nobody knew existed.

You might be surprised to hear that we had one of the best workshops I have ever participated in that week. We pulled everything apart and built a new foundation for the team.

We learned more about each other in a couple of hours than we had bothered to learn in months. Half of the team didn't even like hot drinks. I could see a path emerging for us to truly become the best team we could be, and I finally understood what my role in the team needed to be.

When you apply Delivery Management, your work is defined by the people around you. Being able to understand who you are working alongside, and what they require to be effective, is the key to unlocking relationships and enabling the team.

Everyone you encounter will be unique, so how can you enable such a broad array of individuals? In this chapter, we will consider how knowledge of distinct roles and capabilities can help you to enable people from different backgrounds with defined skill sets. We will also consider how this can help you to develop an awareness of the pressures and expectations they might face, while avoiding many of the mistakes I made.

No matter their accountabilities in the team, everyone has a role to play. You can help to bring groups of individuals together as a cohesive unit. Delivery Management is all about people, so grab your beverage of choice and get ready to discover the people you could be working with.

PRODUCT MANAGERS

One group of people that you will commonly work alongside are Product Managers. They are key people in many teams because they uncover a product that will deliver value. They play an important role in making sure that teams have enough information to be able to work on the right things at the right time.

Product Managers have responsibility for defining the vision and goals for any product that teams will be working to make a reality. Vision and goals should be developed with input from the teams they are part of, alongside insights from other people including users, colleagues, and customers. However, ultimate responsibility should live with the Product Manager.

Each team should only have one Product Manager. This means that in some organisations they support multiple products. Having more than one Product Manager can cause issues with accountability and responsibility. Similarly, having multiple Product Managers in a team can create unnecessary complexity and impediments due to the contrasting directions that two or more people might steer the team in. You should advocate against a multi-Product Manager approach.

The Product Manager will ensure that everyone in the team has high product and organisational alignment. They can achieve this by ensuring that the voice of the user and the organisation is heard. By highlighting priorities for the team, they improve alignment without dictating specific activity. This will help to shape the valuable outcomes the team is working towards.

Many people use the terms Product Manager and Product Owner interchangeably. Product Owner is an accountability that originates in the Scrum framework, as we will discuss further in chapter seven. It can be adopted by a Product Manager, just as someone can apply the Scrum Master accountability. As such, it is easiest to consider Product Ownership as a type of Product Management.

In some organisations without Delivery Management, there is a burden of expectation placed upon Product Managers to remove impediments, coach, and facilitate in order to enable the teams they are part of. Your support ensures that they can focus on defining a strong, clear, and validated direction for the team instead. They can spend their time maximising value.

More often than not, you will find yourself forming an essential relationship with a Product Manager. The clarity that they offer the team makes it easier for you to focus your efforts as an enabler. For example, if an aspect of the product vision will require the team to leverage a complex technology that they haven't used before, you could facilitate engagement with an appropriate enabling team elsewhere in the organisation ahead of time.

When you understand the direction of travel, you have

greater opportunities to provide impactful support. Vision and goals act as a compass for your work that can help you to consider the skills you might need to apply. It is wise to invest in your relationships with any Product Manager to strengthen this alignment. Your effectiveness as a duo will benefit the whole team.

The partnership you establish with any Product Manager will allow you to discover how you work best together, and what you need from each other to be successful. For example, you might agree that in certain conversations, one of you will be an active listener rather than a vocal participant, in order to maintain transparency while retaining specific responsibilities.

This was a situation I found myself in frequently. I would consistently attend customer meetings facilitated by an excellent Product Manager I was fortunate enough to work with. These sessions were an opportunity to listen and learn in order to support the team in the most complete way possible. We gained rich insights from each conversation, but I was always conscious of ensuring the Product Manager, and other members of the team, had enough space to do their jobs effectively. I was a deliberate observer rather than an accidental impediment.

The Product Manager should enable everyone in the team to understand what is needed to bring a product to life and unify around shared goals. They bridge the gap between technology, design, users, and the wider organisation. As a result, the team can create products that people love by solving real problems in a way that keeps the wider business happy.

The type of relationship that the team has with the Product Manager is imperative, and can often be a defining factor of success. Because they are focussed on maximising value, Product Managers will closely consider balancing the needs of the customer or the wider organisation with the needs of the team. You can support the Product Manager to uncover this vital balance and ensure that both perspectives are present through coaching and facilitation. Ideally, both sets of needs will be met, or at least held in balance.

Relationships that the Product Manager cultivates outside of the team can also be influential and impactful. The right colleague or customer conversation can unlock volumes of unrealised value. You can support them to develop these relationships by facilitating sessions where they can focus on content rather than coordination.

An essential relationship the Product Manager should have is with product leaders in the wider organisation. These leaders are the managers of Product Managers. They create a holistic view of the business that ensures a context exists where the team can make effective decisions and do good work. This information can be shared with the team via the Product Manager to develop a picture of how the entire organisational system of work fits together.

You might interact with someone in a product leader role such as a Head of Product if they are key to removing a large scale impediment. For instance, if there are an assortment of dependencies that are limiting the flow of value, or if an inter-team conflict has emerged that is not resolving itself naturally.

Anyone operating in a product leadership role is there to enable Product Managers. They should support a value focussed product culture, a concept we will explore in chapter eight. This culture must help Product Managers to fully embrace their role. Removing ownership and accountability from Product Managers is likely to manifest as an anti-pattern that disempowers them and, as a consequence, disempowers teams.

Marty Cagan highlights how demanding Product Management can be in his book *Inspired*. The time and effort required to be effective is tough to sustain. He articulates that successful Product Managers must be the very best versions of smart, creative, and persistent. However, these skills manifest as the result of a relentless passion to solve customer problems.

It is helpful to understand how these powerful motivating factors can lead Product Managers to burn out. Their level of commitment to delivering value and the broad array of responsibility they carry means unsustainable practices, including working increasingly long hours, can creep in.

You can support them to remain effective and avoid exhaustion by removing impediments that could make their role more challenging, such as bureaucratic governance processes or skill gaps in the team. Coaching techniques can also help them to uncover approaches to work that mitigate some of the potential negative effects of working in such a pivotal role in the team.

Simple conversations became one of the things that Product Managers I have worked with were most grateful for. Outside of removing impediments that we could both see were blocking the team, I made time to touch base with them and check how they were doing. They had an intense and stressful job, so creating space to vent and feel less isolated in their role always seemed to pay off.

Just as you can't be singularly accountable for delivery, neither can the Product Manager. One person might be standing at the ship's helm with a hand on the wheel, but the boat won't sail without the rest of the crew. Although the Product Manager will recommend what should be done to deliver value, the rest of the team will decide how to turn a vision into reality.

It is useful to understand that Product Management extends far beyond the creation of to-do lists or prioritisation of tasks. Product Managers are not there to simply tend to backlogs or capture user stories. Instead, they are enablers that ensure teams are positioned to solve challenging problems and delight users. They are not the boss or owner of the team, but they do help everyone to uncover the route they need to travel.

Your relationship with any Product Manager will be unique, and the combination of your approaches will be distinct. Occasional compromise might be required, but you should ultimately make each other's lives easier. Having a clear and validated route to deliver value ensures that you can invest your time and effort in enabling the team in ways that will have the greatest impact. When you discover how to work together effectively, the whole team will benefit.

ARCHITECTS AND TECH LEADS

Effective teams often benefit from working alongside technical enablers who can support and guide them towards feasible solutions that will deliver value. Tech Leads and Architects are two examples of this function that you are likely to collaborate with.

Their technical insights enable the team to establish a practical course of action to achieve shared outcomes aligned with the product vision and goals. They apply their knowledge of technology to provide options and clarify choices that would impact the way that the team operates.

Tech Leads are experienced Engineers who support teams to deliver value by providing technical guidance. They should help teams to understand the feasibility of the work required to achieve valuable outcomes.

Effective collaboration and communication are key aspects of the Tech Lead role, and they should serve teams by enabling other people's ideas to be surfaced and explored. Communication also enables them to bridge the gap between people with different technical capability levels, including mentoring and supporting other Engineers.

Architects also provide technical guidance to teams, and predominantly come from an engineering background. They undertake analysis in order to support teams by defining technical designs that enable them to have a clearer picture of how they will achieve shared goals that deliver value. Architects can work beyond individual teams to uncover reusable components and design patterns that teams can adopt. They should also have strong communication and collaboration skills in order to support communication of complex and technical ideas with people across the organisation.

It is easy to view architecture as a purely technological challenge, but Conway's Law indicates that the impact of architectural decisions can be felt throughout the organisation; communication structures will mirror technological systems, and vice versa. Therefore, Architects also need to have awareness of the domain they are working in to ensure that the guidance they offer doesn't lead to negative sociotechnical consequences.

Although there are many similarities between these two roles, Tech Leads are typically more practical and continue to undertake engineering work in teams, while Architects operate more strategically, advising and guiding the team through the process of creating technical designs. However, both roles are fundamentally technical enablers that help teams to define how they will achieve valuable outcomes.

Some teams only have a Tech Lead or an Architect, while others have both. This will depend on a number of factors, including the level of support other members of the team require and the complexity of the product the team is delivering. It is important to recognise that the responsibilities of Architects

and Tech Leads can overlap significantly. This is further complicated by the inclusion of Engineering Managers which are
another distinct role.

Engineering Managers are more closely aligned with the
Tech Lead role than the Architect role. However, they are less
likely to undertake practical engineering effort in the way that a
Tech Lead will be expected to. Instead, they will support teams
to discover effective technical practices and ensure that people
are coached and trained in specific skills that will enable them to
undertake their work.

Because Engineering Managers are normally accountable for
people, process, and progress, their role is distinct from other
technical enabling roles. The role is more closely aligned with a
combination of traditional people management and Project
Management, although this varies between organisations. Their
technical knowledge enables them to be a more effective mentor
and coach to the people they manage.

Some teams will have a Tech Lead, Architect, Engineering
Manager, and Product Manager, but these teams are less likely
to require an individual person applying Delivery Management
unless they have a high volume of impediments. Having
someone in the team who is dedicated to facilitation, coaching,
and removing impediments when four enabling roles already
exist could result in duplicated effort. It might also create confusion in the team around who should be undertaking different
activities.

If you work in a team where your role as an enabler is
unclear because of overlapping responsibilities and skills, you
should work to gain clarity as soon as possible. There may still
be valuable activities that you can undertake to support and
enable the team, but if they can effectively deliver value as an
autonomous unit without your contribution, then it is best to

accept this and seek a new opportunity with a different team where you might have a greater impact.

Regardless of how technical enabling roles are implemented around you, the team is likely to benefit from having someone with this focus. Their insight can ensure that the team has a clearer understanding of what they need to do to deliver value, and whether goals are truly achievable. They can actively consider the feasibility of work in the team, ranging from integrability of solutions to the implications of technological impediments. However, this knowledge does not mean that they make all of the technical decisions in the team.

Because Architects and Tech Leads have the opportunity to influence technical decision making in the team, a lot of their work will be detail oriented. As a result, their roles are more closely coupled with the activity of other team members. If an Architect or Tech Lead attempts to work in a way where they are the only person who can make a technical decision for the team, rather than enabling and providing guidance, they are likely to impede the team's ability to deliver value.

Technical enablers, such as Architects and Tech Leads, have an incredible opportunity to help teams uncover effective solutions to complex problems. When they focus on providing insights and guidance, they can ensure that teams have a feasible way to achieve valuable outcomes. You can enable them to assume a supporting function, and help them to be catalysts for collaboration and communication.

TRIUMVIRATE

By examining the role that Product Managers, Architects, and Tech Leads play in teams, you will gain a better understanding of how Delivery Management can be applied alongside other enabling disciplines. Collaboration between these disciplines results in an equilibrium that helps teams to be successful. It creates a supportive structure that accommodates different needs and perspectives.

Incorporating different enabling roles into the team ensures that no single point of view is dominant. This can mitigate a variety of issues. For example, a team that has high technical capability but lacks a product vision and has never considered its ways of working, might burn out in the process of creating a complex system that does not necessarily achieve valuable outcomes.

In contrast, a combination of clear direction, technical expertise, coaching, facilitation, and impediment removal enables teams to work together effectively in order to deliver value. You should help the team to maximise the benefits of these different disciplines by ensuring that communication is happening throughout the team, and that people's capabilities are well understood.

In the book *Sooner Safer Happier*, Jonathan Smart describes three key roles (Figure 6.1) that can be found at different levels of the organisation in order to enable the delivery of value. He proposes them as a Servant Leader Triumvirate: a group of three people providing leadership by serving others. These three equal, enabling roles create balance at each organisational level, whether they work in one team, across multiple teams, or at the most senior level of the organisation.

The three roles are closely aligned with the enabling capabilities we have explored. The Value Outcome Lead can correlate with the responsibilities of a Product Manager, while the Architecture Outcome Lead role aligns well with an Architect or Tech Lead. Similarly, you would fulfil the Team Outcome Lead role by applying Delivering Management.

However, it is useful to consider the balance of three enabling roles, each dedicated to exploring what and how value can be delivered, without presuming these capabilities are specific to a singular job title. For example, an Engineering Manager could function as the Team Outcome Lead in one organisation, while elsewhere, the Value Outcome Lead might be the CEO.

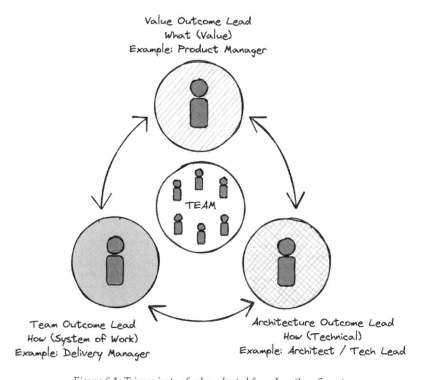

Figure 6.1: Triumvirate of roles adapted from Jonathan Smart

CREATORS

Creation is the core activity for most teams. While it is essential to understand that output doesn't guarantee value, this does not reduce the importance of creation. The majority of teams you are likely to work with will have a handful of roles focussed on enabling, but the rest of the team will be composed of creators. Creator is a broad label, but one that will help you to understand what type of contribution someone will make to the team.

There are many roles that can be aligned with the accountabilities of a creator. By recognising specialist approaches to creation, you can gain an understanding of how people might interact. This enables you to ensure that everyone in the team is able to collaborate and bring together their collective ideas and experience. You should support the team to be on the same page and work cohesively towards common goals so that they can maximise the value of different approaches.

Everyone in an autonomous, empowered, cross-functional team is responsible for their work; therefore, enablers should not reduce the autonomy of creators in the team. Creators should be free to decide what they work on to move the team closer to agreed outcomes. By working together in this way, the team can self-organise and optimise the flow of work in order to deliver value more effectively. Creators in a team are professionals, they do not need to be micromanaged, parented, or babysat.

It is imperative that you are able to support creators of all backgrounds and disciplines. You should understand that different types of creators will have specific needs, but you can facilitate engagement across the team to support the creation of the best possible conditions for them to succeed. They might also face unique impediments related to their role, such as User Researchers only being able to conduct group customer interviews resulting in confirmation bias. Consequently, you should be ready to apply your skills in new ways to remedy distinct challenges.

You must be able to communicate effectively and understand what the team is working on in order to foster the conditions they need to deliver value. Limited clarity, unproductive conflict, and a deficit of learning opportunities are all impediments you can work to remove. You will encounter a lot of variety when enabling creators, but it is important to have the courage, resilience, and confidence to seek support if you get stuck. Rest assured, you don't have to do this alone, and reaching out to your team for help and insight will enable you along the way.

ENGINEERS

Engineers, also known as Developers, are a perfect example of creators. They design, develop, operate, and maintain software. Software engineering is a technical discipline that gained recognition as an engineering field in its own right thanks to Margaret Hamilton promoting it as a distinct set of capabilities during her time working on the Apollo programme at NASA.

In 2011, the entrepreneur Marc Andreessen claimed that "software is eating the world." A claim that has since been proven broadly correct. Software underpins the majority of modern organisations, if not all of them, and will be the backbone of the products delivered by the teams you enable. Having people who can harness software is therefore fundamental to the team's success.

Because of the necessity of software, Engineers will be some of the most essential creators in the teams you support. Their work can bring a product into existence, while ensuring that it is created in a way that prioritises quality and effectiveness. Engineers can also help to ensure that products are easy to use and have a minimal number of problems, often referred to as bugs.

Building relationships with these key team members and taking an interest in their work is always a good idea. It is only by learning about a creator's discipline that you can fully enable them. Understanding foundational principles of software engineering will make it easier to identify and remove impediments, as well as helping you to coach the team to adopt effective ways of working.

Engineers have a highly technical skill set, but this means that people without these skills sometimes distrust the work that Engineers are doing due to a lack of understanding. This can cause an impediment for the team if their work is discounted or challenged, leading to low morale and ineffective colleague engagement. You should manage this challenge by advocating for the work of Engineers and supporting the team, including other enablers, to communicate about value that has been delivered.

In the past, I have seen this distrust cause colleagues to attempt to get constant updates on the progress of work from Engineers because they didn't feel able to engage with technical activity directly. This can be incredibly disruptive, and also has a negative impact on psychological safety. We will consider how you can create clarity around value delivery to mitigate these types of scenarios in chapter seven.

When you trust Engineers, and other creators, to do their job, it makes it easier for them to trust you. Relationships built on trust benefit the entire team as everyone is able to depend on each other to carry their share of the load. This ensures that they will feel able to highlight blockers, such as cross-team dependencies, or fully engage with some of the approaches that you can support the team to adopt, such as retrospectives. We will explore a number of these approaches in chapter seven.

Although Engineers are essential for most teams, they are not the only creators you are likely to work with. For instance, a cross-functional team might include individuals that are focussed on user experience such as UX Designers or Content Designers. By working together in a cross-functional team with a blend of creator and enabler roles, it is possible to deliver every aspect of a product. This enables the team to achieve outcomes without having dependencies on other people to provide additional required skills.

Sometimes, you might work in a team that consists of only one creator type, for example you could support a platform team consisting of Engineers. However, in the majority of teams, creator roles are complementary and enable each other to deliver greater value. This is why it is important to focus on enabling an effective creator environment rather than conditions that only support one discipline. The tools, approaches, and culture we will explore in subsequent chapters will help you to understand what form this environment might take.

CONTENT DESIGNERS

Another set of creators you might work with are Content Designers. They ensure that products are easy to understand and use by leveraging content, including text and images, to solve problems for users. A vast number of products that teams create depend upon effective content, whether people realise it or not.

Cross-functional teams that include Content Designers benefit from having a strong user-centric voice focussed on ensuring the work the team completes is usable and valuable. Usability can often be more focussed on whether technical functions of a product are operational, for instance whether a button performs a designated function. However, this type of technical usability is entirely undermined without considerations of accessibility.

By working with other creators in the team, Content Designers ensure that content is consistent throughout a product, considering an entire end-to-end user journey. However, they do this by making things simpler for users without diminishing the impact and value of content. Simplicity adds value rather than reducing it.

Content Design is not the same as copywriting, in part due to the fact that the written word might not always be the best medium to help users. It is also distinct because it can be seen as a specific way of thinking. In her book *Content Design*, Sarah Winters describes this thought process as being the application of data and evidence to give users what they need, when they need it, as they expect it to be.

Although other creators on the team might be able to create content, this does not mean that they are applying Content Design. Sadly, the skills and knowledge of this discipline are frequently devalued and under-appreciated due to people not fully understanding the specialist approach Content Designers bring to the table.

You can enable Content Designers by ensuring they have adequate opportunities to work closely with other creators in the team and influence the way that the entire product is made. Facilitating sessions that provide them with opportunities to share data and offer their unique perspective can also be valuable. They might benefit from coaching in relation to different ways of working aligned with working in a cross-functional team.

Some of the impediments that Content Designers, and other user experience creators, might face could include having limited access to real customers to conduct research, or not being involved in aspects of product creation. In both of these examples, you should raise these impediments with the wider team in order to see whether the they can collaborate to remove them collectively. Sharing these types of impediments can enable the team to understand each other's roles in greater depth.

UX DESIGNERS

UX Designers are creators that are also focussed on ensuring that products are usable and practical. They are primarily concerned with user experience. This refers to how people interact with a product, for example interacting with a button to switch on a device. Every aspect of that button, from its texture to its shape, has an impact on how you respond to that interaction.

User experience cannot actually be designed, but the factors that influence the experience can be. Having a UX Designer in the team enables everyone to gain a better understanding of the conditions that would elicit a positive interaction, and make the product more valuable to users and customers.

Information architecture enables UX Designers to model interactions and organise different aspects of a product in a variety of configurations to test which variations will be most effective for the user. They create interaction designs, leveraging tools, such as mock-ups or wireframes, that show how different ideas might work at a high level, without too much detail.

The use of information architecture enables the team to get a sense of how the product will work, while also having a foundation that they can build from. This can also help the Product Manager to gather insights that will shape the direction of the product by understanding how users are likely to interact with it. Having a blend of creators focussed on functionality and usability in the team creates a tangible route for the creation of a valuable product.

Some teams have a workflow where UX Designers generate designs which Engineers subsequently have to implement. This forms a type of dual-track model where the team is split and creates a hand-off between discovery and delivery functions in the team. However, this can severely limit collaboration, and reduces opportunities for Engineers to contribute to experiments, or for UX Designers to refine the implementation of their insights. Teams should be able to collaborate fully. This might include UX Designers and Engineers pairing throughout the creation processes.

USER RESEARCHERS

Teams need insights and data in order to achieve valuable outcomes. The team is less likely to deliver value if they do not have a deep understanding of the people who they are creating a product for. User Researchers help to bring the voice of the user into the team.

User Researchers are not creators in the same way as Engineers, Content Designers, and UX Designers, because they do not necessarily create a specific element or aspect of the product. However, they do create research activities and outputs that the rest of the team can leverage to benefit their work.

By conducting interviews and leading studies with users, User Researchers are able to gather data and create valuable insights that will shape the work the team undertakes. This can directly enable the Product Manager to make changes to the goals and vision of the product. It can also help to inform how certain features are implemented by providing additional context for technical enablers and creators to consider.

User Researchers work with the team throughout the creation of a product to ensure that it continues to meet user needs and that the product won't cause problems for users when they interact with it. User Researchers often play a key role in ensuring that the product is moving in the right direction, and provide information that brings clarity to the work that is yet to be completed. Your role as a facilitator can ensure that they are able to easily share their insights.

Teams without a User Researcher might find other ways to gain user insights, but the detail, accuracy, and value provided by having someone that is dedicated to developing this type of knowledge within the team should not be understated. You might support the team to work with a User Researcher on a time limited basis in order to ensure a lack of user data does not become an impediment.

BUSINESS ANALYSTS

Business Analysts are also creators that generate insights and data for the team. However, rather than the specific user focus that User Researchers apply, Business Analysts study trends, data, and patterns that help the team to understand business and user needs. They help to ensure that the team will make better decisions about how they allocate their time in order to maximise the value they deliver.

The insights that Business Analysts provide can help the team to understand whether their work is aligned with the needs of the wider organisation, and enable the team to make informed decisions about how to improve their product in a way that will meet business expectations. This can be especially helpful for the Product Manager who needs to ensure that the voice of the business and user is heard in the team.

The team can benefit from having a creator who is able to produce reports and collate information that will help them to identify areas for improvement, predict future market trends, and understand customer needs and preferences. Business Analysts can help the team to focus on valuable opportunities and invest their efforts on worthwhile experiments.

Unfortunately, Business Analysts are often victims of a number of anti-patterns in teams. It is common for them to end up functioning as a proxy Product Manager, absorbing responsibility and workload related to defining the direction of the team, but without the autonomy that a Product Manager benefits from. This can mean that they are relegated to creating new work items for the team and curating a backlog or to-do list of tasks.

If Business Analysts have a depth of knowledge in other areas, especially technical skills that an Engineer will apply, then they can collaborate with other creators to decompose outcomes into achievable smaller units of value that are easier for the team to deliver. However, this mainly serves to reduce an administrative burden on the team which could be removed in other ways such as limiting the level of detail the team requires in order to start a new task.

I have first hand experience of coaching Business Analysts who did not fully understand where they fit in the teams they were part of. They spent time creating backlog items and reports, but their business knowledge was not being put to good use, and they were predominantly playing second fiddle to the Product Manager. This was disheartening for the Business Analysts as individuals, but it also had a negative impact on the team as it created a divide.

Business Analysts can be helpful, but their skills are often more effective as part of an enabling team focussed on gathering insights in order to create strategic recommendations across the organisation. They could also fulfil a Value Outcome Lead role in a team that does not have a Product Manager; however, this might result in them becoming a Product Manager in everything but name, which would undermine clarity in the team.

BALANCE

"Have you ever noticed the lyrics of "9 to 5" by Dolly Parton?" A strange question for a stag party. I was on the train with my friend Chris. Beers in hand, we were discussing work.

"Seriously, have you ever taken the time to listen to it?" I hadn't. He offered me an abridged version of a talk he had given at a recent conference. A few drinks into the weekend, my mind was blown.

"She's talking about a nightmare company. It's a place where nobody would want to work." Chris walked through the lyrics for me. "Tumble outta bed, and I stumble to the kitchen. Pour myself a cup of ambition, and yawn, and stretch, and try to come to life. She's obviously completely burnt out."

The true revelation came with the chorus. "They just use your mind, and they never give you credit. It's enough to drive you crazy if you let it." Sure enough, this sounded like a horrible place to work. But it felt strangely familiar to the environment of a team I had started working with.

I would tune in to their daily planning call each morning. One or two people would come off of mute to give an update on the day's activities, while everyone else appeared exhausted. Everyone except for the Product Manager.

A few weeks earlier, I had facilitated a retrospective with the team. The tone was flat, and the source of this collective malaise was hard to diagnose. Once again, everyone was borderline silent with the exception of that same single team member.

Although I had suspicions about this dysfunction in the

team, I knew my assumptions alone wouldn't help me to be an enabler. I decided to reach out to the team's Tech Lead.

All became clear between sips of coffee. The team had been a cohesive unit. Working towards a well defined product vision, they had delivered a new application which had achieved record levels of engagement. The countless hours they invested had seemingly paid off.

However, this recognition stopped with one person. The Product Manager. At first, he was invited to speak at an internal conference. Then, he was asked to present to the board. Blog posts and interviews followed. Before the team knew it, he was representing them at an awards ceremony.

This wouldn't have been a problem, except for one thing. Every time the Product Manager had an opportunity to explain the source of their success they failed to mention one, rather essential, factor. The team.

"We felt used." I could sympathise with the blend of frustration and fatigue that the Tech Lead felt. "It was our hard work as a team that got that product completed. He even got a bonus, nobody else did."

As the train journey continued and the other members of the stag party mocked the conversation I was having with Chris, I knew I wasn't going to find the solution to this team dilemma with a can of lukewarm beer in hand.

However, I did know that if things continued this way, most of the team wouldn't be working a nine to five with me anymore. They would be looking for new opportunities to make a living, and Dolly would be right there with them.

Sometimes, it only takes a small misunderstanding to throw a team off balance. Admittedly, taking all of the credit for everyone's work is a fairly large infraction. The team I was working with had lost their stability as a result of one person's selfish actions, regardless of their intentions.

The team had a new form of social hierarchy, and a complete imbalance of passion for the work they were doing. This had left the majority of the team feeling drained and disempowered.

If a team lacks balance, it is unlikely to be able to perform its function in the right way, if at all. Imbalance can be caused by many factors; for example, lacking certain roles in the team while having an abundance of one skill set, having people that believe they are senior to others due to their job title, or having people filling roles part-time leading to dependencies.

It can be difficult to support an imbalanced team, and can lead to a range of problems such as disagreements about why work is not progressing or who should adopt certain responsibilities. This can lead to unhealthy conflict that negatively impacts trust levels.

You should see team imbalance as an impediment that you can help the team to remove. Balance can be restored by working closely with people across the team to develop shared clarity and an understanding of different responsibilities.

While it is beneficial for you to recognise the distinctions between creators and enablers, and the potential relationships and interactions that might emerge as a result of different accountabilities, other people in the team also need to understand each other.

You can adopt a coaching stance, and support individuals to learn about the variety of skills people have in the team, or teach them about roles that they might not have been exposed to in the past. Without this understanding, people might misinterpret their role in relation to others. For instance, an enabler seeing themselves as the team manager.

Because everyone is their own unique person, they will

never be an absolute manifestation of a job description. They will have a life beyond work, and their personal experiences will shape how they apply any discipline. Do not assume that someone's role defines them completely.

Diversity enables teams to achieve valuable outcomes that meet the needs of users and delight customers. The people that use a product are not a singular homogeneous mass, they will also be unique. A diverse team with a balance of perspectives is more likely to understand the needs of users.

Research has repeatedly shown that teams outperform individuals. However, people are inherently complex. There is no guaranteed way to ensure that a team remains balanced, even with a perfect blend of roles or a shared understanding of power structures. You need to help them to collaborate and discover balance in order to unlock their true potential to deliver value as a cohesive unit.

CONCLUSION

When you apply Delivery Management, you will encounter a variety of roles. Having knowledge of different disciplines, and the distinctions between enablers and creators, can help you to support teams to work together effectively.

It is important to recognise that teams should be diverse and balanced in order to meet the needs of users and deliver value. You need to be flexible and adaptable in your approach to support different types of people from a broad selection of backgrounds.

Your knowledge of the roles that you are likely to encounter in multi-disciplinary teams, and the dynamics that can occur as a result of contrasting accountabilities, ensures that you can apply the most appropriate skills to enable others. This will also help you to identify and resolve impediments sooner.

It is important that you are able to see the bigger picture around the team, and help others to understand how different roles can collaborate to achieve valuable outcomes that would not be possible if everyone worked independently.

By being open to new ideas and approaches, you can provide support to multi-disciplinary teams in a variety of contexts. There is something to be learned from every person that you work with, and teams amplify this learning process through active collaboration.

If you are able to apply an open and non-judgemental perspective to any situation, you will be better placed to build trust with others and communicate successfully. Your ability to work as an impediment remover, coach, and facilitator while working with diverse teams depends upon your willingness to invest in relationships.

Your experience of Delivery Management will be shaped by the people around you. The unique cocktail of roles in any team is what enables them to be effective. You have a fantastic opportunity to help others understand each other and develop connections that ensure everyone can deliver value.

Questions for reflection:
○ What are some enabling roles you might work alongside?
○ Can Delivery Management be applied in isolation?
○ What roles might exist in a balanced team?
○ Is any role considered to be the boss of the team?
○ What might you need to consider when enabling creators?

CHAPTER 7
UNIQUE APPROACHES

I remember seeing their board; Team Sparrow. Beautifully arranged post-it notes. Team charter on full display. They even captured the time each work item had been in progress. I was jealous.

Their sprint review was next level. Everyone sat on couches in the meeting space that always seemed to be fully booked. I'd never been able to sit there before.

The whole team spoke up. Engineers discussed pair programming, and their Content Designer chimed in about some front end changes they collaborated on with an Engineer and User Researcher.

Then we had the opportunity to circle the room and examine working elements of their product. Wow. Mind blown. This was impressive. The biscuits they had on offer in the middle of the room sweetened the mood even further.

Then I saw them. Hanging out in a corner of the room. Their Delivery Manager extraordinaire. Their master enabler who must have done something amazing to support this team and get them working like a well oiled machine.

Slowly walking downstairs while returning to my desk, I felt deflated. I was never going to be that good. The team I was part of was working well, but our daily stand ups sounded like flat status meetings, and our board had no magic. I was letting down the team.

Months passed and I kept Team Sparrow and their mythical Delivery Manager in mind. I would read blog posts and scour LinkedIn trying to discover the secret sauce. What would make me that good? How could I ever reach those highs with a team? Would I finally be able to book the hallowed couch filled meeting space?

I got to work and tried to do the best job I could to enable the team. Trying new facilitation techniques, being more proactive with impediments, coaching the team through tough situations. Things were going well, but I was convinced it wasn't enough. Until one day, a chance encounter changed my perspective.

I went along to a community meet up for people working in product teams. Lo and behold, guess who was speaking. It was the uber DM. The superhuman Delivery Manager I had been aspiring to imitate. However, the subject they were talking about was not what I had expected.

"My struggle with imposter syndrome." They began to explain their struggle to find confidence as a Delivery Manager. Having changed careers a few years ago, they always felt like a fraud, doing their best to fit in. They explained how much time they spent reading blog posts and scouring LinkedIn in search of reassurance.

I reached out to them almost immediately. "Can I buy you a coffee?" I expressed my admiration for their work, and how they supported others. I thanked them for helping me to see the kind of contribution I wanted to make to teams.

When we met, we talked for two hours straight. Trading stories about the teams we were working with, exchanging advice on different approaches, and theorising fixes for a variety of organisational issues. Any jealousy I carried had long passed. Now, I was inspired.

The most inspiring aspect of that conversation that I still think about frequently, and continue to share with others, was one phrase. "There's more than one way to do this role." The approaches that I had put on a pedestal had helped at times, but there was no secret sauce, no silver bullet. No singular approach could make anyone the perfect Delivery Manager.

More importantly, I wasn't part of Team Sparrow. I was part of another, equally special team, with unique individuals, our own mix of roles, and a distinct operational context. I needed to uncover approaches that would enable the team I was in to deliver value rather than being solely focussed on what other teams were doing.

There are countless methods and frameworks that teams can apply in order to achieve valuable outcomes, but how do you know which aspects of these will be effective? Are there certain approaches that work consistently? What are some of the under-lying principles that might help you to define your own unique approach?

Delivery Management gives you the opportunity to help teams to discover and apply ways of working that increase their effectiveness. In this chapter, we're going to explore how you can leverage elements of different approaches to work in a way that is appropriate for everyone.

We will consider some of the practices and tools that might inform how you work, and the impact this can have on how you facilitate, coach, and remove impediments. Don't forget, there is more than one way for a team to deliver value, so keep an open mind, and don't worry about perfection. As I learned, you don't need to be in Team Sparrow to be a high-flyer.

KANBAN

Kanban is a methodology that requires transparency and open communication. It originated when Toyota started streamlining its engineering procedures in the late 1940s using a strategy similar to supermarkets stocking their shelves. Supermarkets optimise the flow between the store and the customer by stocking precisely the right amount of items to meet demand.

Toyota used the same method on its production floors with the intention of better matching their inventory levels with actual material consumption. This meant that production was based on customer demand rather than the standard practice of creating an estimated volume of goods and pushing them to market.

Workers would pass a card, or "kanban," to communicate capacity levels in real-time. This enabled a type of "just in time" manufacturing to be introduced. As a result, waste was minimised without sacrificing productivity. This became known as lean manufacturing, or simply, lean.

Teams today can benefit from applying these same principles to their work. Many modern teams leverage kanban boards; a tool used to display work and optimise the flow of it through the team. These boards can exist physically or virtually using a variety of tools such as Trello or Jira.

Openness and transparency allow for better communication and help teams to understand what is happening. When you apply Delivery Management, you can enable teams to consider whether they are working openly and optimising their flow of work. Kanban boards are one tool that supports this by helping teams to visualise work.

Boards are only one aspect of kanban. Having a kanban board does not mean that you are practising the methodology. At its most basic level, a board can show the status of tasks or work items that the team is working on, and they can be used to communicate information without interrupting someone for a status update.

This doesn't mean you should ever consider a board as an absolute replacement for communication. Teams should be constantly collaborating in order to achieve valuable outcomes. However, visibility of work can ensure that conversations are more valuable and focussed on problem solving rather than updates or reporting.

When creating a kanban board, it is important to think about the different stages that work might go through, creating a type of workflow suited to the team's context. This will help to ensure that the board is effective at visualising accurate information that fully captures how a team is working.

The most basic stages of a workflow that are frequently used are: To Do, Doing, and Done. (Figure 7.1) This basic workflow is useful for simple visualisation, but it is unlikely to highlight where work is getting stuck or slowed down. However, detailed workflows can imply a fixed sequence of activity which might not always be appropriate due to non-linear work. We will consider a more detailed workflow later in this chapter.

In a non-factory setting, a team should be supported to accept that work might go back and forth between workflow stages. This is because a lot of work that teams do is complex. You should coach the team to understand that something might return to their to-do list if they uncover new information that makes a work item unachievable at that time.

You can support the team with the process of setting up a kanban board to help them understand what is being worked on currently and where they should focus their efforts. You might do this by facilitating a workshop and coaching the team on what their board could include. The board could also be shared beyond the team boundary, with their consent, to make work visible to colleagues.

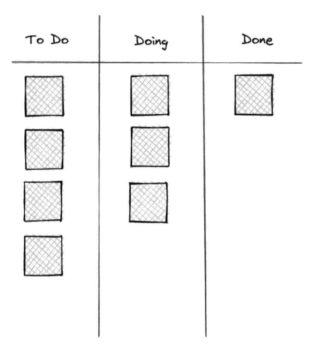

Figure 7.1: Stages of a basic workflow

Ultimately, the board should reflect the system of work that the team is using. If the team is working in a truly cross-functional way, then a detailed workflow with a linear sequence might not be appropriate. Instead, a global busy or in progress condition might be more appropriate and reduce hand-offs inside the team as work is viewed with greater collective ownership.

WORK IN PROGRESS LIMITS

If the team is using a board to visualise work, you can help them to build on this foundation and adopt other aspects of kanban such as work in progress (WIP) limits. WIP limits are a way of limiting the number of tasks, or units of work, that are in progress at any one time. This helps to ensure that the team is not overloaded and that they can focus on completing work before starting something new.

People are often surprised to hear this, and it may feel counterintuitive, but it is often true that doing less gets more done. In the simplest terms, if ten people try to fit through a doorway at once, everyone will get stuck, but if people pass through sequentially, their goal will be accomplished one person at a time.

This aligns with a belief that work can only be valuable once it is done. What is the point of having a full doorway when it means nobody can enter the room. Therefore, completing work items is inherently more important than having many things underway at any given time.

You can teach the team about WIP limits and help them to define their own limits during facilitated events. Limits can be applied to the entire system of work, or to different workflow stages on their board. (Figure 7.2)

When helping a team to establish WIP limits, it is important to think about the true capacity of the team. It can take some time to ascertain how much work should be in progress. Some teams set a maximum WIP limit that is equal to the number of members plus or minus one, but this should be refined over time.

Understanding how much capacity the team has for specific activities should influence how limits are developed in a system with a more detailed workflow. For example, if a team defines a large limit in the development stage but they create a small limit for testing capacity, it is likely that there will be a build-up of incomplete work items. This will create a bottleneck at the testing stage and restrict the delivery of value.

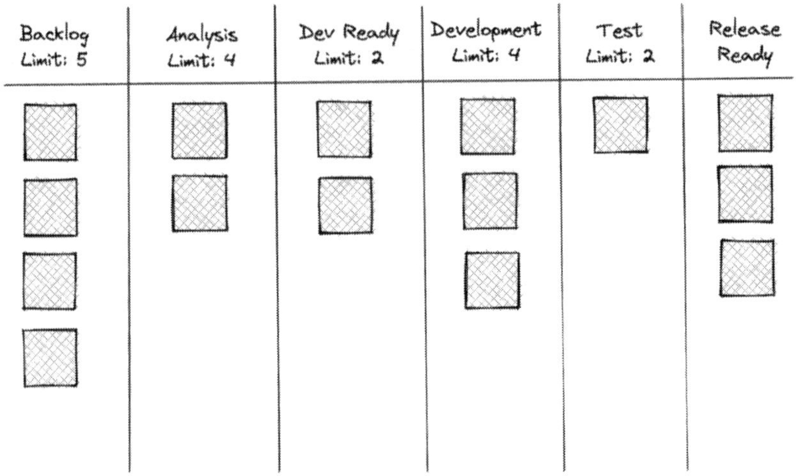

Backlog Limit: 5	Analysis Limit: 4	Dev Ready Limit: 2	Development Limit: 4	Test Limit: 2	Release Ready

Figure 7.2: Workflow stages with individual work in progress (WIP) limits

WIP limits can help to optimise the flow of work by minimising dependencies, bottlenecks, and delays. When it is clear where work is getting stuck, everyone is able to focus their efforts to support work to flow through the entire system and reach completion. If the team is able to accept collective responsibility for their work, a defined workflow with distinct WIP limits can drive collaboration.

WIP limits can also highlight siloed working in less mature teams. For example, if they believe that specific individuals are responsible for each stage of the workflow, and hand-off work between stages rather than collaborating, they are likely to become blocked, or exceed the WIP limit. This can enable you to rapidly identify impediments that you can support the team to remove.

Adopting a process of constant work in progress (CONWIP) can alleviate the risk of hand-offs and siloed thinking found in a system with stage limits. CONWIP was developed by Mark Spearman and Wallace Hopp in 1990. It applies a limit to the entire system, suggesting a maximum volume of work that should be in the workflow at any one time. This can be a simpler way to realise the benefits of limiting WIP, especially in a complex environment with non-linear activity.

You need to accept that WIP limits should be assessed and modified as a result of changes to the team, the work, or the environment, because of the impact these factors have on how work flows. However, any changes to WIP limits should be decided by the whole team and constantly inspected and adapted to optimise for a sustainable, consistent flow of value.

INFORMATION RADIATORS

Kanban boards, and the details contained in them, are an example of information radiators. They provide an accessible and visual source of data that is easy for people to understand. They allow individuals to see the status of work at a glance, and should avoid being unnecessarily complex.

This can help people to stay informed and makes it easier for them to have effective and valuable conversations. Having a better understanding of what is happening leads to an increased ability for everyone to feel engaged and contribute to decision making.

In their most simple form, information radiators are any type of big and visible display. They can be physical or virtual, containing drawings, text, images, or any other visual representations of pertinent valuable information. They should be updated frequently and easy to interact with.

Although kanban provides practices that can help a team to visualise their work, there are a broad range of tools and techniques that can also enable fluid communication both inside and outside of the team that you can incorporate into an information radiator.

An example of this might be creating a highly visible now, next, later roadmap that people in the wider organisation can engage with, supported by a list of recently delivered valuable outcomes. You can provide the team with templates, tools, and resources that will help them create content that is suited to their work and context.

By facilitating the creation of information radiators in workshops, you have the opportunity to help the team consider other opportunities where this approach might enable them to work in the open. This could include coaching them to use information radiators as a way to communicate more effectively beyond their team boundary and influence colleagues.

SCRUM

Scrum is a framework for team collaboration. It is structured so that teams can adjust naturally to changing circumstances and embrace complexity. Scrum promotes self-organisation and the application of empiricism to learn through experiences and improve continuously.

It is a simple framework that can be used in a wide range of situations to solve complex problems. However, Scrum is not a complete guide for how to work, so it requires complementary practices; for example, it can be applied alongside various elements of kanban.

Scrum helps people to work together effectively by defining a set of values and practices that enable teams to develop trust. This aligns with the idea of having a self-organising team that can manage their own work. As a result, the team can decide what they need to do, and how they are going to do it, within the boundaries established in the Scrum Guide.

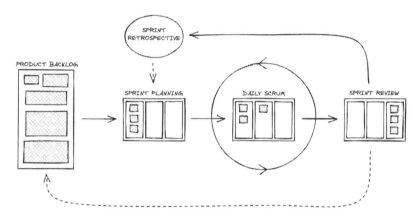

Figure 7.3: Scrum in action adapted from the Scrum Guide

The Scrum Guide is the first place you should look if you want to learn about the framework, and it is equally the best starting point for teams that are interested in exploring and applying it to help them work together. It describes the framework, including its events, artefacts, and accountabilities, alongside the way that these pieces slot together. (Figure 7.3)

Scrum encourages teams to break work into smaller slices of value in order to deliver incrementally. These valuable, useful increments are delivered in a short, time-boxed period known as a sprint. Sprints encourage a frequent release cycle aligned to the delivery of sprint goals; however, a team does not need to wait until the end of the sprint to release something. They also create a cycle for inspection and adaptation in relation to how and what the team is doing.

Although the Scrum Guide is not long, it can take time to fully understand, especially if the team is more accustomed to traditional delivery approaches. If they decide to adopt Scrum in order to foster iterative and incremental ways of working, you can support them to understand and enact the framework. This might include facilitating Scrum events, teaching them about complementary practices, and removing impediments that would limit their progress.

There is a large amount of training available for people who want to learn more and apply the different Scrum accountabilities of Developer, Product Owner, and Scrum Master. You are well placed to adopt the accountability of Scrum Master in the team because it aligns with your skills as someone who can coach and support others, so you might choose to seek training in this area.

It is essential to understand that a short training course does not prepare someone entirely to apply tools and tactics in the real world. There is no equivalent for working with others to try ideas, inspect results, and learn from what you find. Training is only ever a starting point on a journey towards implementing different approaches.

Many of the individual concepts within Scrum can help teams transition towards transparent and agile ways of working. However, Scrum has a level of rigidity that might limit a team from becoming truly agile when applying it. This is because any immutable framework will restrict elements of an agile mindset, including the ambition to constantly improve.

Because Scrum does not attempt to specify how every facet of a team's work should happen, it frequently attracts criticism, especially in relation to its lack of prescribed technical practices. However, because of the generalised nature of the framework, teams are encouraged to discover appropriate practices for themselves.

One source of various technical practices that many teams choose to apply is Extreme Programming (XP), an agile software development framework. XP is focussed on improving software, and the life of the teams that deliver it. It includes a number of concepts and tools that can enable people to collaborate successfully. Gaining an understanding of different technical practices, including those found in XP, will help you to coach and support the team more effectively.

Being able to help teams to apply methodologies and frameworks, such as kanban and Scrum, in different contexts is a valuable skill. If you invest time in familiarising yourself with the Scrum guide and learn about how to use it in a variety of practical settings, you can enable others to benefit from the different practices it describes.

Scrum is used by teams in a broad selection of organisations, but is rarely found in large scale technology companies. This is generally because big tech benefits from high performing teams that do not require the structure of a predefined framework to deliver value on a frequent basis. Many also function in contexts that enable empirical, iterative, and incremental approaches by default.

ADOPTING NEW APPROACHES

When you support teams to adopt new practices and define ways of working, it is important to focus on the outcomes that they will generate rather than perceiving the effective application of an approach as the desired result.

Approaches such as Scrum and kanban can help a team to deliver value, but perfecting the practices they prescribe does not guarantee that they will achieve valuable outcomes. Meaningful work requires more than having a kanban board or working in sprints.

Considering the true reasons for adopting new ways of working is essential, and critical thinking should be applied to any approaches in order to assess whether they are appropriate.

For instance, many organisations adopt Scrum because they have heard the openly debunked idea that it can enable teams to do twice the work in half the time; this is not true. Even if it were true, seeking this type of efficiency boost is counterintuitive to the consistent, sustainable delivery of value, especially when prioritising outcomes rather than output.

Many organisations attempt to implement agile and lean practices because they understand that other successful businesses have adopted this approach. However, fixating on cultivating an agile appearance misses the point. The goal is to deliver value; agile methods can help to make this possible. Perfect agility is not the goal.

Methodologies and frameworks can be a catalyst for teams to shift their mindset and adopt values that enable them to deliver value. They do not constitute the way that teams have to work, nobody should be constrained to one approach. This is why it is illogical for organisations to force an approach on teams, as this action undermines the culture required for teams to be effective.

Instead, teams should be able to inspect and adapt their approach according to the context they operate in and the work they undertake to achieve valuable outcomes. You can facilitate this process of reflection and coach the team to adopt practices that closely align with the way they want to work.

Although a specific methodology or framework might be suitable for the team, there are a number of practices that can be used outside or alongside these approaches. One useful resource for uncovering practices is the Open Practice Library; an open source, community-driven library of tools, and techniques.

The Open Practice Library was established in 2016 when Red Hat Open Innovation Labs identified a chance to codify the open practices and principles they applied throughout client engagements. The library can help you to facilitate conversations or consider different ways to enable individuals, teams, and organisations to discover the optimal ways to deliver value.

Your approach to Delivery Management will be distinct, and this can help to inform the unique approaches of the teams you enable. You should be able to work beyond a single methodology or framework, and apply the most suitable tactics to the environment you are in. However, there are reasons that some practices are more common than others, so it can be useful to gain an awareness of techniques you might consistently advocate for.

TEAM REVIEWS

Team reviews, sometimes referred to as show and tells, are one example of a practice that many teams choose to apply. They are events that allow team members to share what they have been working on with the rest of the team, although a wider audience can also be encouraged to participate in order to gain constructive insights.

An equivalent event found in the Scrum framework is the sprint review. Sprint reviews enable the team to inspect the outcome of a sprint and consider what they want to do in the subsequent sprint. Any type of review event allows the team to assess their progress and ensure they are working towards valuable outcomes.

Team reviews create a feedback loop that helps the team to keep everyone informed of what they are doing. This supports a process of making work transparent in order to inspect and adapt accordingly. As a result, they can gain a deeper understanding of their work and prioritise what they will do next.

The team might choose to demonstrate working examples of a product, or present user research they have gathered. The content of the event is their choice. However, they should be transparent about what they have done. A review structured around glossy presentations disguises the actual impact of delivery.

You should support the team by encouraging them to maximise opportunities to reflect on what they have achieved, and uncover feedback that will enable them to increase the value they deliver. You could also enable the team to experiment with their review structure or audience, using coaching techniques to help them to consider how this type of practice could be more beneficial.

In some contexts, you might facilitate a team review. This can involve helping people to be prepared prior to the review and knowing what they are going to demonstrate, or coordinating the session by introducing people and capturing questions. However, it is wise to avoid becoming an impediment by attempting to own these events, or reducing the self-organisation of the team.

RETROSPECTIVES

Retrospectives are another practice that creates a feedback loop for the team. They are also an event that provides an opportunity to reflect on the past in order to improve the future. However, they differ from team reviews as they are concerned with the people in the team and the processes they apply, rather than the product or outcomes they are working to deliver.

In a retrospective, the team takes a look at what has happened during a fixed period of time or in relation to a specific piece of work. They should consider positives and negatives in order to identify ways that they can learn and improve. This allows them to recognise any potential problems and course-correct if necessary while making changes to how they operate.

Many team's adopt Norm Kerth's prime directive in retrospectives to help them maintain a blameless environment for reflection. "Regardless of what we discover, we understand and truly believe that everyone did the best job they could, given what they knew at the time, their skills and abilities, the resources available, and the situation at hand."

Due to the skills you have as a facilitator, you are well positioned to support the team with retrospectives, enabling open communication and fluid collaboration in a psychologically safe environment. This should help the team to reflect on how they are working, and increase both quality and effectiveness.

You could facilitate a retrospective for the team if they are happy for you to adopt this stance. In order for them to get the most benefit from this event, you might want to consider a structured approach to running the session. (Figure 7.4) Many facilitators also leverage different themed templates to add variety and fun to retrospectives.

Teams shouldn't wait for a retrospective to highlight challenges or resolve conflicts; it's best to discuss problems as they arise. However, they can be a useful way to guarantee that reflection occurs within the team. Establishing a regular cadence of events can also reinforce a culture of openness as they send a message to the team that proactive reflection is prioritised.

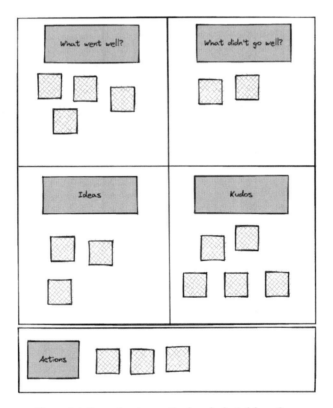

Figure 7.4: Example retrospective board adapted from Greg Holt

You can also use retrospectives as an opportunity to assess whether your own contribution to the team is helping them to be effective. The insights that you gain from people's reflections can determine if you should make changes to the enabling approach you are employing to support them.

Don't forget that you are also a member of the team, so you should have the opportunity to contribute your perspective to retrospectives. This can be challenging if you are facilitating as you will be performing a dual role, but it is important to share your insights and reflect with others.

DAILY PLANNING

Many teams have adopted the practice of using a short, daily event to help them to plan their day. You can support teams to consider how this type of interaction can support their work. These events are often referred to as Daily Stand-Ups, Daily Scrums, or a Daily 15 due to lasting fifteen minutes.

Daily planning allows the team to stay aligned and ensures that everyone is aware of what is happening. They can use these sessions to structure their work and check that they are moving in the right direction on a daily basis. Providing an update on current progress can support this process, but it is not the focus of these events.

You can support the team by ensuring that they are able to easily inspect their work together, and adapt their course of action as a result. Some impediments to this process can include not having a physical or virtual place to visualise work, or a lack of team participation. You should work to remove anything that restricts the effectiveness of this practice.

The team should have complete ownership of daily planning. It is essential to recognise that it is not a status meeting, and it should never be used for team members to report on their progress to an individual outside of the team such as a Project Manager or Team Lead.

This aligns with a risk that can arise if you work as a facilitator during these short sessions. If people in the team are used to traditional ways of working that involve giving frequent updates to someone in a coordination role, they might revert to telling you what they have done or plan to do rather than self-organising and collaborating.

Finding a balance between being present during daily planning to support the removal of impediments, and enabling the team to self-organise and work autonomously can be challenging. You could coach the team outside of these events to adjust how they structure their time without hindering their autonomy.

Teams that work closely together and communicate frequently might not need this type of event. Ideally, all teams should talk more than once a day for fifteen minutes. Without ongoing collaboration, it is challenging for a team to avoid operating as a group of individuals. Nonetheless, having a dedicated opportunity to create a plan for the day in order to achieve valuable outcomes can be useful in any scenario.

WORKSHOPS

Spring 2011 in upstate New York, the writer and artist Austin Kleon is preparing to deliver a talk to students at Broome Community College about the list of things he wished he had been told when he was growing up.

One statement captivated the audience and quickly went viral online. Steal like an artist. This opening declaration of his creative manifesto later became the title of a best selling book.

It turns out that plenty of artists steal. Some of them might prefer to use the word borrow, but how often does anything they have taken get returned? Indefinite rental of ideas feels a lot like stealing to me.

One of my personal favourite examples is "Come As You

Are" by Nirvana. The song has an opening riff that takes me back to being a long haired teenager. It is distinct and memorable, but quite probably stolen.

The precursor to "Come As You Are" was "Eighties" by Killing Joke. A slightly faster version of the riff makes it no less obvious how alike the elements of both songs are. But as with every great heist story, there's a twist.

Before "Eighties" was released, another song existed with the same guitar opener. "Life Goes On" by The Damned. Undoubtedly, The Damned pinched it from somewhere first. It's highly unlikely that a sequence of notes with so many derivatives could have a true original source.

The amazing thing about all three songs is that none of them suffer from sounding alike. They are all loved by countless fans around the world based on their own merit. If anything, I've listened to more Killing Joke than ever before since I noticed that Nirvana felt they were worth stealing from.

Artists steal freely, but they do it in pursuit of creating something new. Enriching the foundations that they are building upon with ideas and reinterpretation of what has gone before. Everything comes from something, nothing is truly original.

So if nothing is original, then why not steal freely? Maybe steal is a loaded word. Learn freely. Absorb everything you can and create wonderful unoriginal things that enrich other people's lives. Use what you discover.

Having read Austin's book and heard him speak at a conference, the idea of stealing like an artist captivated me. It reframed my thoughts on the replication and modification of other people's work, which has led me to facilitate some of the best workshops and retrospectives I have experienced.

Attempting to generate entirely unique and original ideas for how I might facilitate events often tangled me in knots. In contrast, building on existing practices and leveraging other people's ideas enabled me to support effective collaboration and communication with teams and beyond.

Workshops are the perfect opportunity to steal like an artist and leverage approaches that have worked elsewhere. In a workshop, a group of people meet to discuss a specific topic or explore various concepts. You can support these sessions by providing a structure containing engaging activities and practices.

There are many different ways to facilitate a workshop, but creating a safe environment where people are engaged and feel able to contribute is fundamental. In a team context, workshops allow everyone to explore new ideas, examine challenges, or make decisions about the direction of their activity.

Offering your abilities as a facilitator and teacher alongside knowledge of different approaches can result in workshops that people find highly valuable, and ideally enjoyable. It is important to remember that you can only invite participation in a workshop, or any event, you cannot force it upon people without their consent.

Workshops provide an opportunity to enable the team to come up with solutions to problems they are experiencing. Additionally, workshops can be used to educate the team on new practices or techniques. Developing your abilities as a workshop facilitator can ensure that the team gets the most out of the process.

Resources like Sharon Bowman's *Training from the Back of the Room* can be incredibly helpful, and enable you to develop awareness of a variety of different facilitation approaches. However, facilitation is often best learned through experience. As such, participating in training that is focussed on maturing this skill set could prove to be valuable.

SHARED VALUES

The approaches and practices that teams adopt should be applied in the service of achieving valuable outcomes. As we have established, value cannot deliver itself, only people can deliver value. Therefore, any approach should serve people.

An effective approach should have a positive impact on the ability of individuals to interact and collaborate. It needs to influence behaviour within the team. However, behaviour is largely driven by our values. This is why any successful approach will be underpinned by a set of shared values.

Having an agreed set of values enables the team to be more aligned and collaborate as a collective unit. This is due to the increased levels of trust that people experience when they share purpose and direction. Values also manifest in our behaviours, so they can reduce unhealthy conflict and miscommunication if this would be contrary to the team's shared principles.

You can enable the team to discover and agree on a set of values by facilitating collaborative sessions that enable them to consider how they would like to work. This could take place in a designated workshop, or as part of a retrospective. It is important that you do not dominate discussions about team values and that they are owned collectively.

Many teams choose to create a documented set of agreements or a type of charter in order to codify the behaviours and expectations of the team, as we will explore in chapter nine. Social contracts are an example of this that can be found in the Open Practice Library. The team should agree to hold each other accountable to this contract if they create one.

You can also coach the team to remain aligned with their values by asking open questions about whether they might be applicable in different scenarios. It is not your role to police values or force anyone to adhere to them, but you can ask whether they are still appropriate and applicable.

This is especially important if the team decides to incorporate a specific framework or methodology into their approach, such as Scrum. The Scrum Guide requires teams that apply the framework to adopt a set of five values:

- Openness allows the team to be transparent and honest with each other. This helps them to build trust and prevents any misunderstandings from occurring.
- Respect enables the team to feel valued and appreciated. This can help to motivate them and keep everyone working together towards the same goal.
- Courage allows the team to face challenges head-on and encourages them to persevere even when things get tough.
- Commitment ensures that everyone is dedicated to delivering value and reaching shared goals while supporting each other rather than prioritising independent work that isn't aligned.
- Focus helps the team to stay on track and concentrate on achieving valuable outcomes.

Educating the team about values from frameworks such as Scrum can be a fantastic way to start a conversation about how they would like to work, and whether they want to adopt or add to a predefined set of values. This can also complement the wider organisation's values. For instance, Red Hat advocates Freedom, Courage, Commitment, and Accountability.

Shared values are a significant contributing factor to psychological safety. They can reinforce the sense of trust and mutual respect between individuals that teams depend upon.

PSYCHOLOGICAL SAFETY

In 2012, Google embarked on a study to discover what set successful teams apart from the rest. After two years and over two hundred interviews, they discovered five key dynamics; psychological safety, dependability, structure and clarity, meaning of work, and impact of work. They found that psychological safety was the most important of the five.

When the team has ownership of their approach, they have an opportunity to cultivate psychological safety. It enables them to influence factors that are fundamental to their success, such as feeling comfortable with taking risks, showing vulnerability, and being able to speak honestly without fear of retribution.

You can enable the team to be more effective by working with them to define an approach that supports psychological safety. This can be done by promoting transparency and honesty, as well as challenging behaviour that could be seen as threatening or harmful. It is essential that this includes your own actions. Your individual approach should be inclusive and respectful if you want to support the team to adopt equivalent behaviours.

Events such as retrospectives create safe spaces for people to be honest about how they are feeling and enable them to acknowledge their energy levels. Team check-ins are another practice that can have a similar effect, but are more lightweight than a dedicated session for reflection. In their simplest form, you can ask everyone how they're doing at the start of a meeting or workshop.

These practices build trust in the team and make people more comfortable with working in the open and being transparent about any challenges they are facing. They are more likely to acknowledge mistakes, collaborate, and take on broader responsibility when they feel safe. Google even found that teams with higher psychological safety had better retention, enabling teams to be long-lived.

Helping the team to reflect upon their shared values and the goals they are working towards can cultivate and nurture psychological safety. One powerful technique you can apply involves asking open questions about intent or the outcomes someone wants to achieve if they attempt to take actions that you believe could undermine psychological safety.

It is important to consider the impact that different approaches can have on psychological safety. If the team adopts new events to enable empiricism, they might be overwhelmed with pre-existing meetings they don't feel able to decline, or they might be struggling to feel comfortable with working in the open when leveraging information radiators for fear of being misaligned with the strategy of the wider organisation. These factors can lead to unease and low trust, so you should approach them as impediments that could be removed through coaching practices.

Many of the factors that impact psychological safety exist beyond the team, as we explored in chapter five. If the culture of the organisation, or the approach of senior colleagues, impedes the effectiveness of the team leading to sporadic delivery, you should work to mitigate the impact they have.

This could involve coaching people outside of the team to consider the effects of their behaviours, or sharing evidence of defects that have emerged as a result of a high-pressure environment. Your communication skills are essential for influencing others to support a sustainable culture that prioritises people as an enabler of valuable outcomes.

Not everyone will be used to working in high trust teams, so this approach can take time for people to adjust to. Openness and showing yourself for who you are can be a frightening prospect for many people. You should provide support for everyone in the team to express their concerns, even if they aren't forthcoming with their trust. Everyone is different, and it can take some people more time than others to build these types of relationships.

CONCLUSION

Applying Delivery Management effectively extends beyond your ability to support teams with their adoption of specific frameworks or methodologies. Making a valuable contribution to the team is not just about the events you are able to facilitate or the specific practices you advocate.

Adopting a stance where you listen to the team and truly understand their needs before offering your insight and knowledge will enable them to be autonomous and self-manage. Adopting new ways of working can be challenging, but trust and psychological safety provide a solid foundation for teams to agree upon approaches that will enable them to be successful.

If you can help a team to build trust and respect alongside adopting shared values, then they will be in a strong position to collaborate and work openly while frequently inspecting and adapting their work in order to maximise the value they deliver.

Remember that no ready-made framework or pre-defined methodology has been adapted for your context. You need to be prepared to do the hard work to ensure that any practices the team adopts will be suited to their needs and enable them to achieve valuable outcomes. Your role as an impediment remover, coach, and facilitator is pivotal in the process of the formation of a unique approach.

Questions for reflection:

○ How can you support the team to define their approach?

○ How could you gain facilitation experience?

○ What makes a team psychologically safe?

○ When have you felt psychologically safe?

○ How can different practices support openness and transparency?

CHAPTER 8
INSIDE THE SYSTEM

"The human skeleton has two hundred and six bones, which provides the structure for six hundred and fifty muscles. Within those muscles are organs, and tissue, and liquids, and millions upon millions of cells."

Filmmaker Beau Miles had deconstructed the majority of a house when he said those words. "Wood to a house are the bones to a human." He had managed to salvage metres of high quality beams from destruction.

Beneath all of the layers of decades old building materials, there was still value to be uncovered.

Amongst something that had been deemed worthless and ready to be removed, Beau discovered materials that could create something new and useful, possibly even beautiful, if given the opportunity.

From the outside, organisations are a lot like buildings. They exert their presence as rigid structures, with formal identities, and well defined boundaries. Much like the house that Beau encountered, many of them exist on the brink of demolition.

Underneath the facade, every organisation is actually a complex, adaptive system. They are like us, with layers of intricate working parts, each interacting to stay alive.

That's why it's remarkable that so many people only see the rigid structure. They rarely look beyond the skeleton and see the layers of life that coexist around it. People see that something looks old or tired and decide to bring in the wrecking ball and the bulldozer.

"From next week, every team will be using the Scaled Agile Framework." I remember how everyone responded to this new diktat. Our existing culture had been deemed not fit for purpose. We were getting bulldozed.

It wasn't necessarily the choice of framework we took issue with, it was the fact that it was mandatory. There would be no opportunity to scavenge anything valuable before demolition commenced, regardless of how useful or beautiful parts of our structure were.

Seeing an attempt at rapid systemic transformation fail over the course of weeks and months made it abundantly clear that the only way to enable teams to deliver value is to understand their place within a complex, adaptive system, rather than a rigid structure.

But is inspection sufficient? Do you need to manage the system as well as understand it? How can you deal with the systemic challenges that the team will encounter? In large organisations, you might feel like one of millions of cells, but you can play a vital role in ensuring everybody can achieve valuable outcomes.

In this chapter, we'll consider the impact of operating as part of a broader system and some of the limiting factors that can restrict value delivery. We will explore challenges you might face that risk raising your blood pressure, and a selection of the ways that you can ensure that teams are able to put their grey matter to good use.

SYSTEMS THINKING

A system can be defined as a collection of components or elements that are linked together in a way that generates a unique pattern of behaviour. Systems thinking provides a framework for understanding how the system is constructed and the interlinkage between its constituent parts.

Organisational theorist Russell Ackoff espoused the importance of understanding this interlinkage. He stated that "A system is never the sum of its parts; it's the product of their interaction." Therefore, any desired improvement depends upon a holistic understanding of a system.

Systems thinking is an approach that helps you to make sense of complexity by considering the big picture rather than smaller slices of information. This is broadly achieved through a process of mapping and analysis that can enable you to recognise the structures that support the complex, adaptive nature of organisations.

Any visualisation that captures systemic data, such as the distinctions between structures and processes, or objects and relationships, can constitute an aspect of systems thinking. For example, creating maps of team types and interaction modes using *Team Topologies* as described in chapter five.

You could work beyond the team to gather data and create maps, or facilitate workshops with them to gain the benefits of other people's perspective. Whether you create maps collaboratively or independently, you should work openly to ensure that everyone is on the same page. This will increase the likelihood that your outputs will provide valuable context to the team in order to support the way they operate.

This process of mapping and analysis, resulting in simple models, should provide you with an understanding of the flow of value inside of the system. Once you have created a picture that captures flow, you can consider how to optimise it. In many circumstances, optimisation involves recognising the largest impediment to delivering value, and removing it.

When the flow of a system is impeded, it can be referred to as a bottleneck. This narrowed section of a value stream is comparable to an obstructed river, where progress towards a destination is limited. Many factors have the potential to create a bottleneck in the wrong circumstances, including dependencies and short term decision making, both of which we'll explore later in this chapter.

Once you recognise bottlenecks, you can work to remove the impediments that are causing them. Sometimes, these blockers can be resolved by the team; for instance, it might be possible to avoid a hand-off between teams by absorbing responsibility for an activity that causes delays.

If a bottleneck is being caused by a large-scale organisational blocker, you will need to work beyond the team to influence colleagues and advocate for change. You might need to seek support outside of the team, but your application of systems thinking should ensure that you have evidence to support your request.

Systems thinking can help you to inspect the broader context around you, and understand how work is interconnected across the organisation. You can create clarity by sharing this perspective with the team. Having a holistic view of the organisation can influence the practices and approaches they apply. It can also make your efforts as a coach and facilitator more impactful as your own approach will be adjusted to work inside the system.

BUILDING ON SYSTEMS THINKING

The three ways of DevOps described by Gene Kim provide a model to consider the ways that teams can build on a systems thinking approach. (Figure 8.1) This set of patterns highlights three modes of operation for delivering value that each apply increasing levels of detail and engagement with systemic, context specific information.

The first way is the application of systems thinking. It demonstrates a big picture perspective of flow where the team can perceive bottlenecks in order to optimise the system of work and consistently deliver value. However, it shows that systems thinking is only applied in one direction and is more focussed on whether an outcome will be achieved, rather than maximising the value of that outcome.

The second way is the amplification of feedback loops. It highlights how the team should sense and respond by listening to the needs of users once they have achieved an outcome in order to improve the flow of value. This pattern incorporates iterative improvement, emphasising that the team should be able to inspect and adapt their approach.

The third way is continual experimentation and learning. This pattern leverages continuous feedback loops to gather insights rapidly through constant experimentation. This implies that the ability of the team to deliver value is influenced by a culture of growth and learning.

The three ways of DevOps is a useful model to consider some of the additional approaches that will be needed to gain detailed insights that build on the information you can gain from systems thinking. Many of the practices described in chapter seven support the process of creating feedback loops and creating a culture of continuous learning and experimentation.

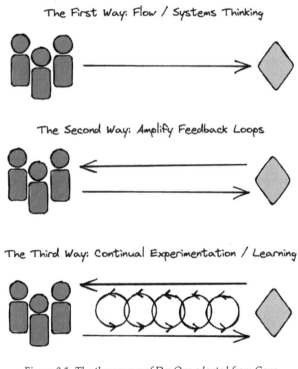

Figure 8.1: The three ways of DevOps adapted from Gene Kim

It is important to recognise the distinctions between these patterns as each of them can be valuable in different scenarios. Sometimes, having a high level view of the system of work will be more helpful than a detailed perspective gained from shorter feedback loops. For instance, systems thinking could help you to identify a potential dependency before it becomes an impediment.

WASTE

When you apply the three ways of DevOps to uncover bottle-necks and impediments that restrict the flow of value, you are likely to encounter waste. It can be defined as anything that does not help to deliver value, but still consumes time, effort, or materials.

Waste can take the form of unnecessary steps in a process, or activities that use up time but do not produce anything useful. This might include unnecessary meetings, or over-planning. For instance, I have been involved in countless recurring planning sessions where a fixed timeline was reworked almost daily to incorporate new information that rendered the existing plans meaningless.

Lean approaches, such as kanban, are centred around the elimination of waste. Working in the open and limiting work in progress are both examples of practices that support this process. They demonstrate that when waste is removed, the team is left with an approach that requires less time and effort to achieve valuable outcomes.

You can enable the team to identify and eliminate waste by coaching them to adopt practices that support inspection and adaptation, such as the application of feedback loops. This will enable them to frequently assess factors such as excessive aspects of their work. This should also include consideration of the reasons behind waste in order to minimise the impact that it has in the right way, especially where people might need reas-surance in order to accept change.

One way to identify waste is to look at the way people interact with other parts of the organisation. For example, you can examine whether they are following a process that is designed for effectiveness, or doing things the way they have always done them regardless of whether the processes are help-ful. If people are following a process that is not designed to add value, then there is likely to be waste in the system.

A lot of processes and systems have unnecessary complexity. Sometimes, this might be as a result of bureaucracy that has accumulated over time, or it might be due to the implementa-tion of ineffective solutions. One factor you should consider is that waste can also occur as a result of self-preservation where people are worried about what will happen if something changes.

Another practice that can support the identification of waste is value stream mapping. It enables people to create a map of the actions required to add value to a user which can then be used as a tool to help guide improvement efforts. This technique can be used to visualise and improve the flow of value through a process by increasing efficiency or limiting hand-offs.

When using these practices, the team might identify burden-some procedures, or layers of reporting and approval that slow down decision making. This presents an opportunity to reduce waste. In this situation, it's important to have a clear under-standing of the goals of the organisation and the team. For example, if a process is no longer supporting them to accom-plish goals, it's likely that it can be removed without having a negative effect.

However, it's important to remember that not all processes can or should be eliminated. Sometimes, a process is necessary for the team to function effectively, even if its value isn't imme-diately obvious. Don't jump to conclusions. It might provide safety measures that only become apparent when things go wrong.

This type of process isn't waste if it actually enables the team to work in a less cautious way and deliver value sooner in the knowledge that measures exist to protect them. In these cases, it's important to find ways to improve the process so that it doesn't slow down the team during normal circumstances. Continuous feedback loops could help this process, as a series of short experiments could qualify the necessity of the process.

Many organisations seek quick fixes for waste. Unfortunately, this often means that people adopt tools rather than considering underlying ways of working; it's easier to change a toolset than a mindset. It is important to understand that tools do not automatically correlate with the application of helpful practices. In many circumstances, it can have a negative impact on a team's ability to deliver value and generate more waste.

Waste can be a complex aspect of a system. Creating alignment around what constitutes waste requires clear and open communication, especially within the team. What might appear unnecessary to one person could seem essential to someone else. This contrast in perspectives is usually emphasised between stream-aligned teams delivering a product, and enabling teams that have an awareness of governance or risk management.

You can facilitate communication with the team and the wider organisation so that everyone has clarity around waste and the ways that it can become an impediment. Be mindful that excessive discussions about waste elimination can, ironically, become a form of waste. Nonetheless, it is a valuable concept for everyone to understand in order to identify the factors that might reduce flow.

DEPENDENCIES

Dependencies are an inevitable aspect of working within a complex, adaptive system. They can reflect relationships between teams, individuals, or work items that are reliant upon each other to deliver value. Systems thinking can help you to identify dependencies by visualising these relationships.

Many organisations understand the importance of managing dependencies, and as such, they accept that visualisation can be beneficial to support this process. However, it can be more productive to focus on the minimisation and removal of dependencies rather than simply tracking them. This is because dependencies frequently become an impediment to the delivery of value.

Dependencies can take a number of forms, although they are often caused by a reliance on a single individual or team. When that person or team is unavailable or unable to do their job, the rest of the team or organisation is unable to continue working. Even at a team level, this can create significant issues.

This type of dependency can lead to a single point of failure, a term that is used to describe a component or element of a system that, if it fails, will cause the entire system to fail. In most organisations, technology itself is less likely to become a dependency if people and processes have been engaged effectively. For example, training to ensure that multiple people can use a complicated subsystem would mitigate this risk.

Single points of failure can be especially dangerous in organisations where a team is crucial to the delivery of value; for instance, in single team start-ups or teams with ownership of a core platform. It is unsustainable to operate in an environment where people cannot continue to work if one team, or a single member of that team, is unavailable.

You should help the team to mitigate anything that could cause these types of issues and prevent them from reaching their goals. As a first step, consider ensuring that the team has redundancies where necessary. Help them to explore whether information could be shared more openly and whether people can learn about each other's skill sets to provide options that reduce single points of failure.

Removing dependencies can also result in the elimination of bottlenecks and waste. For instance, a dependency on another team to make changes to a platform before work can be completed will likely require time to be spent on communication and cause a bottleneck while the team waits. Removing this dependency by collaborating on the platform could accelerate the flow of work through the system.

Sometimes, a dependency is a legacy artefact that no longer needs to exist, such as managerial sign-off requirements that have remained in place regardless of new ways of working being adopted. In this instance, the dependency and waste could be removed by stopping activity that no longer enables the delivery of value. You might support the team by working to highlight the redundant process, or influencing a colleague to work in a different way.

SILOED WORKING

You should aim to break down the barriers that can stop a team from working effectively. One of these potential barriers is siloed working. Functional silo syndrome was defined by Phil S. Ensor in 1988 as a way of describing non-integrated information structures, reflecting how information can be figuratively trapped in a container in a similar way to grain trapped in a silo.

Silos emerge when teams or individuals operate in an isolated way and don't share information or collaborate with other people and teams. This can cause a number of problems. The lack of clarity created by siloed working limits flow and restricts knowledge which can prevent people from being able to work effectively.

They can manifest in a number of ways, and at different scales. The largest silos could include entire business units that refuse to share information. At a smaller scale, isolated functional teams restrict communication and collaboration across disciplines, leading to hand-offs which limit the delivery of value. This type of functional silo can also occur within a team or group. (Figure 8.2)

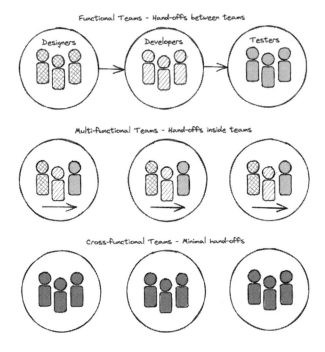

Figure 8.2: Example of functional silos outside and inside of teams

For example, if one person in the team does all of the development work for a product and refuses to let anyone else learn about what they are doing, this would create a silo. If something were to break when that person was ill or on holiday, then there would be issues with resolving the problem.

Equally, if they don't manage their work-in-progress effectively, they might risk building-up more work than they can realistically complete, but nobody else would be able to help or support them. Teams and people that operate in silos can cause problems for the entire organisation as they increase the likelihood of impediments and dependencies emerging.

When people are aware of what is happening around them, they can make informed decisions. As such, you should ensure that information is accessible; openness is the first step in ensuring that people can collaborate to find solutions. However, it is important not to overload everyone with information or burden them with problems that might not be relevant.

This will impact cognitive load: the total amount of mental effort being used in someone's working memory, as defined by psychologist John Sweller. When we ignore cognitive load, people can become overwhelmed as they attempt to hold too much information in their brains. If everyone is expected to be involved in everything all of the time, it can cause a broad array of impediments, such as burnt out team members and low motivation.

Explicitly thinking about cognitive load can be a powerful way of avoiding various pitfalls, such as excessive context switching. One element of this is recognising that healthy boundaries can exist within an organisation. The difference between a healthy boundary and a silo is the fluid transfer of information, enabling collaboration and effective interactions. Open information systems ensure that people have the ability to choose what they consume.

Many organisations initially increase the volume of meetings and workshops they organise to increase information accessibility. However, being solely dependent upon these forums can be restrictive. Asynchronous communication, through the use of tools such as information radiators, can be a far more effective method of enabling engagement.

You should be able to recognise silos and ask questions to discover what is causing them to occur, alongside helping people to understand the issues and dysfunction that they create. Coaching teams and individuals to consider whether their actions are limiting the flow of information and value can have a significant impact on overall effectiveness.

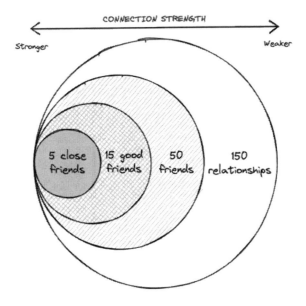

Figure 8.3: Dunbar's number

TEAM SIZE

Some organisations attempt to remedy siloed working by creating large teams where everyone attempts to work together. While silos can create a lack of clarity across an organisation, this can also generate issues. When a team becomes too big, it can be difficult for them to communicate effectively and collaborate.

This aligns with the theory of Dunbar's number that suggests that there is a limit to the number of social relationships a human can have. (Figure 8.3) The theory proposes that a human can only maintain one hundred and fifty social relationships at any one time. After this number, people start to lose some of the social skills needed to maintain connections.

Large teams are also impacted by increased network complexity due to the volume of connections that exist between each person. This can be demonstrated by Metcalfe's law, which originated in relation to telecommunications devices. It states that the value of a network is proportional to the number of connected users of a system.

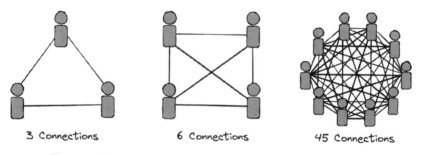

3 Connections   6 Connections   45 Connections

Figure 8.4: Increasing complexity with bigger teams corresponding with triangular numbers

By applying Metcalfe's law in an organisational context, it is possible to see that connections in teams correspond with triangular numbers that increase in a similar way to squared or cubed numbers. You can calculate the number of connections in a team using the formula $(n)(n+1)/2$ where n is equal to the number of people in the team. (Figure 8.4)

You should help the team to avoid becoming too big and operate at a sustainable, small size that enables them to work effectively. A small unit of people with high trust and strong relationships combined with the necessary skills to get work done is more likely to be able to achieve a lot together.

Much like the adoption of specific practices or ways of working, a certain team size does not guarantee the delivery of value. It is a factor that should contribute to the overall success of the team when applied appropriately, but it should not be the primary focus of your efforts.

Trying to fix team size at a certain number is less important than ensuring that people have the ability to work together in a psychologically safe and sustainable way. It is normal for the number of people in a team to change over time, what is important is to ensure that you help them to recognise when changes can become an impediment, and to inspect and adapt how they work accordingly.

TECHNICAL DEBT

Systems thinking enables us to see how operating as part of a broader system can impact the way that value is delivered. However, these effects can manifest in a variety of forms including waste and dependencies. Another consequence is technical debt.

Technical debt describes the result of depending on short term, simple-to-implement solutions at the expense of long term value. Much like taking out a loan, technical debt has to be repaid, whether this occurs gradually over time or in one substantial payment. Teams borrow their future time and effort to deliver sooner.

It can occur as a result of many systemic factors, such as the team needing to make rapid decisions about what to prioritise in order to satisfy colleagues, especially if they are working to an enforced deadline. As a result, their work becomes constrained and they are forced to compromise aspects of their approach with the understanding that it will incur a cost.

As a result of the debt, the amount of value delivered can be disputed because further investment will be required to resolve the cost of faster delivery. Consequently, it is difficult to assess whether a valuable outcome has actually been achieved if the team's work will need to be remediated in future to maintain the stability and reliability of the product.

Some of the negative consequences of technical debt can include reduced testing, lower quality, worse design, increased costs, and future delays. However, technical debt is not inherently bad. How it is managed will determine the impact that it has on the team, especially if they accrued debt unintentionally.

Technical debt can become an impediment to the delivery of value, so you should work with the team to reduce or remove it. You can teach the team about the risks associated with technical debt and work as a coach to enable them to inspect how certain decisions could carry unseen costs.

You could also work beyond the team to teach colleagues about technical debt and support them to consider how their approach might be having a negative effect. For example, helping them to examine whether unnecessary deadlines could make the product less reliable and stable.

A large amount of technical debt can be managed effectively if everyone has the opportunity to understand it, and assess whether it is causing impediments. Visualising existing debt and addressing it through practices such as retrospectives and team reviews can help to highlight the impact it is having.

If the team has accrued technical debt, you should support them to consider whether they can allocate time to paying it back. Some teams dedicate a specific percentage of their time to debt related activities, such as bug fixing and code refactoring. You can enable the team to reduce the impact of technical debt by helping them to adopt an approach that actively acknowledges its existence.

DECISION MAKING

Having a bottleneck in the team isn't fun. Especially if your alarm doesn't go off and you're due to attend a product assessment that morning. On those days, a bottleneck can create a negative feeling that hangs over you like a dark cloud.

Product assessments had a reputation in our team. There was even a special GIF reserved for the lead assessor. Whenever their name cropped up, an ominous repeating image of Darth Vader would appear. You could almost hear the imperial march at the thought of being assessed. Prepare to have your efforts picked apart.

Fortunately, this assessor lacked the ability to force choke anyone, but our work needed to be in perfect order to pass. Based on how my day had started, I wasn't feeling overly optimistic.

I liaised back and forth to get the date pinned down so that the team didn't have to juggle development work and bureaucracy. After the stack of paperwork I had taken off of the team's hands, I was ready for the process to be finished. I could feel myself creeping into bottleneck territory as I accumulated essential jobs that nobody else wanted to touch.

The assessment was due to start. Vader's theme started playing in my head while I waited to join the call. We kicked off with a fantastic pitch from our Product Manager. The vision was clear, the outcomes were tangible, we knew where we were going. One box ticked.

On to the technical details. Engineers who had invested weeks into the product stepped up. Steering masterfully through in-depth questions, it seemed we had gained the high ground. We even got an apprentice in our team to talk about the code that they had refactored.

That was when disaster struck. "Well nobody has shown this to me." Like a bolt of lightning from nowhere, our Tech Lead chimed in. "I haven't reviewed this so I don't know why we're trying to release it." I could feel the presence of the lead assessor as his left eyebrow raised in response. The imperial march started booming in my mind.

Questions followed about whether the product was fit for purpose. "Is this really suitable for release if your Tech Lead doesn't support it?" It was only one small task that hadn't passed through the critical view of our Tech Lead, but it was enough to sabotage our assessment efforts. A bottleneck in the team had caused our hopes to be dashed.

Frustration hung in the air. I could sense our Product Manager's anger growing as the call came to a close and we were offered a slightly hollow "Better luck next time." The hours that followed offered us an opportunity to reflect on why things hadn't gone to plan. After some blunt conversations, one word was at the centre of our diagnosis: Trust.

Our Tech Lead accepted that they couldn't be the arbiter of every piece of work, and if they tried to be, it would continue to slow everyone down. Ultimately, the whole team needed to be trusted to make decisions. We didn't get the result we were looking for in the product assessment, but the opportunity to change our approach ultimately offered the team new hope.

Decision making can be a significant source of impediments and dependencies in teams. If nothing can progress until someone has offered their approval, or people aren't aligned around how decisions get made, it can limit the flow of value. Time spent waiting for decisions can also constitute waste.

Traditionally, decision making was closely aligned with hierarchy. In a worst case scenario, someone would seek a decision from their manager which would then be escalated up the management ladder until a decision could be made at what was deemed to be an appropriate level of seniority. This string of dependencies had the potential to cause multiple impediments.

Once a decision had been made, it had to be communicated back down the chain. This meant that a long time could pass between someone making a decision and people finding out about it, leaving them unable to act until they were given the necessary information. Delays and deadlines create a dangerous combination, often resulting in technical debt.

Self-organising, cross-functional teams require a shift away from this type of approach. If the system is structured in a way that disempowers the team by removing responsibility for decision making, then they are likely to struggle to deliver value in a consistent, sustainable way.

The team I was part of during the product assessment learned this lesson the hard way. Our Tech Lead felt an immense pressure to oversee everything the team did. They believed that they were solely responsible for the quality of everything we produced because the system retained hierarchical decision making and ownership.

They were equally afraid that anything less than a perfect decision would undermine their role as a Tech Lead: a position that they had been aspiring to gain for a number of years. The system was structured in a way that rewarded linear thinking rather than a continuous learning environment, so they modelled their behaviours around work as an individual contributor.

As with many behaviours, the majority of their actions were motivated by a blend of factors, including past experiences. Previous Tech Leads and Architects they had worked with had been micromanagers, pushing everyone to follow specific instructions. They saw themselves as team managers rather than enablers.

These systemic factors all feed into the complex and adaptive nature of organisations. External context can influence the way that teams work more than you might realise. Most of which boils down to a question of where power truly resides in an organisation. Can the team make decisions for themselves in order to achieve valuable outcomes?

I worked closely with the Tech Lead for a number of months after the product assessment. I used some of the professional coaching techniques we discussed in chapter four to help them to examine their interactions with the team. Over time, everyone learned to fully trust each other, and psychological safety increased. The Tech Lead became an outstanding mentor to others and adopted a servant leadership approach, regardless of the cultural pressure the system created.

Coaching and facilitation are two of the best ways to remove impediments related to decision making. Creating transparency around decisions, and applying systems thinking to identify where restricted decisions are causing bottlenecks and dependencies are some of the ways that you can enable the team.

If you support the team to use open and direct communication, they can forge a stronger culture of collective decision making. This will enable them to apply a unified approach when they interact with the wider organisation, even if the system is structured to reinforce traditional hierarchy.

The success of self-organising teams can provide evidence that you can share with other people, including senior colleagues, who might want to consider adopting a new decision making approach to improve the broader system of work.

OUTPUTS VS OUTCOMES

When you operate as part of a wider system, it can have a significant influence on how value is delivered. From inter-team dependencies to decision making approaches, it can have an impact on everything the team does. There is a defining characteristic in any organisation that can amplify these effects: whether they focus on outputs or outcomes.

As we have previously established, outputs are the building blocks that result in outcomes. If our customer were a child celebrating their birthday, the output could be cake but the desired outcome would be a happy kid. The output should ensure that the outcome is achieved.

Organisations consistently aspire to deliver value; however many of them are fixated on traditional objective setting approaches that optimise the system to efficiently deliver predefined outputs. This aligns with linear planning approaches that fix scope with a belief that they will create something valuable. However, in this scenario, the outputs are not serving an outcome; they are the end rather than the means.

Teams operating in an output focussed system can end up creating products which turn out to be of no use or value because they are forced to reach a predetermined conclusion. This normally requires the team to define and deliver within a fixed scope. As a result, time is often seen as the most variable factor in delivery, leading to efficiency being prioritised ahead of effectiveness.

To use our previous example, if a cake is the output, then without a defined outcome, we could make any type of cake and achieve the goal. Therefore, a basic flavourless cake with no decoration would meet the criteria.

Why not create it as quickly as possible? When the system is optimised for outputs, everything has to be explicitly qualified, and anything unqualified will be deemed non-essential and a source of delays.

When the team is focussed on getting things done as quickly as possible, rather than achieving a valuable outcome, they are more likely to create technical debt, leading to issues when they need to pay it back. An output focussed context can result in a short term focus, with reduced consideration for how work undertaken today might affect work in the future.

In contrast, when teams focus on outcomes, they aim to deliver value in the form that is most appropriate for users, customers, and colleagues. The number of features released, or work items completed is inconsequential if they don't deliver value. There's no point making a birthday cake if the kids won't enjoy it.

Systems thinking can help you to assess whether you are operating in an environment that prioritises outputs or outcomes. By mapping actions that people plan to undertake alongside the results they hope to achieve, you can visualise whether the system is optimised for pre-defined conclusions or adaptive solutions.

You should help the team to focus on outcomes rather than outputs in order to minimise waste and improve the flow of value. Jonathan Smart, author of *Sooner Safer Happier*, describes this shift in thinking as "swapping fixed milestones on fixed solutions for outcome hypotheses." What value do we believe we can deliver, and what will be required to help us achieve this?

Rather than being focussed on whether an output has been

delivered, you should enable the team to reflect on what they have learned, how they measure value, and what steps they can take to achieve valuable outcomes. You can do this by adopting the practices we discussed in chapter seven that leverage your skills as a facilitator and coach.

Even when you work in a system that prioritises outputs over outcomes, you should support the team to shift away from this mindset. This can bring pressure as people are often more comfortable when they have a sense of certainty, even when it doesn't deliver value. Therefore, you need to help people embrace uncertainty in pursuit of valuable outcomes.

You can work beyond the team to teach people across the organisation about the benefits of focussing on outcomes, including a reduction of risk, and the maximisation of value. This should be complemented by working in the open to ensure that people can see the outcomes the team delivers for themselves, and, hopefully, start to support this approach.

CONTINUOUS VALUE DELIVERY

Sisyphus was a dangerous mix of prosperous and tyrannical. His idea of a party was putting visitors to the sword. This was not an act that the gods looked kindly upon, regardless of the crown on his head.

As King of Ephyra he led his people to glory, but his own hubris would be his downfall. Sisyphus managed to strike a crafty deal with a river god. He would betray Zeus in return for a new natural spring in his city.

Zeus was enraged. He ordered Thanatos, the physical manifestation of death, to chain Sisyphus in the underworld so he couldn't cause any more trouble. But this king was more crafty than Zeus expected.

Sisyphus asked for a demonstration of the chains, and in the process, bound Thanatos before escaping to the world of the living. As a result of death being trapped, nobody could die, causing chaos and suffering.

The gods freed Thanatos, and Sisyphus knew his days were numbered. So he plotted again. When he died, he asked his wife to forego tradition and cast his body into the river.

When he reached the Underworld, he asked for a chance to return to the world of the living to scold his wife and request a proper burial. Persephone, the Queen of the Underworld, was convinced. However, he had to promise to return.

Needless to say, Sisyphus did not come back. The gods had seen enough. He had twice escaped death through cunning tricks. There would not be a third time. Zeus summoned him.

His final punishment would be a simple task. Roll a boulder up a hill. On the first day, Sisyphus started his ascent, and as the sun moved across the sky, the boulder moved upwards.

As night fell, he lost his footing. The boulder slipped. He could only look on as the boulder rolled all the way back down the hill. The gods were cruel.

As day two came, Sisyphus was determined to conquer the slope. But, as darkness came, he lost his footing again, and the boulder tumbled down. Day three, four, and five were all the same. He was destined to roll this rock up hill for eternity.

Many people can empathise with the struggle of Sisyphus. Condemned to endlessly repeat a seemingly impossible task. But what the gods did not consider was the purpose and meaning he would find in this daily pursuit. At least, that is the assertion of Albert Camus in his 1942 philosophical essay.

Each day Sisyphus would get further up the hill, growing a little bit stronger, slowly mastering the art of climbing. Camus theorised "The struggle itself is enough to fill a man's heart. One must imagine Sisyphus happy."

Delivery Management is centred around enabling people to deliver value. However, value is not a one-time goal, it is not a mountain peak to be conquered or a finish line to be sprinted through. It is a journey of continuous value realisation. This endless pursuit is its own process of purpose and mastery.

Continuous delivery can feel daunting for a lot of teams, with an endless cycle of work bringing the threat of fatigue. However, relentlessly churning out a huge volume of stuff is no guarantee of value. Delivering value continuously depends on quality, usability, and sustainability.

The system the team operates in can have significant implications on their ability to work effectively for a long period of time. People often only discuss this when they are already drained, and retroactively examine the factors that caused them to lose motivation. Awareness of these topics will ensure that you can enable the team to avoid various pitfalls that frequently cause failure.

Fundamentally, if people aren't okay or feel exhausted, they are unlikely to be able to do their best work and make significant contributions within the team. This is especially important in modern organisations undertaking knowledge work because they are reliant upon people's capacity to use their minds.

Many organisations gauge the success of delivery by how fast people get things done. A focus on speed can create the wrong incentives and reinforce a focus on output rather than value. What is the point in building the wrong thing twice as fast as it would take to build the right thing?

If the focus of the team is on getting things done quickly, they may be tempted to cut corners and deliver work that is not high quality. It can also lead to the prioritisation of work that delivers minimal value if it is easier to complete.

This can lead to poor outcomes for the team and the organisation as a whole. The team will also need to remedy these issues later down the line if they are expected to achieve certain goals, so although something might look like it saves time in the short term, additional effort will need to be invested in the future. Re-treading the same ground can quickly become monotonous.

Prioritising pace can also rapidly burn out a team. If they are expected to do things faster, they might compromise their own wellbeing to make it happen. You should support the team to avoid fixating on how quickly they are completing work, especially if it compromises their ability to deliver value.

It is important for the team to fully understand the issues that a focus on speed might create. There is no benefit in an environment that supports one or two weeks of work before exhaustion kicks in. You can help them to discover a sustainable pace for delivery that enables them to gain frequent feedback and learn rapidly in order to consistently achieve valuable outcomes over an extended period of time.

Delivering value on a one-time basis as a team is great, but it has a greater impact when it becomes habitual. The positive effects of repeatedly achieving goals as a collaborative unit begin to compound. Certain activities will become more familiar, relationships can grow stronger, and trust should increase.

Continuous delivery enables the team to uncover purpose and mastery within their work. You can enable them to recognise the proof of what they have accomplished, and the evidence of their growth. When people see progress towards their goals, they are more likely to become personally invested and motivated; this leads to fulfilment.

An overarching sense of fulfilment, in combination with sustainable working practices, is complemented by a system that supports self-organisation and autonomy. When people have a sense of agency, they will harness their motivation to apply new ideas, and manage their time in a way that supports longevity and consistency.

CONCLUSION

Sustainable, consistent value delivery requires a system that is optimised to make the most of the time and effort that people invest. It's not about making stuff for the sake of it. Stepping away from traditional approaches can result in a more psychologically safe environment, where people feel trusted to make decisions and self-organise in order to achieve valuable outcomes.

Understanding the system around the team can enable you to apply Delivery Management more effectively. Every environment you work in will be different, and the challenges you encounter will be varied, but if your approach allows you to visualise the system, and remove restrictive impediments, you can make a huge difference to the people you are working with.

The system around the team will be the source of many constraints, from dependencies to technical debt, but it can also be an enabler. Working with managers to access training for team members in order to remove a bottleneck, or liaising with other teams to change a process and reduce waste are just two examples of how the wider organisation can provide solutions.

You might feel like a small cog in a big machine when you work as part of a wider organisation, but your knowledge and skills will enable you to contribute new approaches that remove single points of failure, create feedback loops, and focus on outcomes. The tools in your toolbox will help the team to experiment with different practices in order to optimise for the fast flow of value.

Questions for reflection:
- How can you improve the flow of value?
- What are the benefits of working towards outcomes?
- What are some dependencies you might encounter?
- How can you apply systems thinking?
- How could you reduce waste?

CHAPTER 9
CREATING A FOUNDATION

As the President walked into the room, a line of employees stood to attention. Gradually working his way down a row of suits, his hand finally reached someone in entirely different attire. "So, what do you do?"

Right hand outstretched, left hand occupied by a broom, John F. Kennedy had some idea what the answer might be from the person in overalls. "I'm putting a man on the moon, Mr. President."

During the May prior to his visit in 1961, Kennedy had addressed Congress. "This nation should commit itself to achieving the goal, before this decade is out, of landing a man on the moon and returning him safely to earth."

This vision had captivated four hundred thousand NASA employees. Nobody talked about emptying bins, changing light bulbs, or cleaning toilets. Everyone was there to contribute to one mission: put a man on the moon.

The next year, Kennedy spoke in Houston, Texas. "Why, some say, the moon? Why choose this as our goal? And they may well ask why climb the highest mountain? Why, thirty-five years ago, fly the Atlantic? We choose to go to the moon."

This was not an isolated vision. It had become the goal of everyone at NASA, and an entire nation. "Space is there, and we're going to climb it, and the moon and the planets are there, and new hopes for knowledge and peace are there."

Many people would leave the story there, but as we've already discussed, Delivery Management doesn't advocate hero leadership. If Kennedy had delivered his messages to an empty room, the USA would never have reached the moon.

Without a doubt, the President helped to catalyse the energy of the nation around an ambitious goal that many thought was impossible. He asked what the entire nation could achieve together by converging around a larger purpose: a new age of human advancement.

However, the key element of that offer was that people were given an opportunity to own this accomplishment. It would be the American people reaching the moon, not just one man.

Kennedy knew that without the knowledge, effort, and commitment of hundreds of thousands of NASA employees, this vision would never be brought to life. He also knew that funding such an ambitious programme would require the support of citizens.

In many ways, the most important person in this story is not JFK. Instead, think about the first person who had the confidence to assert that sweeping floors was an essential aspect of space travel. That type of message catches like fire.

The race to the moon was captivating not simply because it was an opportunity to go where nobody had been before. Instead, it was a way to be part of something larger than oneself.

John F. Kennedy created the spark for a thriving culture where everyone could see their contribution towards a singular valuable outcome. The bond between everyday activity and a vision of space meant that nobody was working in isolation. Even the mundane became meaningful.

Fostering this type of culture takes time, effort, and belief. Creating the right blend of these components is more challenging than mixing rocket fuel. If the vision isn't right, then the team won't find purpose, and if the environment isn't safe, the team won't trust each other enough to collaborate.

Every spaceship needs a launch pad. It tethers the explosive mass of the rocket to the ground for long enough to develop thrust, and provides a stable surface for a safe journey towards the atmosphere.

Creating a foundation for teams is like providing a launch pad. It creates the environment for them to develop momentum as they start to deliver value. They need a level of stability as they delve into realms of complexity, and embark on new adventures.

So how can you support the team to create an appropriate foundation? What should the team consider when building a launch pad? And what are some of the foundational practices that can help the team to achieve valuable outcomes?

In this chapter, we will explore what your role should be in enabling the team to create an effective environment that sets them up for success, including consideration of a variety of techniques and cultural indicators. Most importantly, we will discuss how your approach can help the team to own their foundation and understand how everyone can contribute.

Aim high, shoot for the moon. In the words of Norman Vincent Peale, "Even if you miss, you'll land among the stars."

SHARED VISION

How often do you embark on a journey without considering where you're going? Even the most adventurous explorers tend to pick a direction and use this to inform their decisions. It ensures that they avoid walking in circles. Vision provides this direction for teams.

However, just like explorers, the teams you enable will often be working with many unknowns. Vision is not about drawing the entire route that will be travelled and asking others to get on board. Instead, it should inspire them to embark on the journey towards a valuable outcome.

Vision should provide a common understanding of the direction the team wants to move in, generating alignment in the process. It underpins the rest of the work that the team will do, and provides motivation to invest effort. It is the team's why, and it is foundational to their success.

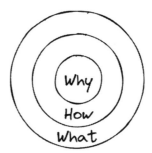

Figure 9.1: Golden Circle adapted from Simon Sinek

In his book *Start With Why*, Simon Sinek suggests that starting with why taps into our innate drive to align information with our values and beliefs. Being able to put a why into words creates emotional context for decision making. It is what our brain looks for first before deciding how or what, as reflected in Simon Sinek's golden circle. (Figure 9.1)

The person who is most commonly accountable for the team's vision is the Product Manager, or someone inhabiting a Value Outcome Lead role. They should establish what positive change the team's work will bring about. This needs to be specific enough that it is tangible, while broad enough to adapt to emergent information. It will commonly take the form of a short statement that can then be decomposed into smaller goals by the team over time.

However, it is essential that the Product Manager does not work in isolation. The team has to own the vision together. If there is not a level of adoption and ownership around a vision, then it will be far less effective. Working on something you don't believe in is highly unlikely to inspire you.

This is one area where you can provide support through enabling practices. Helping the Product Manager to examine whether they are pitching a picture of the future that nobody is buying into by asking powerful questions or inviting opinions in a retrospective can turn a dead-end scenario into an opportunity.

Equally, good ideas can come from anywhere in the team. There might be important reasons to make changes to the vision that people aren't aware of yet. If you're in the car with other people, and someone spots a sink hole that's big enough to swallow the vehicle and everyone inside, it's wise to hit the brakes and consider turning around. You don't carry on regardless just because your hands are on the wheel.

A shared vision helps to ensure that everyone in the team has a common understanding of their work. It becomes a foundational element of effective communication because everyone knows where they are going, which unlocks conversations about how they want to work, and what they need to accomplish to fulfil their vision.

The challenge of creating a stable foundation for the team becomes much easier when they feel confident that their work is valuable. People are significantly more willing to invest effort and build trust if they know it will help them to accomplish something important. However, this highlights why vision crafting will often require a specific set of skills in order to weave a narrative that truly resonates.

In order to fully enable the team, you must be able to understand and clearly communicate the vision. Not only will this ensure that your approach is appropriate for the context you are working in, but it can also help you to take the position of a critical friend within the team. Your understanding will enable you to play devil's advocate in a constructive way that improves decisions and results.

If any member of the team does not fully understand the vision, it can create impediments. This could take the form of an individual doing work that is misaligned with everyone else's effort, or it could result in miscommunication across the organisation. Confusion is terrifyingly contagious among groups of people, so I'm sure you can imagine the impact of a rogue team member describing a vision that stands in stark contrast to reality.

You should enable the team to remain aligned with the wider organisation. Supporting them to work in the open and establish feedback loops will ensure that they have ways to engage with different teams and colleagues. This provides them with the opportunity to gauge the clarity of their vision and ensure that they are contributing to broader business objectives.

The team's vision should be broad enough that it inherently has a level of resilience; however every element of the team's foundation should be flexible and adaptable enough to accommodate change. If the team discovers that their vision is no longer directed towards valuable outcomes, it is appropriate to review and update it. An inspiring vision that is not aligned with value is deceptive; the world doesn't need more snake oil.

FACILITATION

Once the team has established a clear direction, conversation is likely to rapidly steer towards how they want to work, and what they need to do to accomplish their vision. In fact, some teams will be tempted to forego this process and dive straight into the creation process.

In his blog post "Spotify's Failed Squad Goals", Engineering Manager, Jeremiah Lee, describes some of the flawed ways of working he experienced at Spotify. One observation he offers is that collaboration was an assumed competency in the organisation. However, this resulted in teams blindly tweaking their approach in the hope of uncovering the secret ingredient they needed to deliver value.

Jeremiah notes that "Collaboration is a skill that requires knowledge and practice." Although the team will need to collaborate to establish a vision, much of this process involves high level conversations sparked by the imagination of one person. It is not a guaranteed indicator of whether they will be able to collaborate and communicate effectively. Sadly, it doesn't come naturally to all teams.

However, they're in luck: you're here to help. Delivery Management is perfectly tailored to supporting teams with the process of creating a foundation. As a leader who serves the team, you can apply each of the aspects of enablement to help them establish the approach, environment, and culture they need to be effective.

In many ways, the most important aspect of enablement that you can bring to the table during this process is facilitation. It is a fundamental element of Delivery Management that unlocks communication in teams and across organisations, while generating the space for ideas to flow and for people to be heard. It ensures that the team can leverage their collective intelligence to define a foundation.

Communication is often constrained by hierarchy, processes, and the types of tasks that people have to undertake, but you can remove these restrictions through facilitation. It can enable teams to avoid being hindered by the dictatorial style of command-and-control approaches and support open and fluid engagement instead. In that vein, facilitation is not about chairing meetings, or being an event organiser.

One of the fundamental goals of facilitation is to support transparency. Any event that draws information out of people's heads and makes it visible for others to see will enable shared understanding. Open communication encourages interaction with ideas, and enables individuals to become aligned. (Figure 9.2)

Facilitation can be beneficial in many different settings. From workshops and meetings, to almost any type of discussion between people. You can facilitate in almost any situation because you are not required to make a contribution to the content of these sessions. Instead, you are there to provide structure and process in a way that enables others to share their thoughts freely.

When the team is establishing a foundation, the structure and process you provide can take the form of different activities or collaborative practices. These might be used to help the team codify expected behaviours or express and clarify their approach to work. We will explore some of these practices later in this chapter.

In some facilitation scenarios, it can be appropriate to contribute your thoughts and ideas. For instance, it would be counterproductive to facilitate a discussion about core working hours and avoid telling the team that you won't be available when they are. However, it's important to understand that making a contribution to a session is distinct from facilitating one. If you intend to do both, you should be mindful of the impact of blurring this boundary, such as inadvertently dominating conversations.

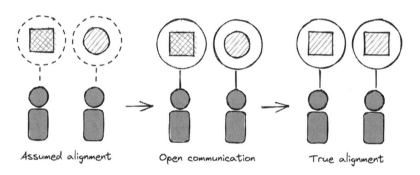

Assumed alignment   Open communication   True alignment

Figure 9.2: Open communication enables alignment adapted from Jeff Patton & Luke Barrett

It can be challenging if people don't understand what to expect from you as a facilitator, especially if it causes someone else to attempt to lead or chair the session as a result. You should help others to understand the contrast between facilitators and contributors, and support them to consider how they can engage effectively during a session. Communicating your intent can help to ensure that everyone is on the same page.

Over time, this might lead to opportunities to apply your

coaching skill set, and support the team to learn about different facilitation approaches. You could also teach them about different practices, and give them opportunities to gain facilitation experience as another way to enable self-organisation. This can help them to understand what they should expect from you as a facilitator.

When you facilitate any type of event, you should confirm that context is clear for everyone involved. This means ensuring that people understand why a workshop, meeting, or discussion is taking place, and what is expected of them. If this information doesn't exist, it is worth trying to gather it as early as possible, or make a decision about whether a session should go ahead.

An agenda can help to generate transparency before a workshop or meeting, and keep the discussion aligned to a target outcome. It does not have to cover all of the content that might be explored, but it is important to articulate why an event is happening and what people hope to achieve. If an agenda has not been defined beforehand, you can incorporate activities into the start of the session to develop a structure in collaboration with the participants.

This is especially useful when the team is establishing a foundation as they are unlikely to have collaborated with you previously in similar sessions; transparency enables collective understanding. In contrast, when you are part of a long-lived autonomous team, they might need less context prior to an event you facilitate as they should be more familiar with your approach.

Another method that you might choose to apply is timeboxing. A timebox is an agreed period of time within which something can take place, such as a piece of work or a conversation. They can apply to a segment of a session, or the entirety of an event. Timeboxes can help the team to avoid rabbit holes and enable them to stay focussed on an agreed outcome, such as reaching a consensus. They are a constraint that should encourage productive and valuable discussion rather than limiting it.

It can be helpful to remind people of the timebox, or use a visual reference such as a timer, in order to keep discussions on track and ensure that everyone is mindful of giving others a chance to participate. Although the timebox should be respected, there must also be a degree of flexibility to extend it if there is agreement in the session that ending a conversation early might be unhelpful.

Every session should result in an outcome. This could be reflected as actions, decisions, or artefacts, but the outcome should be clear regardless of how it is communicated. Everyone should understand what has been explored and what they need to do next. If a workshop or meeting is unlikely to achieve an outcome, then the value of the session should be questioned.

Some events might generate a different outcome than expected; for instance, a planning session could result in changes to the team's ways of working. However, it's important that an event doesn't only generate unproductive conversation.

Discussing ideas and sharing information can lead to a valid outcome; such as increased alignment, but it is important to make this goal explicit so that people can agree on whether a session will be a valuable use of their time.

When you facilitate specific practices that support the creation of the team's foundation, there are likely to be well defined outcomes, such as decisions on how the team will work, that can be captured in different artefacts.

However, at points in this process, it can be beneficial to facilitate conversations that avoid tools and visuals in order to support the creation of stronger human connections. Because collaboration is often an assumed competency, people forget how important it is to cultivate fertile soil for trust and healthy relationships to bloom.

In many teams, facilitation itself ends up becoming part of the team's foundation. This should not result in you becoming a dependency, as you do not need to be their sole facilitator, it is a hat that anyone can wear. However, it can be helpful to acknowledge and incorporate the value of having someone who can play an active role in enabling communication and supporting diverse voices to be heard. The contrast between sessions with facilitation and those without becomes obvious to many people once they have fully experienced it.

There are many foundational practices that you can facilitate with the team. A valuable resource that can enable you to support this process is the Open Practice Library. It includes numerous tools and activities aimed at cultivating an open and collaborative environment that supports technical effectiveness. Don't be afraid to experiment with different practices and share them with the team if you think it will support the formation of their foundation.

WORK AGREEMENTS

One foundational practice that many teams apply is the creation of work agreements. These are often known by many different names; from team charters, to social contracts. Professional Scrum Trainer, Christiaan Verwijs, describes them as "Team-agreed expectations on how you will behave, interact, and deal with certain scenarios."

Some people might have had negative experiences with work agreements in the past. In his blog post "How To Create Better Work Agreements For Your Team", Christiaan is explicit about the fact that some people might consider them to be immature or unhelpful. Not all work agreements are created equal. This is why your skills as a facilitator are so valuable in the process of creating a foundation. You can ensure that the team has the best opportunity to produce something valuable.

Work agreements can span many aspects of how the team will work. From psychological safety and conflict management, to goal definition and experimentation. These are topics that we will explore in further detail later in the chapter. Creating work agreements is a way to ensure that everyone is mindful of how they will collaborate in pursuit of value delivery aligned to their shared vision.

This practice also reinforces the autonomy of the team and their ability to self-manage. It supports a key foundational element of long-lived, empowered teams as they have the opportunity to define their own expectations and shape their approach. As such, it is essential that everyone has the opportunity to contribute to agreements, and revise them if changes happen in the team.

The easiest way to create work agreements is to facilitate a workshop and create a space where people can capture the outputs from the discussion. This could involve a virtual whiteboard, or post-it notes spread around a room. The information can then be synthesised into a single artefact.

As a facilitator, you can spark the process of creating work agreements by asking open questions such as "What do you think an effective culture looks like?" or "What should we avoid as a team?" Because agreements should also include your views, you might invite someone else to facilitate the session, or work with a co-facilitator to ensure that you can contribute without undermining the effectiveness of the event.

One activity that many teams employ is the process of

reaching consensus around elements of their agreements. This can be achieved by using a Liberating Structure, as acknowledged in chapter two, such as *1-2-4-All* which enables the team to capture ideas individually before sharing in pairs, then groups, followed by an open conversation. If the team cannot reach consensus around a specific topic, then it should not be included in their work agreements.

Although a physical version of the work agreements can be a helpful artefact for the team to cite, while also enabling them to radiate information about their approach with other teams or colleagues, Christiaan Verwijs suggests that the primary place for work agreements to live is in the minds of everyone in the team. They should be something they refer to on an ongoing basis in order to be valuable rather than a gesture.

The team's work agreements are likely to be the most visible indicator of their foundation. However, it will tend to be a concentrated and concise version of the values, ways of working, and overall approach they apply. Their true foundation will be broader than work agreements. Nonetheless, the process of creating agreements can do a lot to increase alignment, build trust, and catalyse collaboration.

TRUST

There are few things that impact teams as much as trust. It forms the backbone of human relationships, and sets the stage for people to collaborate effectively. Sadly, it is easily taken for granted. Just as collaboration is an assumed competency in many organisations, people frequently presume that trust will emerge effortlessly.

Any team that is committed to delivering value and accomplishing their vision should think about how they can nurture trust and psychological safety as early as possible in the process of creating a foundation. It is an important topic to consider when creating work agreements, but it can also be helpful to have additional in-depth conversations about fostering a high trust, psychologically safe environment.

A practice that can help to strengthen this part of the team's foundation involves inviting them to visualise the worst environment they can imagine. Humans have an in-built safety mechanism, known as a negativity bias, that causes our brains to fixate on bad experiences and interactions in order to avoid threats in future. As such, it should require less effort for people to recall negative environmental factors.

Once people have contributed their thoughts they can start to discuss the things they would like to avoid. The ease of being able to identify elements of a bad environment usually leads to people feeling more assured about their ideas, and therefore they feel less vulnerable sharing with others.

As a result, this practice often reveals common ground in teams, even when people don't know each other very well. In most contexts, you will find that people identify similar negative traits, such as micromanagement, blame culture, and low trust.

After sharing their perspectives on how they wouldn't want to operate, you can provide the team with the opportunity to flip the exercise on its head and invite them to consider what an effective environment would look and feel like instead. For many people, this will involve qualities that depend on high trust and psychological safety.

It can be difficult to understand what a high performing team, built on trust and respect, truly feels like without experiencing it first-hand. Because many people haven't worked in this type of environment in the past, it can present a challenge when enabling people to define their foundation. Starting with negatives might seem counterintuitive, but it sets the stage for aspiration. They might not be able to describe an environment they have never experienced, but they can articulate what they want to avoid.

By inviting everyone to be explicit about what they feel would constitute negative and positive work environments, they have an opportunity to incorporate their views into the foundation of the team. Rather than assuming that everyone is aligned on how they want the team to operate, this activity creates clarity, and ensures that people can commit to fostering the environment they need.

At one time, I worked with a team that believed an effective environment would involve having influence over how they worked and what they did each day. Self-organisation and autonomous decision making were deemed to be essential, partly in opposition to negative past experiences with command-and-control managers; as such, they needed to feel safe taking risks and communicating openly.

One way that this manifested was a formal agreement across the entire team that they would signal intent rather than asking for permission. When anyone in the team believed that they could do something that would deliver value, they committed to letting others know what they planned to do, and started experimenting in order to validate or disprove their hypothesis rather than spending time and effort on a proposal for someone to approve.

Overall, this aspect of the team's approach had a number of benefits as they were able to focus on high value activities without delay, while also actively reducing technical debt, and achieving valuable outcomes that might otherwise have been overlooked. This would not have been possible if the team had not been explicit about how they wanted to work and ensured that their foundation would cultivate high levels of trust.

At first, a few team members were sceptical about the potential of this approach succeeding, but they could see how it contrasted with prior unpleasant experiences, and could provide mitigation to factors that limited their capability. Over time, these individuals experienced the magic of an empowered team, and thrived in a high trust environment built around intent based leadership. High performance became a collective state of mind that allowed everyone to achieve more than they thought possible.

Rather than assuming that everyone has the same needs, effective teams dive into focussed conversations about what they require to be successful before they embark on their journey to deliver value. Trust and psychological safety need to be nurtured, so helping the team to consider whether they are taking steps to ensure this happens is an important step in creating a foundation.

IMPEDIMENTS

In the build up to a bout between Mike Tyson and Evander Holyfield, Tyson was asked whether he was worried about his opponent's plan for the fight. He replied; "Everyone has a plan until they get punched in the mouth."

Preparing for calm waters only works if you can guarantee that the weather won't change. Every team will encounter issues at some point in time. It's borderline inevitable, especially when we work with high levels of complexity. So what happens when the shit hits the fan?

I have seen many teams dive straight into delivery without any consideration for how they will handle problems along the way and overcome impediments. Some of them managed to create a high trust environment where strong relationships carried them through, but it is remarkable to see how team dynamics change when things go south.

Having this conversation when defining a foundation in the team is not pessimistic; it is rational. Impediments are inevitable, so they cannot be ignored. However, many people jump straight to the detail of how they will fix technical issues, what they could do if someone is ill, or who they might speak to if a process is broken. While these types of impediments will arise, the most important thing to consider is not the specifics of each challenging scenario, but rather how the team will band together when times are tough.

Establishing how to navigate conflict and disagreements is often the best way to bolster trust, and ensure that the team can be effective, even when things don't go to plan. It can form an important element of their foundation, whether this is captured in work agreements, or even in the form of a charter. One team I enabled had a special "break glass in case of emergency" document that everyone had committed to.

Many teams imagine themselves being highly aligned at all times, partially because individuals rarely think that their opinion might be wrong. However, conflict is a natural part of human interactions. It would be strange for everyone to agree all the time, and if anything, this could be an indicator that the team lacks perspective and diversity.

In contrast, productive disagreements, or healthy conflict, can help the team to maximise the value they deliver. It can lead to a more productive and cohesive team, and enables them to develop a deeper level of trust in each other. Teams that listen to each other and continue to collaborate to achieve valuable outcomes, even when they aren't perfectly aligned, are far more effective than those who down tools at the first sign of disagreement.

The team should be able to disagree when things are on track in order to ensure that they are taking the right course of action, but it becomes far more difficult to depend upon politeness and general decency when the pressure is on.

Being explicit about how to work through difficult situations before they happen can save a lot of pain down the line. This especially can mitigate the negative effects of passive aggression that slowly eat away at a team, breeding resentment and undermining trust.

You can facilitate a conversation about this topic in the process of creating work agreements, or as a separate workshop depending on whether the team feels they have enough to discuss. As part of this process, they can agree on conflict management techniques they might employ, such as talking through a problem from another person's perspective first, seeking mediation for disagreements, or using empathy maps. It is important for the team to agree on what is and isn't acceptable.

Conflict and disagreements are often resolved through consensus. As such, many teams incorporate methods of finding common ground and reaching agreement into their foundation. This can include simple consensus decision making practices such as asking someone to make a proposal on a decision and getting people to vote with thumbs up if they agree, or thumbs down if they want to amend the proposal.

Using a foundational practice such as delegation poker, created by Management 3.0, can support the process of consensus decision making and develop clarity around assumptions related to the delegation of responsibility. Conflict can arise around impediments when people presume that someone else will take care of an issue; delegation poker removes this ambiguity. The game involves a set of cards that signify seven levels of delegation that are used to reach consensus by voting on who has what level of influence over pre-defined cases or scenarios.

If the team chooses to incorporate facilitated consensus decision making into their foundation, it can help to ensure that everyone is able to contribute during discussions by default, but it might mean that you will be relied upon as a facilitator in a broader set of scenarios. As a result, you will need to be prepared to function as a neutral element of the team when conflict and disagreements arise.

You need to be able to facilitate productive discussions without taking sides during debates or arguments. You should help the team to consider whether they are keeping their discussion on track, or whether they are going down a rabbit hole, especially when disagreements arise between a small portion of the team.

If you ensure that everyone has a chance to participate in discussions, you will often find that diverse views emerge and debates become less binary. By remaining neutral, you can help to maintain an environment where people are able to engage fully and reach a healthy consensus.

Although you can play a key role in helping others to negotiate conflict, it is worth remembering that you are part of the team as well, so you will have your own thoughts and opinions that you might want to share.

Asking someone else to facilitate a session for the team can ensure that you are clear about adopting a less neutral stance during a conversation rather than attempting to contribute while facilitating. The team's foundation can include recognition that external facilitation might be required in certain scenarios.

Ultimately, the way that the team negotiates stressful situations should be a reflection of the way that they interact at all times. Being explicit about expectations, such as having space for everyone to share their thoughts, being comfortable challenging behaviours that undermine other people, or using consensus as a way to move forward, all impact day to day elements of the team's environment.

Being prepared for difficult situations increases people's ability to work effectively as they will have less fear and anxiety about things going awry. Incorporating an approach to negotiating conflict and disagreements into a foundation ensures that the team will be resilient, even when there's a fist flying towards their chin.

EXPERIMENTATION

During my time working in government, I grew to love an image of a little anthropomorphised dog wearing a hat. The dog attempts to reassure himself by saying "This is fine" as everything around him is engulfed in flames.

This image perfectly captured the feeling I often had when something was clearly not right, but I felt compelled to nod along with certain decisions as a result of political pressure or senior management. I knew I had to pick my battles, and sometimes it was better to accept one decision in order to influence another.

However, someone that I worked with explained that they always thought of that little dog as the directors and managers we worked with. Continuing on their merry way as they ignored the burning inferno around them.

Government Communications Headquarters, better known as GCHQ, published an influential report in 2016 titled *Boiling*

Frogs. The paper draws attention to many of the root causes and consequences of "This is fine" leadership in government.

The title originates from a tale about frogs and hot water. Supposedly, if you drop one of our amphibian friends into a saucepan of cold water and slowly raise the temperature, the frog will gradually adapt to the heat until at forty degrees, it will drift off to sleep.

Unfortunately for the frog, as it enters into a sweet slumber, it too believes "This is fine" without realising that the water will continue to climb towards boiling point. As the water reaches one hundred degrees, the frog will boil in the pan and never wake up.

However, this GCHQ paper wasn't simply offering a lesson in French cuisine. Instead, it was attempting to highlight that situational awareness is frequently overstated. When a frog is dropped into a pot of boiling water it will immediately jump to safety. It knows everything is not fine.

People are often reluctant to leap out of the fire. It's warm and comfortable. Who wants to be out in the cold? These same people might even believe their settled state in a challenging scenario means that they are resilient and adaptable. What they have failed to recognise is the need to find the exit if they want to survive for longer than a sleeping frog in boiling water.

Although this anecdote about boiled frogs has been proved untrue many times, the metaphor remains powerful. It is easy to become complacent in a complex, adaptive environment. GCHQ indicated that countless individuals risk being blissfully unaware of the dramatic changes in the world around them, and that their approach is no longer fine.

So what can you do about it? Well, for starters, when the house is on fire, sound the alarm. People might not decide to exit the building, but at least you can let them decide whether they are okay with reality. You will be amazed at how many people didn't even notice that the lovely orange hue around them was a sign of impending immolation.

Clarity is frequently taken for granted. People regularly assume that they will be able to make informed decisions by default. They often overlook the fact that it is easy to make assumptions and overcommit to ideas.

For example, individuals have a tendency to suffer from the sunk cost fallacy. They will ignore reality and plough on with a specific course of action if they have invested their time and effort, even if their activity becomes increasingly unlikely to deliver value.

Being open and honest about what is happening has been a vital part of many high performance environments I have had the pleasure of working in. An effective foundation should enable the team to gain clarity in relation to the work they are doing and the world around them, then respond accordingly. However, it is hard to overstate the importance of codifying what this means for the team.

In the process of establishing a foundation, it is wise to examine how to develop a clear picture of reality on a continuous basis, and implement appropriate changes. For many teams, this might consist of making a commitment to experimentation and learning as one aspect of their work agreements, but it can also be important to apply additional foundational practices that can help the team to respond to what is happening around them.

Creating a culture of experimentation is a logical response to the inherent complexity of the work the team needs to undertake to deliver value. There is no way to predict the exact course of action that will be needed to accomplish their shared vision, or to plan precisely for the unknown. As an element of the team's foundation, it supports the application of iterative and incremental ways of working alongside numerous aspects of an agile or lean approach.

When teams commit to embracing experimentation, they are accepting that their work might not deliver desired results, but it will always provide an opportunity to learn. The only type of failed experiment is one that is poorly implemented. If it is conducted with meaningful intent, then it cannot be considered a failure, regardless of the outcome.

Leveraging multiple small experiments rather than committing to one large piece of work enables the team to test ideas and consider whether they are worth pursuing further, while being able to change direction rapidly without investing huge amounts of time and effort in something that might not deliver value or help them to accomplish their vision.

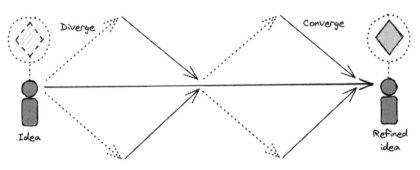

Figure 9.3: Cycles of divergence and convergence adapted from cnpatterns.org

Experimentation as a foundational practice can take the form of multiple cycles of divergence and convergence; when the team conducts experiments followed by the integration of feedback and learning. (Figure 9.3) This also reflects the Double Diamond model created by the British Design Council, building on the work of Béla H. Bánáthy, demonstrating a process of discovery, definition, development, and delivery.

The process of divergence and convergence supports the delivery of smaller units, as work is gradually refined into slices of value. These slices can be delivered early and often, generating greater clarity than work that is bundled into one enormous release because of the opportunity to learn continuously.

Another foundational practice that complements continuous experimentation is the introduction of a "stop the world" event. At any point in time, anyone in the team can stop what everyone is doing. They might do this for a number of reasons, such as an experiment revealing important information that will shift the team's course of action. This ensures that even when conducting small experiments, the team has a mechanism to avoid wasting time and effort, or make important course corrections.

You can support the team to consider how their foundation can generate clarity in the process of creating work agreements, or as part of other events you might facilitate aligned with the team's unique approach, such as planning sessions or retrospectives. Some people struggle with the idea of experimentation rather than generating predefined outputs, so if the team decides to incorporate these practices into their foundation, they might benefit from coaching.

Teams that build experimentation and learning into their foundation are generally more able to try new things, take risks, and minimise unhealthy conflict. All of which reduces the fear of failure and blame culture that can restrict a team's effectiveness. This has a significant impact on their broader environment as they have defined a clear set of expectations related to an empowered, self-organising, autonomous approach to work.

DEFINITION OF DONE

Another foundational practice that generates clarity while mirroring many elements of work agreements is the creation of a definition of done. This artefact also codifies expectations for the team, but it relates to criteria that work items must meet before they can be considered complete. A definition of done increases transparency by providing explicit instructions for quality validation.

Discussing what done means when creating a foundation can feel strange to some teams. Like jumping ahead in a novel, or starting at the end. However, establishing a common understanding around the concept of done creates alignment and a sense of what good looks like. This can become a guide for how the team will work, and clarifies what the team must do to achieve valuable outcomes.

Until something is done, it constitutes work in progress, and therefore it has yet to deliver value. A half built boat won't get you very far across the ocean. As discussed in chapter one, iterative and incremental ways of working attempt to combat this issue by supporting the frequent delivery of valuable outcomes on a regular basis that accumulate over time. In order to achieve this, effective inspection and validation of completed work is essential.

A definition of done usually takes the form of a list of consistent criteria that need to be met in order for a work item to be considered finished. This can include functional and non-functional criteria, such as being able to pass through automated quality checks, or meeting a defined standard of accessibility. It can also include tasks such as peer review.

You can help the team to create their definition of done by facilitating a workshop where they are able to share ideas about what criteria something needs to meet to be considered complete, and reach a consensus, as they would with work agreements. One person's definition of done is unlikely to be the same as someone else's, so it can be challenging to draw together different perspectives, but everyone needs to be comfortable with the criteria they capture.

A shared understanding of done will increase alignment, and ensure that everyone has the same picture of what has actually been completed. For example, many teams include criteria related to integrability in order to validate that work contributes to the wider product. Without this criteria, some people might consider unintegrated work to be complete, while others see it as work in progress or technical debt.

It is worth noting the distinction between a definition of done and acceptance criteria. A definition of done applies to all of the team's work, whereas acceptance criteria are specific to individual work items. It is possible for something to meet a set of acceptance criteria, but not meet the definition of done; as such, the work is incomplete. Many teams specify that their work must fulfil agreed acceptance criteria as part of the definition of done.

The team's definition of done should be another living artefact that is inspected and reviewed frequently, whether this happens in standalone sessions or in established events such as retrospectives. It is essential that the entire team is familiar with it to ensure that it is applied consistently, and that everyone feels a sense of ownership and responsibility. Over time, it should become more comprehensive, enabling the team to continuously increase the quality of their work, and reduce risk in the process.

Creating a definition of done is a foundational practice not only because it helps to paint a unified picture of high quality work, but also because it can help the team to rapidly uncover dysfunction. If they are struggling to meet their own criteria on a frequent basis when working iteratively and incrementally, it could highlight issues such as high work in progress, skill gaps, or bottlenecks.

It is also a valuable aspect of the team's foundation because it helps them to optimise for completion, as opposed to only considering how they can get work underway. In other words: stop starting, start finishing. This supports many aspects of the approach they might choose to apply such as feedback loops, limiting work in progress, and flow. By frequently meeting their definition of done, the team can ensure that they are delivering value early and often.

GOAL SETTING

Once the team has established a vision, created work agreements, and produced a definition of done, in combination with other foundational practices, they should have a shared understanding of why they are working together, and how they want to work. However, it is important that they consider how their foundation can support them to define what they need to do to accomplish their vision and start delivering value.

There are a number of foundational practices that can support the process of defining what the team needs to do. Practices that enable them to define goals, or objectives, are potentially the most important.

Goals provide a focus on a specific outcome aligned with the team's vision, while retaining the flexibility to implement the insights gained from iterative and incremental ways of working, further leveraging experimentation.

Just as the team's vision should not be created in isolation by any one individual, their goals should be developed collectively as well. As such, the best place to start with goal related foundational practices is usually a conversation. Bringing the team together to think about how they want to define goals moving forwards doesn't require a workshop, but it can be beneficial if you are able to facilitate a session that outlines different practices they can apply.

A prevalent goal setting practice that many teams employ is the creation of Objectives and Key Results, or OKRs. They are designed to guide people towards desired outcomes while generating alignment, supporting learning, and fostering commitment. Creating OKRs should be a collaborative process that enables the definition of measurable goals.

OKRs generally capture a goal as an objective followed by three to five measurable key results. This can be captured as a written statement; for example, "We will deliver a highly available shared platform for the entire organisation as measured by 97% up time, adoption by six of seven business units, and weekly code deployments."

The objective is a simple articulation of what the team hopes to achieve. It should be aspirational, significant, and tangible. More than anything, they must be clear. Key results are indicators of progress towards the objective. They should be specific, verifiable, and measurable.

OKRs are commonly paired with a designated timebox in order to track whether key results have been fulfilled. An objective can exist beyond the designated timebox, but key results should either be accomplished, reviewed, or removed. They are designed to evolve over time as the team learns more in pursuit of accomplishing their shared vision and delivering value.

Two key resources that can help you to support the team with the application of OKRs are the books *Measure What Matters* by John Doerr and *Radical Focus* by Christina Wodtke. It can be beneficial to familiarise yourself with OKRs in greater depth as they are easily abused. This is because they serve as a vehicle for goals whether they are good or bad, so it is possible to apply them in ways that might negatively impact the team such as emphasising output over outcomes or command-and-control behaviours.

An alternative to OKRs that aligns more closely with an experimentation based environment, and addresses a criticism of OKRs' lack of detail about the path to implementation, are Goal Experiments Measures, or GEMs, the creation of Kathy Keating. Developing GEMs is a similar goal setting foundational practice that the team can employ, but they also involve the definition of experiments.

Just as the team would start creating an OKR by defining an objective, GEMs start with the articulation of a goal. However, this is then followed by an ideation process that should indicate how we might achieve the goal. At this stage, the ideas do not need to be measurable, which should encourage creativity and ambition.

Once the team has captured a number of ideas, they can then refine them into actions that they feel will be the most achievable. Kathy suggests that "Confidence is great, and it can lead us in helpful directions, but I still have not met a single person that could accurately predict the future. Since we cannot accurately predict the future, all these ideas are simply experiments. Some of these ideas will get us toward our goal, and others will not."

With a list of goals and experiments at hand, the team can now consider how they will know that the experiments were successful in moving towards the goal. These are the measures. They should be time-bound, clear, and, most importantly, measurable.

Building on our previous OKR example, the GEM could be

"We will deliver a highly available shared platform for the entire organisation by deploying OpenShift, creating CI/CD pipelines, enabling self-service access to the platform, and offering out of hours support as measured by 97% up time, adoption by six of seven business units, and weekly code deployments."

Our goal and measures can remain the same, but now there are experiments for the team to conduct in order to achieve the desired valuable outcome aligned with the vision. The beauty of experiments in GEMs is that the team can chop and change them as necessary. If something isn't moving the measure, it can be exchanged for a different experiment, or another experiment can be added to accelerate progress towards the goal.

You can support the creation of OKRs or GEMs through asynchronous collaboration, which you could facilitate by creating a digital workspace for the team, or by organising a workshop. It can be beneficial to co-facilitate this session with the Product Manager as they are likely to be well versed in goal setting and able to contribute to the creation of effective goals and measures, while the team should have the requisite creativity to consider experiments.

It is important to avoid vanity measures or unrealistic goals, especially because this will not support value delivery. Goals should align with valuable outcomes; therefore, the team needs to understand how their work integrates with the broader priorities of the organisation and the needs of users. This is another area where they can leverage the insight and knowledge of a Product Manager.

Having the ability to set goals is fundamental to any team's success, which is why it constitutes an aspect of their foundation. The goal setting process ensures that everyone is on the same page and working towards shared outcomes, which, in turn, helps to cement other aspects of the foundation such as trust between team members.

FORECASTING

If the team is able to confidently leverage their foundation to articulate their why, how, and what, then the one remaining piece of the puzzle that their foundation should support is the ability to answer the unenviable question "When?"

In the words of Daniel Vacanti, author of the book *When Will It Be Done?* "If you have ever been asked [that question], then you have been asked to make a forecast. My guess is that when you were asked that question, you struggled mightily to answer it." He surmises that any prediction is likely to be wrong. So how can the team ensure that they are able to competently forecast their work?

In his book, Daniel articulates the ways that people misunderstand forecasting, and fail to incorporate information related to the various pitfalls of complex work. Forecasting and planning are activities that many teams do not consider when they are creating a foundation, but this leads them into a trap of providing impossible imaginary timelines when they are eventually pressed to provide dates.

It is common for information captured in plans to be presented as factual when it has yet to be validated or critically assessed. Without being explicit about the fact that many plans and forecasts involve guess work, the information is taken as a commitment to do something by a fixed point in time.

A forecast is an estimate of what might happen, while a commitment is often seen as a promise to do something. Forecasting can be a valuable practice for the team, but they must be careful not to communicate in a way that blurs the line between forecasts and commitments. Just as the weather is forecasted rather than promised, these predictions can also change.

Plans and forecasts often create a sense of safety, but it is vital to understand how to apply them appropriately, and their limitations. Many organisations are still hooked on fixed, linear plans such as Gantt charts. However, linear plans that are spread over a long period of time, while trying to reflect complex work, often require a lot of best guesses and depict milestones that cannot be guaranteed due to the volume of assumptions required to give the illusion of predicting the future.

Unfortunately, precision planning in a traditional waterfall context does not guarantee that new information won't come to light that requires plans to change. In fact, the 2020 Chaos report estimated that less than 30% of waterfall projects are delivered on budget, on time, and within scope. The forecasts illustrated on these plans are therefore inaccurate over 70% of the time.

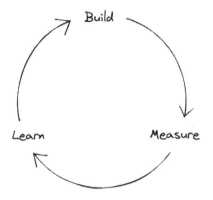

Figure 9.4: Feedback loop adapted from Eric Ries

Iterative, incremental approaches acknowledge the inaccuracy of plans and forecasts up front and attempt to factor this into the ways of working that the team will apply. The work that a team undertakes in a complex domain should not be set in stone.

Through experimentation and continuous learning, there is a commitment to change scope in order to maximise the delivery of value. Work should change and develop over time as the team learns more about what they need to do. (Figure 9.4)

There is a common myth that teams working in an iterative and incremental way do not plan and forecast, but this is not the case. Teams that work in this way simply require an approach that is different to the ones that people might be more familiar with in traditional environments. Work in the complex domain requires flexible and adaptable plans. (Figure 9.5)

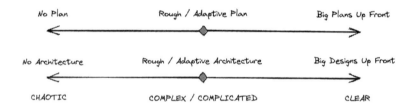

Figure 9.5: Planning in complex or complicated domains adapted from Henrik Kniberg

Planning in complex environments is more rigorous than many people believe, with a vision, goals, and experiments all articulating what the team will do, enabled by various foundational practices. If they incorporate artefacts such as a product backlog into their unique approach, or adopt a framework such as Scrum, then they will inevitably have a number of information radiators that demonstrate this plan.

One foundational practice that many teams employ, often facilitated by a Product Manager, to support their planning approach and provide an information radiator, is the creation of a now, next, later roadmap. This is a type of plan that shows what the team is aiming to do in the short, medium, and long term, with an acceptance that the plan will be less specific the further into the future it gets.

A related practice that can also reflect the work that the team still needs to do is user story mapping. This is an activity where the team uses visual tools such as sticky notes or sketches, possibly on a physical or virtual whiteboard, to outline the interactions that need to happen over time to achieve an outcome with progressive levels of detail under each interaction.

Story mapping is an opportunity to put your facilitation skills to good use in order to support the team's process of capturing work and creating an information radiator that visualises essential activity.

Discomfort frequently arises in organisations because these types of plans and roadmaps do not tend to display with fixed dates. Instead, they reflect valuable outcomes that still need to be achieved in order to accomplish the vision of the team. They are prioritised on the basis of value, and can articulate key dates or deadlines when absolutely necessary, but many people are still inclined to seek more information about when work will be completed.

When Will It Be Done? advocates the use of probabilistic forecasting. This foundational practice can enable the team to provide greater clarity on how long work might take to be complete. It can help them to consider the variability and complexity of their work when making predictions by using statistics to observe trends.

Probabilistic forecasting is the practice of predicting a range of outcomes and assigning a probability to them. By acknowledging a wide array of possible outcomes, the team can develop a better idea of what might happen in the future. This allows them to make more informed decisions, and provide a level of assurance to colleagues.

By using a simulation method such as Monte Carlo, it is possible to use the historical data of how much work has been completed over the course of a fixed period of time to calculate how many work items the team are likely to complete in a certain number of days.

For example, if data for the last ten sprints showed that the team completed between 3 and 14 work items consistently with an average completion rate of 1 work item every 1.6 days, a simulation of 1000 sprints shows that the team would be 91% likely to take 6 sprints to complete a backlog of 35 work items, with an average completion rate of 1 work item every 1.7 days.

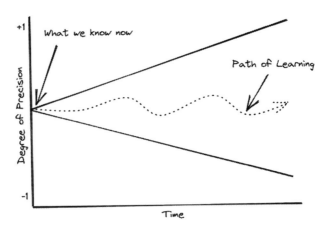

Figure 9.6: Cone starting with high confidence adapted from Dave Berardi

However, even probabilistic forecasts have their limits. All forecasts and plans are created at a fixed point in time with a limited amount of information. Once new information emerges as time passes, it is possible for a forecast to become irrelevant as the assumed path of learning might not prove to be accurate. (Figure 9.6)

This is why it is important to be transparent about the assumptions involved in this process and be clear about the lack of precision when forecasting further into the future.

With that being said, all plans and forecasts start at a point of high variability due to the large volume of assumptions the team are working with at the point of forecasting. (Figure 9.7) As time passes, the team will learn more through iterative and incremental value delivery enabled by experimentation, helping them to reduce their assumptions over time and increase the accuracy of their forecasts and plans.

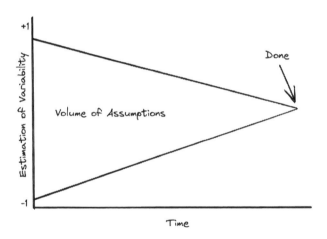

Figure 9.7: Cone starting with assumptions adapted from
Steve McConnel

Another limitation of probabilistic forecasting is that it is most effective when the team is able to slice their work into similarly sized items to increase the consistency of the forecasts. This requires a certain level of maturity in the team related to work item sizing and their ability to limit WIP to improve the smooth flow of value. The team's foundation should support this, especially if they are fostering an environment that benefits from GEMs.

However, even if the team have consistently sized work items and have optimised their environment for fast effective flow, probabilistic forecasts will only be able to say how long it should take to complete known work. It will be possible to provide a probability that one work item will take x number of hours or days, but it might not be possible to suggest how long it will take to achieve a valuable outcome unless the goal has been completely and accurately decomposed into work items and captured on a to-do list or backlog.

It is important to be mindful of the fact that focussing on the completion of individual work items can lead the team to prioritise output rather than outcomes. Shifting focus towards experimentation with variable scope and well defined time horizons for measurement mitigates the risk of artificially locking in arbitrary dates related to output.

Nevertheless, probabilistic forecasting introduces a more scientific empirical method for answering the question "When will it be done?" that contrasts with the inaccurate guess work of traditional waterfall planning. Although a forecast can never be a guarantee in a complex setting, it can still be helpful.

You can support the team to apply these practices over time as an aspect of planning activity or team reviews. The person who is most likely to seek support in generating this information is the Product Manager or someone in a Value Outcome Lead role as they will be corresponding closely with key colleagues who might seek this insight.

Forecasting can be a daunting topic, but it is important for the team to be able to consider their approach before someone else attempts to define how they plan and predict their work. Incorporating planning and forecasting practices into the team's foundation will ensure that they are able to operate in an environment that minimises assumptions and provides transparent data led assurance.

CONCLUSION

The team's foundation supports every aspect of their work. From their culture to the way that they collaborate. Without a stable foundation, the likelihood of achieving value delivery is decreased. This is why it is so important to support them in the process of establishing an effective environment.

Facilitation is an invaluable aspect of this process. Not only does it help the team to engage with each other, but it also fosters trust and creates clarity. As such, it enables you to support others to consider numerous aspects of their foundation, such as their shared vision, work agreements, and a variety of foundational practices. This in turn helps the team to establish the why, how, what, and when of their work.

By having the opportunity to shape the environment they want to work in, the team is able to be explicit about what they need and set themselves up for success. Considering the impact of topics such as trust and psychological safety prior to diving into delivery will increase effectiveness and ensure that the team can work through impediments.

When people feel safe, they're more likely to take risks and think creatively, leading the team towards better outcomes. Healthy conflict, in particular, can help team members come together and reach a consensus. This element of their foundation will enable them to find a path through disagreements in a productive way that promotes cohesiveness rather than discord.

With a strong foundation, the team should feel assured that they are able to try new things, which aligns perfectly with the spirit of experimentation. Keeping work small, and setting clear goals, will enable the team to deliver value early and often, allowing them to develop a clearer picture of when they can expect to accomplish their vision.

Ultimately, the process of creating a foundation should be one that allows the team to forge their ideal environment. Your contribution as an enabler can help them to uncover foundational practices that could significantly shape their ability to achieve valuable outcomes. As a result, they can discover the magic of working in a high performing team where they are respected and valued.

Questions for reflection:
- What is the worst working environment you can imagine?
- What is the best working environment you can imagine?
- What practices can support the creation of a foundation?
- Why is it important to consider why, how, what, and when?
- How would you facilitate the creation of work agreements?

CHAPTER 10
BECOMING A DELIVERY MANAGER

So, do you still like the sound of Delivery Management?

Hopefully at this point you feel like you have a good sense of what it involves. It's not always easy, it requires plenty of effort, but it can be incredibly rewarding.

In order to successfully help teams to deliver value, you will need a variety of skills and knowledge, including the ability to apply each of the aspects of enablement: coaching, facilitation, and impediment removal.

This can seem like a lot to ask of one person, but you don't need to be perfect; nobody is. If you don't have all of these abilities from day one, I am certain that, through the application of a growth mindset, you will find plenty of opportunities to learn.

If you're eager to undertake a career in Delivery Management, you might still be wondering what else you need to know? Where can you find support? How can you get started?

This chapter will talk about some of the first steps you might want to take in your Delivery Management journey.

However, if you're already a Delivery Manager, use this as

an opportunity to consider how you can support other people who want to explore this discipline. Equally, contemplate your own development path and think about how you can find areas for personal growth.

We might be nearing the end of the book, but there is still plenty to explore, including one of the best aspects of Delivery Management: that anyone can embark on this adventure.

YOUR KNOWLEDGE

When it comes to learning about Delivery Management, there is no one-size-fits-all approach. It is essential that you bring your full and authentic self to the role and make it your own. The underlying skills and capabilities that you will use can be applied in many different ways.

The best way to learn more about the topics we have explored is to search for books and articles related to the subject, discuss these ideas with people around you, and experiment with new methods and practices in your own context. This will help you to develop the knowledge that you need to apply Delivery Management successfully.

Some good places to start might be seeking information on topics such as:

- Product Management
- Psychological Safety
- Agile and Lean
- DevOps
- Coaching
- Servant Leadership
- Scrum and Kanban
- User Experience

By reading about these subjects, you will gain a better understanding of the principles behind Delivery Management, and how they can be applied in your own work context.

This will also help you to develop an understanding of the roles and responsibilities of people who might be in the teams you support. You can use this knowledge to develop your own approach to Delivery Management, while continuing to discover that there are many ways of doing things, each with their own strengths and weaknesses.

The knowledge you have gained while reading this book can be applied in a variety of contexts. If you want to apply any of the skills or ideas we have considered, one of the most important things to remember is the value of clear communication. This means taking the time to understand the needs of people around you, and ensuring that everyone is on the same page with respect to what you are doing and why.

It is also important to be flexible in your thinking, and be willing to try new things in order to find what works best for the context you are in. This involves being open to change, and being able to adapt as needed. If you are looking to develop your Delivery Management skills further, you could consider taking on additional responsibilities in your current role that align with your interests. This can help you to test different approaches and gain beneficial experience.

Being open to feedback from people you currently work with can make this even more valuable. It can help you to see things from a different perspective, and enable you to adopt approaches that are more effective. It is important to ensure that people feel comfortable giving you feedback, and that they know it will be used in a constructive way to help you on your Delivery Management journey.

MENTORING

If you are working towards becoming a Delivery Manager, it can be beneficial to learn from people who have already been successful in the role. By studying what has worked well for others, you can experiment with similar practices in your own work. Mentoring is one way to benefit from an experienced Delivery Manager's insights and guidance.

Having a mentor is incredibly valuable. They can provide support and advice that is substantiated by their own experience and knowledge. There are also opportunities for them to act as a sounding board for new ideas, helping you to gain the confidence to experiment with different approaches, tools, and practices.

Finding a mentor can be tricky, but there are many ways to do it. Reaching out to someone is usually the first step, although many mentoring relationships emerge organically over time. You should look beyond the people who manage you as it's best to find a third party for mentorship who can offer a different perspective without bias.

It is important to find a mentor who is compatible with you and that you feel comfortable talking to. You need to trust them and feel that you can learn from them. Your mentor doesn't have to be someone senior; they can be at your level or even less experienced than you are in some areas, so long as they can support your development.

YOUR PLAN

One of the best ways to reach a target is to be clear about what you want to accomplish. This will allow you to focus on what is important, and help you to apply the right mindset. It can be easy to become bogged down by doubt and anxiety, but focussing on what you want to achieve will help you to keep your eye on the bigger picture.

Defining a plan of action can help you to be successful. Using a flexible approach like a now, next, later roadmap will enable you to map out the goals you are setting for yourself while avoiding the pitfalls of a fixed, linear plan that might limit learning.

Breaking your goals down into smaller steps and going through a process of prioritisation will make it easier to stay on track, while preventing you from becoming overwhelmed, especially if you encounter any setbacks.

A key factor in achieving your goals that many people miss is the importance of getting started. Most people have ambitions, but very few will take the first steps towards them.

Don't wait around; start employing an incremental and active approach instead. Put your plans into action rather than waiting for something to change around you. Maybe you already have by reading this book?

SUPPORT

When you are trying to achieve any goal, it is helpful to have support from other people. This is especially true when you are working to accomplish something challenging that may require a lot of time and effort.

On your journey to becoming a Delivery Manager, having support from those around you can make all the difference.

One way to get this support is to share your goals with people you respect and value. This allows them to understand what you are working towards, and provides an opportunity for them to offer assistance. It also helps to develop a sense of commitment; once you have stated your intentions to someone, you can ask them to keep you accountable.

Sharing your goals with current Delivery Managers can also be an effective way of gaining support from a broader community of people who will be willing to help you to fulfil your ambition. There are many ways to engage with the community of existing Delivery Managers, such as social media platforms. For example, Twitter and LinkedIn have a large number of people who are interested in Delivery Management, and actively learn from each other on a daily basis.

These platforms provide a space for discussion and collaboration with a diverse audience of people working in a broad array of organisations. They also regularly offer the chance to explore Delivery Management further, whether this is through an event or opportunities to apply for a new role. Staying engaged with others can accelerate your progress exponentially.

GAINING EXPERIENCE

On the path to becoming a Delivery Manager, you will want to gradually gain greater amounts of experience in applying the different aspects of enablement.

Opportunities to practise facilitation exist all around you, from volunteering to teach people about a new topic, to work meetings you already attend. The secret to gaining facilitation experience is being willing to just dive in.

Starting to remove impediments can be a bit more intimidating. It's the kind of work that a lot of people avoid because it truly involves getting your hands dirty. However, the broad impact that you can have by actively reducing the effect of impediments is enormous.

If you want to start removing impediments, solve one

problem with the people around you, and then do it again, and once more after that. When you start finding ways to solve problems consistently, you will develop the skills required to be an excellent impediment remover.

Coaching is arguably the most challenging aspect of enablement to gain experience in. Learning how to effectively adopt a coaching stance is vital to becoming a Delivery Manager. It will help you to develop trusted relationships with team members, and can enable others to feel supported and appreciated.

Helping people to unlock their full potential is one of the most rewarding aspects of Delivery Management, but coaching also mitigates the risks of adopting the stance of a traditional manager. This means avoiding micromanagement, and being focussed on enabling others to be effective instead.

Staying away from command-and-control behaviours can be challenging if you are attempting to develop your Delivery Management skill set while working in a more traditional organisation. However, even in a traditional context, the application of the aspects of enablement can help to build trust with the people around you.

COLLABORATION

An important part of becoming a Delivery Manager is understanding the value of collaboration. Working with teams in any context provides a valuable learning opportunity to apply the aspects of enablement and support people's efforts to deliver value. However, this will require you to be flexible in your thinking, adaptable in your approach, and open to new practices.

Working in teams enables people to achieve more than they would individually. They are able to share ideas, learn from each other, and develop a better understanding of how they can achieve valuable outcomes. Experiencing this with any type of team is good preparation for becoming a Delivery Manager because time spent working with other people can provide a strong foundation for your growth and development.

By examining your current experience through the lens of Delivery Management, you should gain a clearer understanding of how your knowledge is relevant to the role. Discussing this experience with existing Delivery Managers will help you to understand what will be required from you.

Developing awareness of how your experience of working with teams relates to this discipline will enable you to be more prepared when the right opportunity arrives. This should give you the confidence to start applying for roles and seeking feedback on which areas of knowledge you need to develop further.

PROGRESSION

Within the Delivery Management profession, job titles can vary significantly, and will usually only hold relevance within a specific organisation. Sometimes, these roles will reflect the scope of influence someone has or the level of responsibility they carry. They are not always indicators of someone's proficiency or skill level.

I have known people operating with a "Senior" job title that demonstrated skills and knowledge far beyond that level. Similarly, I have met some "Leads" who I would suggest weren't applying Delivery Management, and might have been better suited to working in a different role.

Nonetheless, having an understanding of the different levels that you can expect to operate at can be beneficial both from the perspective of establishing goals on your career journey and defining the level of capability that you should be aiming to achieve.

Although this structure might not align with Delivery Management opportunities you will pursue, it should give you a sense of the roles you might be able to progress into.

My experience of Delivery Management has predominantly come from working for the British government where there are normally five different levels of Delivery Management:

- Associate Delivery Manager - You work closely with another Delivery Manager to learn the ropes. You might shadow them to gain experience and help to enable a team to deliver value.
- Delivery Manager (working level) - You enable a team to deliver value by removing impediments, facilitating, and coaching.
- Senior Delivery Manager - You enable a team to deliver value in a context involving an increased level of complexity.
- Lead Delivery Manager (equivalent to Principal) - You oversee the entire delivery process for a product. You are likely to work with multiple teams. This is a high-level role, and it requires a lot of experience and expertise.
- Head of Delivery - You are an experienced practitioner who exemplifies what 'good' looks like across the delivery roles. This includes setting the example for effective communication, collaboration, and problem solving.

YOUR JOURNEY

It is important to remember that everyone's career journey looks different. (Figure 10.1) There is no singular route to achieving your goals, and sometimes you might find that the thing you have been working towards isn't actually what you were hoping for. In my experience, establishing career goals has enabled me to define a direction for what I wanted to achieve, but I have rarely ended up in the precise destination I planned.

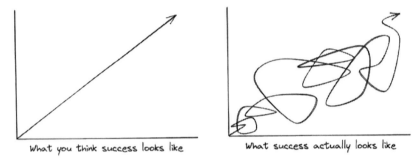

What you think success looks like   What success actually looks like

Figure 10.1: The picture of success adapted from Emily Freeman

Equally, I have had a mix of experiences that felt insignificant at the time but turned out to be career defining. These experiences stand in contrast to achievements that ended up not meeting my expectations in the long run. You never know what might come your way. In many senses, the journey is the destination when it comes to your career.

It is worth taking time to reflect, possibly even using a retrospective template, in order to consider what you actually enjoy doing and what is shaping your goals. Personally, I have found that pursuing roles that are part of an accepting and open culture have been better for me than seeking a job with the most senior title.

Consider what success really means to you; is it about the

salary you take home, knowing that you are doing something worthwhile, or simply feeling okay at work?

If you are looking to pursue a career in Delivery Management, I'm optimistic that you will have found this book to be a helpful starting point. However, it is important to remember that reading about ideas will only ever be the beginning of a journey. The application of ideas is how they become knowledge. That's when they really start to take root in your life and have a tangible effect.

There are many things that can help you to succeed as a Delivery Manager. The best way to find them is by getting experience and continuing to learn. The joy of being part of a team and achieving goals together is hard to describe, but the fact that an entire Delivery Management community exists, that is full of people who are passionate about enabling others to deliver value, should be an indicator of how rewarding it can be.

CONCLUSION

I'm not one to punch walls, but after another meeting where I saw Delivery Managers being scolded for their lack of ability to micromanage teams and produce Gantt charts full of feature focussed milestones, the wall in my office looked pretty appealing. One hit and I reckoned I'd feel better.

I became a Delivery Manager because I was inspired and excited in equal measure by the sound of autonomous teams creating products and doing impactful work. Experiencing it for myself was a revelation. A whole world opened up before my eyes.

That's why I was so disheartened to see multiple colleagues being pressured to adopt command-and-control behaviours and push outdated Project Management approaches on teams full of highly capable and intelligent adults. It's fair to say that when I started writing this book, I had a lot of frustrations about the state of Delivery Management.

Organisations sadly have a tendency to overlook the inherent complexity of the world and struggle to accept the reality that not everything can be planned or controlled. As a result, the focus in many businesses is not on people but on output.

It can be a challenge to change mindsets and get managers to consider alternative approaches, especially when many of them have become successful by doing the same thing repeatedly. However, it is not difficult to see how investing in others and helping them to realise their full potential can lead to incredible outcomes.

After reading this book, you should understand why having a people-focussed approach to work leads to greater successes; including the delivery of value.

Through engagement and collaboration, people can achieve amazing things together. That has always felt like common sense to me, and writing about Delivery Management has exposed why I have those beliefs.

IMPACT

I hope that these chapters have clarified some ideas for you and also inspired you to think of new ones. Even if they are thoughts on how you are going to prove me wrong!

One of my biggest aspirations for this book is that it will spark new conversations and help people to reconsider perceptions they might have of Delivery Management. It might even lead to some less prescriptive job adverts and nudge organisations to consider how they can improve their culture for everyone, regardless of role.

I am incredibly motivated to help people have better experiences with their teams and organisations after a mix of highs and lows throughout my own career. Delivery Management has provided me with many opportunities to do precisely that.

If you are on your own Delivery Management journey, I would love to hear about the impact you are able to have on the people around you, and hope that you will consider what you can do to help other people that might be interested in becoming a Delivery Manager, even if they don't know it yet.

As someone who was an aspiring Delivery Manager at one point, I understand that it can be difficult to know where to start. This book has been written as one type of starting point, but it is important to remember that there is always more to learn.

GROWTH

A true growth mindset means that this book should only be a platform for more learning. It is essential to be constantly expanding your knowledge; it is the only way to ensure that you can fully support the people around you, and enable them to be successful.

In my experience, the best way to gain knowledge is by getting your hands dirty and discovering things along the way. I think the world would be a richer place if everyone had the opportunity and willingness to be constantly learning, so I hope that this inspires you to explore further.

There are many things to discover about Delivery Management, some of which can't be taught, but the journey of learning in this role is engaging, vibrant, and a lot of the time, really fun. I hope I have helped you to see the potential of a career in Delivery Management, and that you are now motivated to start uncovering even more about the discipline.

For existing Delivery Managers, I hope that this book has enabled you to reflect on the journey that you took to get where you are. I am certain that none of you have travelled exactly the same path, but your effort to become a Delivery Manager deserves to be celebrated.

I would love to see you using this book to help other people that are also interested in this discipline, and leverage it as a tool to improve other people's lives.

Whether you share this content with a senior manager or someone who has just started in the team you support, my ambition is that it helps to demonstrate what Delivery Management is about and why you wanted to be part of this community.

If you feel willing and able, I would urge you to share your thoughts with the wider community of Delivery Managers in order to provide new perspectives and ideas for others, including how your approach differs from what you found in this book. I believe that this will help to further develop this field.

GETTING STARTED

In many ways, Delivery Management is still in its early stages, and there is plenty of room for it to grow and develop, especially alongside emerging approaches such as DevOps. I believe that Delivery Management has the ability to change the way that organisations operate, and increase their ability to achieve valuable outcomes.

Thank you for investing your time in what I've written, and in your own Delivery Management journey. I appreciate your interest in exploring this discipline, and hope that you can apply the knowledge you have gained to support others to accomplish great things.

Delivery Management gives you the opportunity to make a real difference in the world.

Imagine if every reader of this book could help a team to deliver value. Think of the cumulative effect we could have. If that sounds good, why wait? Let's get started.

ACKNOWLEDGMENTS

Where do I start? The process of writing this book has felt like a marathon, but in all honesty it was more of a consistent light jog with a few 5km races in between.

Much like when I started running, there were times where I would talk myself out of challenging my limits, or underestimate the amount I could do. Of course, I also overestimated how much I could do at certain points in the process, and inevitably ended up needing to rest up for a few days.

The person who listened to me moan about editing, blurt out ideas on leadership and micromanagement, and voice my anxieties about whether I was going to be able to write about certain topics was Claudia. She consistently gave me the space to pursue this project, and helped to keep me on track. I am incredibly grateful to her, including her reminders that I have a tendency for verbosity when I write.

This gratitude also extends to Claudia's mum, Dawn, and sister, Annie. Our Friday night dinners have always been the perfect opportunity to joke about the latest hair brained scheme that I'm tinkering away on, but even when we're laughing about me becoming a virtual estate agent for a few months, tackling ambitious DIY projects, or weighing a career move, I always feel supported.

Without Dawn there is no way I would be where I am. Having a confident voice telling me that I can accomplish more than I know has helped me beyond words. To share a slice of Dawn's wisdom: There's rarely a good reason not to pursue an opportunity.

The person who has probably had the biggest direct impact on the book has been Annie. She has diligently edited and refined my words, helped me to be concise, and enabled me to say team less than twenty times in every paragraph. Beyond that, she has been an excellent advisor whose opinion I value greatly.

It's equally fair to say that this book would not be what it is today without the help of my good friend Laura. Not only was she able to coach and guide me towards creating something unique that truly reflected my lived experiences, but she also generously shared her professional knowledge, enabling me to benefit from her expertise as founder of Derbyshire Writing School.

I'm very fortunate to have the ongoing love and support of my parents and siblings. I owe my Mum and Dad a lot of thanks for teaching me the value of education, the importance of hard work, and the power of knowledge. Without them, none of this would have been possible. My brother, Adam, and sister, Francesca, constantly inspire me to be more creative and pursue opportunities that require imagination.

The Delivery Management, Agile, and DevOps communities are deserving of my unending thanks for providing inspiration and direction for this book. My writing has been guided by countless blog posts, LinkedIn debates, and books written by people with incredibly deep knowledge about topics that fascinate me without limit.

From this community I should give a special mention to the beta readers of some of the many drafts of this book. Al, Chris, Emily, Emma, Hannah, Himal, Jac, Jason, Laura, Maarten, Marty,

Matt, Matthew, Nick, Richard, Sam, Stefan, Steve, and Tom, thank you all for taking the time to make my writing so much more impactful than it would have otherwise been.

I also owe a lot of credit to the excellent teams and individuals I have worked with at the Department for Work and Pensions, Homes England, and Red Hat. They inspired plenty of these stories, helped me to grow, and shaped my perspective on team enablement. Special thanks to Barry, James, Matt, Nick, Karl, Bob, Allison, and a multitude of Steves for their support.

One person who shaped many aspects of my writing was Nick. What started as a mentoring relationship while working at DWP has turned into a friendship, and it has been amazing to see him flourish in his career. He informed much of what I felt might help people to explore Delivery Management.

Looping back to the start of this book, I want to offer my thanks to Ben and Steve at The Hometown Group for helping to teach me what a team really looks like when I was first finding my feet in the world of work. Not only have they created an amazing business, but they are also an incredible professional partnership. Ben has been an especially impactful mentor to me over the years; thanks Errey.

The final acknowledgment I'd like to offer is to you, the reader. Thank you for taking the time to read this book. Its creation has been a process of growth, with highs and lows along the way, but knowing that you have invested your curiosity to see what I've written makes it all feel particularly worthwhile. I can't wait to see the value you go on to deliver.

REFERENCES

1. Adkins, Lyssa. *Coaching Agile Teams*. Addison-Wesley Professional, 2010.

2. Álvarez-Huerta, P., Muela, A. & Larrea, I. "Disposition Towards Critical Thinking and Student Engagement in Higher Education." *Innov High Educ*, March 2022. https://doi.org/10.1007/s10755-022-09614-9

3. Andreessen, Marc. "Why Software Is Eating The World." *WSJ*, 20 Aug. 2011, https://online.wsj.com/article/SB10001424053111903480904576512250915629460.html.

4. Bastow, Janna. *Twitter*, https://twitter.com/simplybastow/status/1168531672335343616. Accessed 21 June 2022.

5. Baynham Hughes, Chris. "GEMs: An alternative to OKRs" *Open Practice Library*, 14 Dec. 2021, https://openpracticelibrary.com/practice/gems/.

6. Beattie, Tim, Mike Hepburn, Noel O'Connor, and Donal Spring. *DevOps Culture and Practice with OpenShift*. Packt Publishing Ltd, 2021.

7. Berardi, Dave. "Agile and Dealing With The Cone of Uncertainty." *AKF Partners*, 8 July 2018, https://akfpartners.com/growth-blog/dealing-with-the-cone-of-uncertainty-with-pdlc.

8. Berg, Cliff, Kurt Cagle, Lisa Cooney, Philippa Fewell, Adrian Lander, Raj Nagappan, and Murray Robinson. *Agile 2*. John Wiley & Sons, 2021.

9. Bittner, Kurt. "If You Want to Go Faster, Try Empowering Your Teams..." *Scrum.Org*, 6 Apr. 2022, https://www.scrum.org/resources/blog/if-you-want-go-faster-try-empowering-your-teams.

10. Bowman, Sharon. *Training From the Back of the Room!* John Wiley & Sons, 2008.

11. Bruce, Lizzie. "The Value of Content Design." *Content Design London*, 20 Feb. 2020, https://contentdesign.london/content-design/value-of-content-design/.

12. Cagan, Marty. "INSPIRED, 2nd Edition." *O'Reilly Online Learning*, https://www.oreilly.com/library/view/inspired-2nd-edition/9781119387503/c19.xhtml. Accessed 21 June 2022.

13. Cagan, Marty. "The Delivery Manager Role." *Silicon Valley Product Group*, 13 July 2014, https://www.svpg.com/the-delivery-manager-role/.

14. Cagan, Marty. *INSPIRED*. John Wiley & Sons, 2017.

15. Cartigny, Lauren. "Holding a Safe Space: What Is Coaching?" *LinkedIn*, 5 Nov. 2019, https://www.linkedin.com/pulse/holding-safe-space-what-coaching-lauren-cartigny.

16. Catmull, Ed. *Creativity, Inc.* Random House, 2014.

17. Chan, Tian. 2019. "When Individuals Are More Innovative Than Teams." *Harvard Business Review*. December 31. https://hbr.org/2019/12/when-individuals-are-more-innovative-than-teams.

18. Cialdini, Robert. *Influence, New and Expanded*. HarperCollins, 2021.

19. Cleff, Andy. "Navigating Complexity Aka Cynefin for Dummies." *Andy Cleff*, 12 Sept. 2017, https://www.andycleff.com/2017/09/navigating-complexity-aka-cynefin-dummies/.

20. Clinton, Christina. "What Does a Leader-Leader Culture Look Like?" *PRCA*, https://www.prca.org.uk/What-does-a-Leader-Leader-Culture-look-like. Accessed 21 June 2022.

21. CoachHub. "Professional Coaching: Everything You Need to Know in 2022." *CoachHub*, 18 Feb. 2021, https://www.coachhub.com/blog/professional-coaching-everything-you-need-to-know-in-2022/.

22. Crain, Anthony. "Projects to Products: What It Means, Why It Matters | TechBeacon." *TechBeacon*, https://techbeacon.com/app-

dev-testing/projects-products-what-it-means-why-it-matters.
Accessed 21 June 2022.

23. Crain, Anthony. "Projects to Products: What It Means, Why It
    Matters | TechBeacon." *TechBeacon*, https://techbeacon.com/app-
    dev-testing/projects-products-what-it-means-why-it-matters.
    Accessed 23 June 2022.

24. Cutler, John. "12 Signs You're Working in a Feature Factory."
    @johncutlefish's Blog, 17 Nov. 2016, https://cutle.fish/blog/12-
    signs-youre-working-in-a-feature-factory.

25. de Saint-Exupéry, Antoine. *Citadelle*. Sodis, 2000.

26. Ding, Oliver. "Curativity Theory: Table of Contents and Related
    Articles." *Curativity Center*, 2 Apr. 2022, https://medium.com/the-
    art-of-bagging/curativity-theory-9660e73f367.

27. Doerr, John. *Measure What Matters*. Penguin, 2018.

28. Dominguez, Jorge. "The Curious Case of the CHAOS Report
    2009." *Project Smart*, 10 Oct. 2021, https://www.projectsmart.co.
    uk/it-project-management/the-curious-case-of-the-chaos-report-
    2009.php.

29. Drumond, Claire. "Is the Agile Manifesto Still a Thing?" *Atlassian*,
    https://www.atlassian.com/agile/manifesto. Accessed 21 June
    2022.

30. Dweck, Carol. *Mindset*. Constable, 2012.

31. Eckfeldt, Bruce. "How to Play Devil's Advocate in a Productive
    Way." *Inc*, 22 May 2020, https://www.inc.com/bruce-eckfeldt/
    how-to-play-devils-advocate-in-a-productive-way.html.

32. Edmondson, Amy. *The Fearless Organization*. John Wiley & Sons,
    2018.

33. Evans, Beth. "Becoming A Delivery Manager". *Paper Studio*, 15
    Nov. 2021, https://paper.studio/2021/11/15/becoming-a-
    delivery-manager/.

34. Fatokun, Abisola. "Relationship between a Product Manager and a
    Delivery Manager." *Medium*, 9 June 2015, https://medium.com/@

abisola/relationship-between-a-product-manager-and-a-delivery-manager-9e5138b587b6.

35. Forsgren, Nicole, Jez Humble, and Gene Kim. *Accelerate*. IT Revolution, 2018.

36. Fowler, Martin. "Bliki: StranglerFigApplication." *Martinfowler.Com*, 29 June 2004, https://martinfowler.com/bliki/StranglerFigApplication.html.

37. Fowler, Martin. "Continuous Integration." *Martinfowler.Com*, 20 May 628, https://martinfowler.com/articles/continuousIntegration.html.

38. Fox, Erica. *Winning from Within*. Harper Collins, 2013.

39. Freeman, Emily. *DevOps For Dummies*. John Wiley & Sons, 2019.

40. GCHQ. "GitHub - Gchq/BoilingFrogs: GCHQ's Internal Boiling Frogs Research Paper on Software Development and Organisational Change in the Face of Disruption." *GitHub*, https://github.com/gchq/BoilingFrogs. Accessed 18 July 2022.

41. Geraghty, Tom. "DevOps, Psychological Safety and Resilience Engineering." *Tom Geraghty*, 20 May 2020, https://tomgeraghty.co.uk/index.php/resilience-engineering-and-psychological-safety/.

42. Gilad, Itamar. "5 Ways Your Company May Be Misusing OKRs." *Product Coalition*, 1 July 2019, https://productcoalition.com/5-ways-your-company-may-be-misusing-okrs-3d5cdb22aa4e.

43. Gould, Zoe. "Scrum Master Or Delivery Manager – What's In A Name?" *Zoe On The Go*, 3 May 2019, https://www.zoeonthego.org/2019/05/03/scrum-master-or-delivery-manager-whats-in-a-name/.

44. Greenleaf, Robert. *Servant Leadership*. Paulist Press, 2002.

45. Greenway, Andrew, Ben Terrett, Mike Bracken, and Tom Loosemore. *Digital Transformation at Scale: Why the Strategy Is Delivery*. Pearson, 2021.

46. Halvorson, Kristina. *Content Strategy for the Web*. New Riders, 2012.

47. Hane, Carrie, and Mike Atherton. *Designing Connected Content.* Pearson Professional, 2017.

48. Harbott, Karim. *The 6 Enablers of Business Agility.* Berrett-Koehler Publishers, 2021.

49. Hastings, Reed. *No Rules Rules.* Random House, 2020.

50. Highsmith, Jim, Linda Luu, and David Robinson. *EDGE.* Addison-Wesley Professional, 2019.

51. Hinshelwood, Martin. "80% of Communication Is Non-Verbal." *Scrum.Org,* 1 July 2020, https://nkdagility.com/blog/80-of-communication-is-non-verbal/.

52. Hirst, Chris. *No Bullsh*t Leadership.* 2020.

53. Holliday, Ben. *Multiplied.* TPXimpact, 2022.

54. Holub, Allen. *Twitter,* https://twitter.com/allenholub. Accessed 21 June 2022.

55. Hopkins, Jeremiah. "The Scrum Master's Role in Organizational Bottlenecks." *Cprime,* 23 Dec. 2020, https://www.cprime.com/resources/blog/the-scrum-masters-role-in-organizational-bottlenecks/.

56. Hunter, John. "Ackoff on Systems Thinking and Management - The W. Edwards Deming Institute." *The W. Edwards Deming Institute,* 2 Sept. 2019, https://deming.org/ackoff-on-systems-thinking-and-management/.

57. Jain, Ankur. "Output Vs Outcome: Why The Outcome Is More Important Than Output." *LinkedIn,* 30 July 2021, https://www.linkedin.com/pulse/output-vs-outcome-why-more-important-than-ankur-jain.

58. Jones, Andrew, and Don Seville. "Action to Outcome Mapping: Testing Strategy with Systems Thinking." *The Systems Thinker,* https://thesystemsthinker.com/action-to-outcome-mapping-testing-strategy-with-systems-thinking/. Accessed 4 July 2022.

59. Jones, Josh. "Read the CIA's Simple Sabotage Field Manual: A Timeless Guide to Subverting Any Organization with 'Purposeful

Stupidity' (1944)." *Open Culture*, 1 Dec. 2015, https://www.
openculture.com/2015/12/simple-sabotage-field-manual.html.

60. Kalmodin, Mia. "Agile Coaching in a Nutshell." *Dandy People*,
https://media.dandypeople.com/2019/02/agile-coach-in-a-
nutshell-10.pdf. Accessed 21 June 2022.

61. Keating, Kathy. "Get your OKRs out of my GEMs."
KathKeating.Com, 14 Nov. 2021, https://kathkeating.com/get-
your-okrs-out-of-my-gems/

62. Kelly, Allan. *Project Myopia: Why Projects Damage Software
#NoProjects*. Allan Kelly Associates, 2021.

63. Kersten, Mik. *Project to Product*. IT Revolution, 2018.

64. Kim, Gene, Jez Humble, Patrick Debois, and John Willis. *The
DevOps Handbook, Second Edition*. IT Revolution, 2021.

65. Kim, Gene, Kevin Behr, and George Spafford. *The Phoenix Project*.
IT Revolution, 2018.

66. Kim, Gene. "The Three Ways: The Principles Underpinning
DevOps - IT Revolution." *IT Revolution*, 22 Aug. 2012, https://
itrevolution.com/the-three-ways-principles-underpinning-
devops/.

67. Kim, Gene. *The Unicorn Project*. IT Revolution, 2019.

68. King, Jude. "How Great Leaders Communicate Big Vision So That
Others Want To Join In." *Medium*, 29 Nov. 2019, https://medium.
com/@Jude.M/how-great-leaders-communicate-big-vision-so-
that-others-want-to-join-in-d3296e7ca37e.

69. Kleon, Austin. *Steal Like an Artist*. Workman Publishing, 2012.

70. Kniberg, Henrik. *LinkedIn*, https://www.linkedin.com/in/
hkniberg/. Accessed 21 June 2022.

71. Kniberg, Henrik. *Scrum and XP from the Trenches - 2nd Edition*.
Lulu.com, 2015.

72. Kriegenbergh, Arthur von. "Making Better Decisions." *Agile
Arthur*, 25 June 2019, https://www.agile-arthur.com/blog/
making-better-decisions.

73. Ladas, Corey. "CONWIP Systems | Lean Software Engineering." *Lean Software Engineering,* http://scm.zoomquiet.top/data/20091216134521/index.html. Accessed 29 June 2022.

74. Lee, Jeremiah. *Spotify's Failed #SquadGoals,* 19 April 2020, https://www.jeremiahlee.com/posts/failed-squad-goals/.

75. Lencioni, Patrick. *The Five Dysfunctions of a Team.* John Wiley & Sons, 2011.

76. *Liberating Structures,* https://www.liberatingstructures.com/. Accessed 21 June 2022.

77. Lissack, Michael. "Don't Be Addicted: The Oft-Overlooked Dangers of Simplification." *She Ji: The Journal of Design, Economics, and Innovation, Volume 2, Issue 1,* 2016, https://doi.org/10.1016/j.sheji.2016.05.001.

78. Lyden, John. "Creating a One-Team Organization." *Expressworks,* https://www.expressworks.com/wp-content/uploads/2018/03/TeamEffectiveness-White_Paper.pdf. Accessed 2 July 2022.

79. Marquet, L. David. "3 Advantages to Being Curious" *Intent Based Leadership.* July 23 2019. https://intentbasedleadership.com/3-advantages-to-being-curious.

80. Marquet, L. David. *Turn The Ship Around!* Penguin UK, 2015.

81. Miles, Beau. "Saving This House's Wood from Landfill (about $15k Worth)." *YouTube,* 8 June 2022, https://www.youtube.com/watch?v=OkapOJxBmbE.

82. Mitchell, Ian. "Walking Through a Definition of Done." *Scrum.Org,* 31 May 2017, https://www.scrum.org/resources/blog/walking-through-definition-done.

83. Morris, Brad. "Is There a Catfish in Your Life?" *The Post and Courier,* 11 Dec. 2019, https://www.postandcourier.com/georgetown/opinion/brad-morris-column-is-there-a-catfish-in-your-life/article_0daaadcb-55ac-5fde-87f2-97e2c5169b69.html.

84. Morton, Luke. "Defining Your Ways of Working." *Luke Morton*, 28 May 2020, https://lukemorton.tech/articles/defining-your-ways-of-working.

85. Mota, Pedro. "Team Topologies for Data Engineering Teams." *Data Arena*, 16 May 2021, https://medium.com/data-arena/team-topologies-for-data-engineering-teams-a15c5eb3849c.

86. Newboult, Colin. "Greatest Test Sides: England 2001-03 | PlanetRugby." *PlanetRugby*, 26 Mar. 2020, https://www.planetrugby.com/greatest-test-sides-england-2001-03.

87. Orosz, Gergely. "How Big Tech Runs Tech Projects and the Curious Absence of Scrum." *The Pragmatic Engineer*, 21 Sept. 2021, https://blog.pragmaticengineer.com/project-management-at-big-tech/.

88. Overeem, Barry. "From 50% Agile Coach to 100% Scrum Master." *Scrum.Org*, 20 Aug. 2016, https://www.scrum.org/resources/blog/50-agile-coach-100-scrum-master.

89. Overeem, Barry. "Myth 8: The Scrum Master Is a Junior Agile Coach." *Scrum.Org*, 11 Dec. 2017, https://www.scrum.org/resources/blog/myth-8-scrum-master-junior-agile-coach.

90. Overeem, Barry. "Should a Scrum Master Be Technical?" *Scrum.Org*, 30 Aug. 2017, https://www.scrum.org/resources/blog/should-scrum-master-be-technical.

91. Overeem, Barry. "The Scrum Master as a Facilitator." *Scrum.Org*, 3 Aug. 2015, https://www.scrum.org/resources/blog/scrum-master-facilitator.

92. Overeem, Barry. "The Scrum Master as a Manager." *Scrum.Org*, 23 July 2015, https://www.scrum.org/resources/blog/scrum-master-manager.

93. Overeem, Barry. "The Scrum Master as an Impediment Remover." *Scrum.Org*, 7 Apr. 2016, https://www.scrum.org/resources/blog/scrum-master-impediment-remover.

94. Panchadsaram, Ryan. "What Is an OKR? Definition and Examples." *What Matters,* https://www.whatmatters.com/faqs/okr-meaning-definition-example/. Accessed 9 Jan. 2022.

95. Parr, Kealan. "What Is the Strangler Fig Pattern and How It Helps Manage Legacy Code." *FreeCodeCamp.Org,* 15 June 2021, https://www.freecodecamp.org/news/what-is-the-strangler-pattern-in-software-development/.

96. Parris, Denise Linda, and Jon Welty Peachey. "A Systematic Literature Review of Servant Leadership Theory in Organizational Contexts." *Journal of Business Ethics* 113, no. 3 (2013): 377–93. http://www.jstor.org/stable/23433856.

97. Partogi, Joshua. "Scrum Master: The Master of the Art of Facilitation." *Scrum.Org,* 19 Aug. 2018, https://www.scrum.org/resources/blog/scrum-master-master-art-facilitation.

98. Partogi, Joshua. "What is Servant Leadership?" *Scrum.Org,* Nov. 26 2017. https://www.scrum.org/resources/blog/what-servant-leadership.

99. Pellegrino, Anthony. "What Is the Role of a Technical Program Manager?" *Exponent,* 9 June 2020, https://blog.tryexponent.com/what-is-the-role-of-a-technical-program-manager/.

100. Perri, Melissa. *Escaping the Build Trap.* O'Reilly Media, 2018.

101. Pink, Daniel. *Drive.* Canongate Books, 2010.

102. Pratt, Karen. *Transactional Analysis Coaching.* Routledge, 2021.

103. Quast, Lisa. "6 Ways To Empower Others To Succeed." *Forbes,* 28 Feb. 2011, https://www.forbes.com/sites/lisaquast/2011/02/28/6-ways-to-empower-others-to-succeed/.

104. Ries, Eric. *The Lean Startup.* Currency, 2011.

105. Rossingol, Natalia. "Team Topologies Summary - A Faster Way to Making Your Teams Click." *Runn.io,* https://www.runn.io/blog/team-topologies-summary. Accessed 2 July 2022.

106. Rozovsky, Julia. "Re:Work - The Five Keys to a Successful Google Team." *Google,* 17 Nov. 2015, https://rework.withgoogle.com/

blog/five-keys-to-a-successful-google-team/.

107. Russell, Matt. "Strategic Leadership: The 3 Levels of Listening." *The Startup*, 5 Dec. 2019, https://medium.com/swlh/strategic-leadership-the-3-levels-of-listening-e3f0c27f8d01.

108. S. Wuchty, B. F. Jones, B. Uzzi, "The increasing dominance of teams in production of knowledge." *Science* 316, 1036–1039 (2007).

109. Sanchez, Helene. "Product Vision 2020." *Mind the Product*, 16 Nov. 2020, https://www.mindtheproduct.com/product-vision-2020/.

110. Scott, Kim. *Radical Candor*. Macmillan, 2017.

111. Seiden, Joshua. *Outcomes Over Output*. Independently Published, 2019.

112. Siegel, Joel. "When Steve Jobs Got Fired By Apple." *ABC News*, https://abcnews.go.com/Technology/steve-jobs-fire-company/story?id=14683754. Accessed 21 June 2022.

113. Sigel, Adam. "Building Trust with Engineers." *Boston Product*, 18 Nov. 2016, https://medium.com/boston-product/building-trust-with-engineers-f933d07d6038.

114. Sinclair, Toby. "Agile Coaching v Professional Coaching." *Toby Sinclair*, 3 May 2021, https://www.tobysinclair.com/post/agile-coaching-v-professional-coaching.

115. Sisney, Lex. "Top-down vs. Bottom-up Hierarchy" *Organizational Physics*, 13 Oct. 2016, https://organizationalphysics.com/2016/10/13/top-down-vs-bottom-up-hierarchy-or-how-to-build-a-self-managed-organization/.

116. Skelton, Matthew and Manuel Pais. "Team Cognitive Load." *IT Revolution*, 19 Jan. 2021, https://itrevolution.com/cognitive-load/.

117. Skelton, Matthew, and Manuel Pais. "Key Concepts." *Team Topologies*, https://teamtopologies.com/key-concepts. Accessed 21 June 2022.

118. Skelton, Matthew, and Manuel Pais. *Remote Team Interactions Workbook*. It Revolution Press, 2022.

119. Skelton, Matthew, and Manuel Pais. *Team Topologies*. IT Revolution, 2019.

120. Smart, Jonathan. "Organisational Agility: Give People a VOICE." *Sooner Safer Happier*, 28 Sept. 2018, https://medium.com/sooner-safer-happier/organisational-agility-give-people-a-voice-5d5e68449aa7.

121. Smart, Jonathan. *Sooner Safer Happier*. IT Revolution, 2020.

122. Squirrel, Douglas, and Jeffrey Fredrick. *Agile Conversations*. IT Revolution, 2020.

123. Stanier, Curtis. "Don't Attribute to Malice What You Can Attribute to Misalignment." *The Startup*, 9 Aug. 2019, https://medium.com/swlh/dont-attribute-to-malice-what-you-can-attribute-to-misalignment-30bf5f9da76c.

124. Stanier, Michael. *The Coaching Habit*. Box of Crayons Press, 2016.

125. Sutherland, Jeff. *Scrum*. Currency, 2014.

126. Swindoll, Chuck. "Tension in the Tank, Part Two." *Insight for Living*, 21 Nov. 2017, https://insight.org/resources/daily-devotional/individual/tension-in-the-tank-part-two.

127. Syed, Matthew. *Black Box Thinking*. John Murray, 2016.

128. Tanner. "Scrum Is Not Agile." *Spikes And Stories*, 28 Nov. 2016, http://www.spikesandstories.com/scrum-not-agile/.

129. *The Prime Directive - Agile Retrospective Resource Wiki*. http://retrospectivewiki.org/index.php?title=The_Prime_Directive. Accessed 21 June 2022.

130. Tkachuk, Kate. "Technical Debt." *Edvantis*, https://www.edvantis.com/blog/technical-debt/. Accessed 4 July 2022.

131. Turnbull, Giles. *The Agile Comms Handbook*. 2021.

132. Vacanti, Daniel. *When Will It Be Done?: Lean-Agile Forecasting to Answer Your Customers' Most Important Question*. 2020.

133. Verheyen, Gunther. "The Value in the Scrum Values." *Scrum.org*, 1 Apr. 2021, https://www.scrum.org/resources/blog/value-scrum-values.

134. Verheyen, Gunther. *Scrum – A Pocket Guide – 3rd Edition*. Van Haren, 2021.

135. Verwijs, Christiaan, Johannes Schartau, and Barry Overeem. "Take Your Scrum Team's Definition Of Done To The Next Level!" *The Liberators*, 28 Feb. 2022, https://medium.com/the-liberators/take-your-scrum-teams-definition-of-done-to-the-next-level-7108e129eb2d.

136. Verwijs, Christiaan. "In-Depth: How To Create Better Work Agreements For Your Team." *The Liberators*, 19 July 2022, https://medium.com/the-liberators/in-depth-how-to-create-better-work-agreements-for-your-team-7738e474ad13.

137. Wadsworth, Don. "Silos For Good Not Evil!" *Jostle*, https://blog.jostle.me/blog/silos-for-good-not-evil/. Accessed 2 Sept. 2022.

138. Warrington, James. "The Future of Project Management." *The Telegraph*, 21 June 2022, https://www.telegraph.co.uk/business/business-reporter/future-project-management/.

139. Watts, Geoff. *Scrum Mastery*. 2013.

140. Webber, Emily. "Building A Progression Framework For A Multidisciplinary Organisation". *Emily Webber*, 21 June 2021, https://emilywebber.co.uk/building-a-progression-framework-for-a-multidisciplinary-organisation/.

141. Webber, Emily. "Explaining The Role Of A Delivery Manager". *Emily Webber*, 29 Jan. 2016, https://emilywebber.co.uk/what-is-an-agile-delivery-manager/.

142. Wester, Julia. "Create Faster and More Accurate Forecasts Using Probabilities." *Scrum.Org*, 15 Jan. 2020, https://www.scrum.org/resources/blog/create-faster-and-more-accurate-forecasts-using-probabilities.

143. Widdowson, Lucy, and Paul J Barbour. *Building Top-Performing Teams*. Kogan Page Publishers, 2021.

144. Winters, Sarah. *Content Design*. 2017.

145. Wodtke, Christina. *Radical Focus*. 2021.

146. Wolpers, Stefan. "Technical Debt & Scrum: Who Is Responsible?" *Scrum.org*, 17 June 2019, https://www.scrum.org/resources/blog/technical-debt-scrum-who-responsible.

147. Yap, Simon. "Why Sport Coaching and Professional Coaching Are Different?" *Simon Yap, PCC*, 2 June 2018, https://minds-senses.com/sport-coaching-and-professional-coaching/.

148. "Agile Retrospectives" *Atlassian*, https://www.atlassian.com/agile/scrum/retrospectives. Accessed 30 June 2022.

149. "BBC ON THIS DAY 2003: England Win Rugby World Cup." *BBC News*, http://news.bbc.co.uk/onthisday/hi/dates/stories/november/22/newsid_3747000/3747398.stm. Accessed 21 June 2022.

150. "Carol Dweck: A Summary of The Two Mindsets." *Farnam Street*, 2 Mar. 2015, https://fs.blog/carol-dweck-mindset/.

151. "Catfish." *Wikipedia*, https://en.wikipedia.org/wiki/Catfish_(film). Accessed 17 July 2022.

152. "Cone of Uncertainty." *Agile in a Nutshell*, http://www.agilenutshell.com/cone_of_uncertainty. Accessed 21 June 2022.

153. "CONWIP." *Wikipedia*, https://en.wikipedia.org/wiki/CONWIP. Accessed 29 June 2022.

154. "Delegation Poker." *Management 3.0*, https://management30.com/practice/delegation-poker/. Accessed 2 Sep 2022.

155. "Engineering Manager Job Description." *Betterteam*, https://www.betterteam.com/engineering-manager-job-description. Accessed 21 June 2022.

156. "Exploratory Experiments." *CN Patterns*, https://www.cnpatterns.org/organization-culture/exploratory-experiments. Accessed 21 June 2022.

157. "Fostering a Culture of Innovation." *Red Hat*, https://www.redhat.com/en/about/our-culture. Accessed 2 July 2022.

158. "How Much of Communication Is Nonverbal?" *The University of Texas Permian Basin*, 3 Nov. 2020, https://online.utpb.edu/about-

us/articles/communication/how-much-of-communication-is-nonverbal.

159. "Introduction to Systems Thinking for Civil Servants." *GOV.UK*, https://www.gov.uk/government/publications/systems-thinking-for-civil-servants/introduction. Accessed 3 July 2022.

160. "Is 'You Built It, You Run It' Living up to the Hype?" *Atlassian*, https://www.atlassian.com/incident-management/devops/you-built-it-you-run-it. Accessed 21 June 2022.

161. "Manifesto For Agile Software Development." *Agilemanifesto.org*, 2001. https://agilemanifesto.org/.

162. "Metcalfe's Law." *Wikipedia*, https://en.wikipedia.org/wiki/Metcalfe's_law. Accessed 23 June 2022.

163. "Open Practice Library." *Open Practice Library*, 2022. https://openpracticelibrary.com/.

164. "Pareto Principle." *Wikipedia*, https://en.wikipedia.org/wiki/Pareto_principle. Accessed 21 June 2022.

165. "Professional Scrum Competency: Developing People and Teams" *Scrum.Org*, https://www.scrum.org/professional-scrum-competencies/developing-people-and-teams. Accesses 24 June 2022.

166. "Project Management." *Wikipedia*, https://en.wikipedia.org/wiki/Project_management. Accessed 21 June 2022.

167. "Software Engineering." *Wikipedia*, https://en.wikipedia.org/wiki/Software_engineering. Accessed 21 June 2022.

168. "Strangler Fig." *Wikipedia*, https://en.wikipedia.org/wiki/Strangler_fig. Accessed 21 June 2022.

169. "Tech Lead Responsibilities." *GOV.UK Developer Documentation*, 5 Apr. 2022, https://docs.publishing.service.gov.uk/manual/tech-lead-responsibilities.html.

170. "The Myth of Sisyphus - Alex Gendler." *YouTube*, 13 Nov. 2018, https://www.youtube.com/watch?v=q4pDUxth5fQ.

171. "The Myth of Sisyphus." *Wikipedia*, https://en.wikipedia.org/wiki/The_Myth_of_Sisyphus. Accessed 5 July 2022.

172. "The Tell Us Once Service - How it works." *Bereavement Advice Centre*, https://www.bereavementadvice.org/topics/registering-a-death-and-informing-others/the-tell-us-once-service/. Accessed 21 June 2022.

173. "This Is Fine." *Know Your Meme*, 12 May 2015, https://knowyourmeme.com/memes/this-is-fine.

174. "Unconditional Positive Regard." *Wikipedia*, https://en.wikipedia.org/wiki/Unconditional_positive_regard. Accessed 30 July 2022.

175. "What Is Agile?" *Agile in a Nutshell*, http://www.agilenutshell.com/what_is_agile. Accessed 21 June 2022.

176. *"What Is An Agile Coach?"* https://www.scrumalliance.org/agile-coaching. Accessed 21 June 2022.

177. "What Is DevOps?" *Atlassian*, https://www.atlassian.com/devops. Accessed 21 June 2022.

178. "What Is Kanban?" *Atlassian*, https://www.atlassian.com/agile/kanban. Accessed 28 June 2022.

179. "What Is Lean? Lean Thinking." *Lean Enterprise Institute*, 13 July 2022, https://www.lean.org/explore-lean/what-is-lean/.

180. "What Is Professional Coaching?" *Flow Coaching Institute*, https://flowcoachinginstitute.com/blog/what-is-professional-coaching/. Accessed 21 June 2022.

181. "What Is Scrum?" *Atlassian*, https://www.atlassian.com/agile/scrum. Accessed 28 June 2022.

182. "What Is Servant Leadership?" *Greenleaf Center for Servant Leadership*, https://www.greenleaf.org/what-is-servant-leadership/. Accessed 21 June 2022.

183. "What Is UX Design? User Experience Definition." *Adobe XD Ideas*, 24 Nov. 2020, https://xd.adobe.com/ideas/career-tips/what-is-ux-design/.

ABOUT THE AUTHOR

Jonny Williams is an Agile Delivery Lead at Red Hat. Prior to this he was Head of Delivery at Homes England.

Having enabled teams to deliver value for over ten years, he now supports organisations to uncover effective modern approaches to work.

Jonny is an experienced community leader in the public sector, having coached and enabled teams and individuals to maximise their potential while working for the UK Government as a civil servant, and in the higher education sector.

His experience as a Delivery Manager enabled him to explore the disciplines of Agile Coaching and Scrum Mastery. This led to Jonny being one of less than one thousand people from around the world certified as Professional Scrum Master III in May 2021.

He lives on the edge of the Peak District in Leek, Staffordshire with his partner Claudia and their two attention loving cats; Peggy and Pip.

YOUR NOTES

Made in the USA
Middletown, DE
16 February 2023